Norwegian Women's Writing 1850–1990

Women in Context

Women's Writing 1850–1990

Series Editor: Janet Garton (University of East Anglia)

This new series provides a survey, country by country, of women's writing from the beginnings of the major struggle for emancipation until the present day. While the main emphasis is on literature, the social, political and cultural development of each country provides a context for understanding the position and preoccupations of women writers. Modern critical currents are also taken into account in relating feminist criticism to recent critical theory.

Forthcoming volumes in the Series include *Women's Writing in Italy* by Sharon Wood (University of Strathclyde) and *Swedish Women's Writing* by Helena Forsås-Scott (Open University in Scotland).

Women in Context

NORWEGIAN WOMEN'S WRITING 1850–1990

Janet Garton

ATHLONE
LONDON & ATLANTIC HIGHLANDS, NJ

First published 1993 by
THE ATHLONE PRESS LTD
1 Park Drive, London NW11 7SG
and 165 First Avenue,
Atlantic Highlands, NJ 07716

British Library Cataloguing in Publication Data
*A catalogue record for this book is available
from the British Library*

ISBN 0 485 91001 2 hb
0 485 92001 8 pb

Library of Congress Cataloging-in-Publication Data

Garton, Janet.
  Norwegian women's writing, 1850–1990 / Janet Garton.
     p.   cm. -- (Women in context)
  Includes bibliographical references.
  ISBN 0-485-91001-2. -- ISBN 0-485-92001-8 (pbk.)
   1. Norwegian literature--Women authors--History and criticism.
2. Norwegian literature--19th century--History and criticism.
3. Norwegian literature--20th century--History and criticism.
I. Series.
PT8415.G37   1993
839.8'2099287--dc20

Typeset by
BIBLOSET

Printed and bound in Great Britain by
The University Press, Cambridge

In memory of Astrid
and for Annegret, Carol and Eli
– and all the others who have shared
the frustrations and the joys

Contents

List of Illustrations

Acknowledgements

I should like to record my thanks to the University of East Anglia for allowing me study leave in order to work on this book. I received invaluable help from Tom Geddes at the British Library and from the University Library and the Nordic Studies Department in Oslo. Norwegian publishers were generous in their assistance with information and material, in particular Eva Lie-Nielsen (Gyldendal), Ivar Havnevik (Aschehoug) and Torleif Grue (Oktober). Many colleagues in Norway provided advice and practical help during my frequent visits; I should like in particular to mention Edvard Beyer, Irene Engelstad, Jorunn Hareide, Leif Longum, Leif and Tora Mæhle, Odd Martin Mæland, Torill Steinfeld, Elisabeth Aasen. Kristin Brudevoll from NORLA was, as always, a great support. Amongst the authors studied in this volume, I received information and helpful comments from Halldis Moren Vesaas, Bjørg Vik and Cecilie Løveid. The historians Richard Evans, Stewart Oakley and Claus Bjørn (Copenhagen) read certain sections and commented on my approach. Any misconceptions which remain are entirely my own.

For permission to reproduce the illustrations I am indebted to the following: Gyldendal norsk forlag (for the portraits of Camilla Collett, Aasta Hansteen, Cora Sandel, Amalie Skram, Sigrid Undset, Halldis Moren Vesaas, Bjørg Vik and Herbjørg Wassmo), Aschehoug (for Gerd Brantenberg, Ragnhild Jølsen, Torborg Nedreaas, Mari Osmundsen, Anna Rogstad) and Cecilie Løveid for her own portrait. The scene from *Two Acts for Five Women* is from the National Theatre archive, Oslo, and that from *Double Delight* from the archive of Oslo Nye Teater.

Finally I should like to thank my parents for their unflagging support and my sons for their forbearance during three long years.

Janet Garton
Norwich

Series Foreword

The aim of the *Women in Context* series is to present a country-by-country survey of women's writing from the beginnings of the struggle for emancipation until the present day. It will include not just feminist writers but women's writing in a more general sense, incorporating a study of those working independently of or even in direct opposition to the feminist aim of greater autonomy for women.

While the principal emphasis is on literature and literary figures, they are placed in the context of the social, political and cultural development without which their position cannot be properly understood, and which helps to explain the differing rates of progress in different areas. The volumes therefore combine survey chapters, dealing with women's place in the public and private life of a given period, with more in-depth studies of key figures, in which attention will be focused on the texts. There is no attempt at encyclopaedic completeness, rather a highlighting of issues perceived as specifically relevant by women, and of writers who have influenced the course of events or made a significant contribution to the literature of their day. Wherever possible, parallels with other countries are drawn so that the works can be placed in an international perspective. Modern critical currents are also taken into account in relating feminist criticism to recent critical theory.

Until quite recently women's writing has been virtually excluded from the literary canon in many countries; as a result there is often a dearth of information available in English, and an absence of good translations. *Women in Context* represents a move to remedy this situation by providing information in a way which does not assume previous knowledge of the language or the politics of the country concerned; all quotations are in English, and summaries of central texts are provided. The general reader or student of literature or women's studies will find the volumes a useful introduction to the field. For those interested in further research, there is a substantial bibliography of studies of women's writing in the country concerned and of individual authors, and of English translations available in modern editions.

Janet Garton

Introduction

Why a volume on Norwegian women writers? Norwegian literature is an area to which not even the most informed general reader has had much access. Ibsen is an internationally acclaimed dramatist (without, often, being much associated with Norway at all); Knut Hamsun is known to some; but of women writers, none but Sigrid Undset has ever achieved noteworthy success in the English-speaking world. Like Selma Lagerlöf in Sweden, Edith Södergran in Finland, Karen Blixen in Denmark, she seems an isolated figure; yet behind each of these writers lies a rich and diverse tradition which is in many cases only now becoming available to English readers through the medium of translation.

The Scandinavian countries are often held up today as models of liberated thinking and radical legislation as regards women's role in the family, in employment and in politics; and the admiration is justified. Yet behind these achievements lies a long struggle, originating in a form of society which in the early nineteenth century was as male-dominated as any in Europe. In Norway the conflict was exacerbated by the fact that the country itself was struggling into independence in the first part of the century. Unlike Denmark and Sweden, with centuries of independence behind them, Norway had been for hundreds of years a protectorate under the Danish crown, and even during the whole of the nineteenth century it was partially dependent on Sweden.

During the years after independence from Denmark in 1814, Norway was gradually evolving its own system of government and its own distinct literary tradition; and the issue of women's rights was one which emerged slowly. The major woman writer in mid-nineteenth century Norway, Camilla Collett, would ruefully compare her own country's progress in such matters with that of Great Britain and the United States, and hold up John Stuart Mill as a model to her own countrymen. In literature too, women were for a long time practically invisible, despite the fact that creative writing enjoyed enormous prestige in the new nationalism of the nineteenth century. Norway's men of letters were regarded not just as entertainers but as representative national figures, guardians of the national spirit. Yet until the last couple of decades of the century, one looks in vain for well-known female literary figures; in an epoch which in English literature produced Jane Austen, Charlotte and Emily Brontë and then George Eliot, there is only one woman writer who is pre-eminent in Norwegian literature, and that is Camilla Collett herself.[1]

The last two decades of the nineteenth century, however, saw the founding of groups dedicated to the cause of liberation for women, and particularly to winning the vote; and women began to play an increasingly public role in literary and cultural debate. Camilla Collett, who came to public attention with her novel *Amtmandens Døttre* (*The District Governor's Daughters*) in 1854–55, became the first of several women writers to contribute both in fiction and in polemic utterances to the debate about women's role in society and about sexuality and the double standard, which reached a pitch of vociferousness bordering on hysteria in Scandinavia as a whole in the 1880s and 1890s.

Once the Women's Liberation Movement in Norway got going, it moved comparatively quickly. It had its share of frustrations, but nevertheless succeeded, without resorting to the extreme measures to which the British suffragette movement was driven, in winning universal suffrage in 1913. Norway was only the second European country to give all women the vote, after Finland in 1906; Denmark followed in 1915, Sweden not until after Britain in 1921. For a time Norway was in the vanguard, acclaimed by American liberationists who did not achieve universal suffrage for the whole of the USA until 1920. (All the Protestant countries of Northern Europe were, of course, much earlier than the Southern Catholic countries in according this privilege to women; countries like France, Spain and Italy had to wait until after the Second World War.)[2]

After the winning of the vote, there was something of a lull in liberationist activity in Norway, as in many other countries; important as was its symbolic significance, it did not radically alter the structures of power or the programmes of the political parties, and women's direct influence in public life did not increase to any marked extent.[3] It was not until 1924 that the first woman was elected to the Norwegian Parliament, and the Church, the legal profession, industry and finance remained solely the preserve of men. Legislation to improve women's social standing, begun in the nineteenth century, proceeded slowly; but the economic depression of the 1930s and the upheaval of the Second World War, with the German occupation, focused attention elsewhere. It was not until the late 1960s that there began the surge in feminist agitation which resulted in a degree of participation in public life at the highest level and a real equality of opportunity in most fields, enshrined in law, which is second to none in the world.

If there was a slackening in the rate of women's political achievements in the earlier part of the twentieth century, the same cannot be said of women's writing; from the 1880s onwards, Norwegian literature has produced a number of literary figures who would be as well known internationally as George Sand or George Eliot had they written in French or English. And the last generation in particular has seen women writers becoming a major force in literary life, responsible for much of the most exciting work being written. The majority are still, as they have always been, writers of fiction; but they have made significant contributions to drama and poetry as well.

Feminist literary criticism has emerged as a discipline in Norway since the early 1970s, and has attracted some of the best talents amongst researchers. The majority of research has adopted the historical-biographical approach, the so-called 'Anglo-American' method, undertaking the task of rewriting literary history in order to rediscover the lost tradition of women writers, along the lines of Elaine Showalter's *A Literature of Their Own,*[4] or re-evaluating the work of well-known authors from a fresh perspective, as in Sandra M. Gilbert and Susan Gubar's *The Madwoman in the Attic.*[5] But there are also adherents of the 'French' school of linguistic criticism, which starts from the premiss that it is impossible for women writers and critics to liberate themselves from the strictures of the male tradition unless they first reinvent language to embody the multiplicity of the feminine.[6]

Little criticism in English about Norwegian women's writing exists, beyond a few articles on authors like Sigrid Undset or Cora Sandel.[7] This makes it difficult to refer English speakers to secondary reading, much of which is in Norwegian. Part of the reason for this has been the lack, until very recently, of any substantial body of translated works. Sigrid Undset is unique in being the only Norwegian woman writer whose major works were translated not long after they were written – no doubt in part due to the award of the Nobel Prize. Twenty-two of her books had been published in English by the time of her death in 1949. Otherwise only Cora Sandel made any impact before the last few years, thanks to the indefatigable efforts of Elizabeth Rokkan, who translated five of her novels in the 1960s.

In the last decade, however, there has been a considerable change, due largely to the enterprise of a few small publishing houses in Britain and America, and to the Norwegian government's policy of supporting the publication of its literature abroad.[8] Nineteenth-century classics like Amalie Skram's *Constance Ring* and *Betrayed*, short stories by Nini Roll Anker, Ragnhild Jølsen, Solveig Christov and others have at last been published in English. Camilla Collett's *The District Governor's Daughters* has just appeared for the first time in English, almost 140 years after its publication in Norway. Halldis Moren Vesaas's *Selected Poems* has also appeared. Contemporary literature is faring better too; the list of recent translations includes Bjørg Vik's *An Aquarium of Women*, *Out of Season* and *Daughters*, Cecilie Løveid's *Seagull Eaters* and *Sea Swell*, Gerd Brantenberg's *What Comes Naturally* and *The Daughters of Egalia*, Herbjørg Wassmo's *The House with the Blind Glass Windows*. The time is ripe for a fuller presentation of these works and their authors in English.

My decisions about which authors to foreground in the following study have been influenced in part by the availability of translations, but also by my own sense of their relative importance in both a historical and a literary context. Of the authors to whom I have devoted a complete chapter, most are principally writers of fiction, but I have included one poet (Halldis Moren Vesaas) and one dramatist (Cecilie Løveid). Because much of the material will be relatively unfamiliar to many readers, I have introduced a fair amount of historical and biographical information, highlighting the tensions which lie behind as well as within the texts. Yet the main emphasis is always placed on the texts themselves. I have been concerned to examine not only what Norwegian women write but the way they write, the rhythms and images of their poetry and prose – to demonstrate that they do indeed have a literature of their own.

PART I
1850–1913

1
Finding a Voice

The Birth of a Nation

It was with the publication of Camilla Collett's novel *Amtmandens Døttre* (*The District Governor's Daughters*) in 1854–5 that the struggle for women's rights in Norway can be said to have properly begun. In order to understand the frustrations out of which the book arose, however, it is necessary to look back to the beginning of the nineteenth century or, more precisely, to 1814, the year in which the modern Norwegian state came into being.

For many hundreds of years before 1814 – ever since the latter part of the fourteenth century – Norway had not existed as an independent sovereign state. The country was ruled by the Danish monarch; and although in theory all (male) citizens of the twin kingdoms were equal, in practice it was Danish administration, language and culture which predominated. The Norwegian civil service was largely staffed by Danes, and Copenhagen was the cultural as well as the administrative centre of both countries. Norway did not have its own university; its scholars studied at the University of Copenhagen and its intellectuals and artists often settled there permanently. The population was small and largely rural. Of the total of 885,000 in 1815, only 9.8 per cent lived in towns; the rest were scattered over a wide expanse of often inhospitable terrain. In comparison with the rest of Europe it was backward; in the eyes of the great powers it was negligible.

The beginning of the nineteenth century brought international conflicts in which Norway became an incidental victim. The British naval blockade of Denmark from 1807 meant that Norway was virtually cut off from its ruler and, more seriously, from its trade links; near starvation followed. In the bargaining of the great powers, Swedish ambitions to take over Norway grew, as it became politically expedient for the Swedes to look westwards to compensate for the loss of Finland to the Russians in 1808–9. The

Swedish crown prince, Jean-Baptiste Bernadotte (later Karl Johan), took advantage of Denmark's vulnerability to threaten Frederik VI into ceding Norway to Sweden.

The union with Sweden, which was to last until 1905, was, however, very different from the utter dependency of the relationship to Denmark. National feeling had been growing in Norway since the late eighteenth century, and the years of isolation from Denmark gave it further impetus. In 1809 a society for the promotion of economic and educational advance, *Selskabet for Norges vel*, was founded, and 1813 saw the foundation of a Norwegian university and plans for a national bank. When news of the cession reached leading Norwegians, they were not disposed to accept their new overlords passively. At a meeting of a hastily organized national assembly at Eidsvoll in April 1814, regional representatives drew up and ratified a Norwegian constitution, which laid down provisions for a national Parliament [*Storting*] to oversee the running of national affairs in collaboration with the king and his ministers. The Swedes saw the expediency in ensuring a peaceful takeover by accepting the constitution, which thus provided a significant degree of autonomy for Norway, and the basis for much future wrangling as the Norwegians progressed towards complete independence during the uneasy century of union.

The constitution confirmed Norway's growing sense of nationhood, which began to make itself felt in all areas of public life during the first decades of the nineteenth century. The *Storting* gradually acquired more confidence in its dealings with the Swedish king, local government was introduced and political parties were formed, until in 1884 full parliamentarianism under Johan Sverdrup's new Liberal administration began the process of dismantling the union.

The building up of the cultural life of Norway, and especially of the capital, Christiania (Oslo[1]), was a vital ingredient in the creation of a national identity. There can be few countries in which there has been such intense interaction between writers and politics, and in which writers' pronouncements have been taken so seriously, as they were in Norway throughout the nineteenth century. The milieu was small, and prominent figures often played many roles. In the 1830s and 1840s, nationalism coincided with Romanticism to produce a National Romantic movement of which the hero was Henrik Wergeland (1808–45), son of one of the founders of the constitution. He has been given the lion's share of the credit for restoring Norwegians' confidence in their cultural inheritance;[2] as well as producing some fine poetry and plays, he was an ardent advocate of education for the people, writing a series of popular textbooks, a furious polemicist and a devotee of the Norwegian line in politics and literature, striving for a native and colloquial tone in his writings. In this he was opposed by a Danophile group which favoured a gradual development of the joint Dano–Norwegian culture which had grown up over the centuries, based on the Danish language as the natural medium of expression. The leader of this group was also a poet, Johan Sebastian Welhaven (1807–73), whose classically restrained verse was as much a contrast to Wergeland's as were his politics.

Reviving the national culture involved looking back to the past – and in Norway's case, to find a heroic past one had to look some way back, to before the Black Death and the collapse of Norwegian autonomy. There was thus a revival of interest in medieval culture during this period (further encouraged by Romantic tendencies, which, in Norway as elsewhere, encouraged a glorification of this half-mythical time). Sagas, ballads and tales of the Norsemen provided material for quasi-historical treatments of Norway's golden age – amongst others, for Ibsen's early historical dramas in the 1850s. Turning to the more recent past, researchers also became aware of the oral tradition which had preserved the folk literature down through the centuries. The pioneers in this field were P.Chr. Asbjørnsen and Jørgen Moe, who travelled around the country collecting *Norske folkeeventyr* (*Norwegian Folk Tales*, 1841–4). These collections are important not only for the tales which they rescued for posterity but also for the language in which they are retold, which attempts to capture the colloquial style of the teller and give them a more native Norwegian form.

The importance of the language question in the development of the modern Norwegian state can hardly be exaggerated; it still raises hackles today in a way which amazes foreigners whose own language development has been a process of gradual growth. During the centuries Danish had become the official written language, differing in orthography and vocabulary from the still spoken Norwegian. A reinstatement of Norwegian became part of the national programme. There were two different schools of thought, however. One advocated a gradual adaptation of Danish to conform more closely to educated Norwegian usage, the other a radical break with Danish and the substitution of a new language form based on the rural language of the people. In the event – and one might say unfortunately, in view of later ramifications – both directions were followed, with the result that two Norwegian languages developed. Dano–Norwegian, which developed into the modern *bokmål* ('book-language'), approximated to urban usage in Eastern Norway, and has always been the language of the majority. However, a significant (but now dwindling) number, among them some of Norway's finest writers, opted for the other language, originally called *landsmål* (national language) but since 1929 called *nynorsk* (Neo-Norwegian). The latter is a language which owes its formation to one man, the philologist Ivar Aasen, who travelled around rural Norway in the 1840s collecting dialects out of which he constructed a dialect norm, publishing a grammar in 1848. In the 1880s *landsmål* was accepted as an alternative language of instruction in schools.

What part did women play in the birth of this modern Norwegian state? In direct political terms, the answer is, not surprisingly: absolutely none. There were no women delegates at Eidsvoll in 1814; both the electors and the representatives they chose were male. So were the electorate for the *Storting*, and the Members of Parliament. It has been suggested that it was a retrograde step for women's participation in public affairs:

> Those tough, strict, responsible men had little ability to understand and value the female mind. There were several women who were well-known and had wide influence in the centuries before the nineteenth. From the beginning of the nineteenth century – or rather from 1814 onwards – there is not a single woman in Norway who is visible beyond the narrow circle of the family. And in the furious politicking which developed in Norway after 1814 we do not hear a single woman's voice.[3]

The men themselves, of course, represented an élite. The franchise was restricted during most of the nineteenth century to men with a property qualification; as late as the 1870s, only 7–8 per cent of the population was entitled to vote. But stranger than the absence of female electors is the almost total absence of women from any form of public life during the early part of this century. This is no doubt largely due to the fact that there was so much emphasis on 'politicking' during this period. Women had no legal status in their own right, could not carry on a trade and had no access to higher education. Bourgeois women were respectable only as members of a family; working-class women toiled at menial tasks for even less pay than their menfolk.

During the first decades of the nineteenth century there were some cautious political reforms which benefited a small number of women. In 1839 the *Storting* decreed that women over forty should be authorized to practise a craft if it was necessary for their own support; in 1842 this right was extended to all unmarried women. There is no evidence that women themselves agitated for these reforms, however; they were seen primarily as a relief to heads of families who had previously had to support unmarried female relatives who were unable to earn their own living, and whose presence in the household was becoming burdensome as labour-saving devices made housework easier and there was less need of their unpaid labours. Yet this was the beginning of a process of reform which gradu-ally recognized women's right to participation in economic and public life.

There was no well-known female writer or artist in Norway in the first half of the nineteenth century. Cultural life too was the preserve of an élite, and flourished mainly in cir-cles connected with the University of Christiania – to which women did not have access. That is not to say that women were not writing before 1850; they had been writing since before books were printed, and the tradition of published wom-en's writing in Norway goes back to the poet and psalm-ist Dorothe Engelbretsdatter in the seventeenth century. But their writing was often of the intimate kind which did not catch the public eye: religious meditations, translations, stories for children, memoirs. Often it was anonymous, and has been overlooked by literary historians.[4] It is also of relevance to note that the novel, which has shown itself to be a form congenial to the talent of women writers, developed rather late in Norway; in fact the realistic novel of family life did not make its appearance in Norwegian literature until there was a woman of sufficient talent to create it. That woman was Camilla Collett, and the novel was *The District Governor's Daughters*.

Two Pioneers

Camilla Collett's novel was the culmination of a long struggle on the part of its author, a cry of protest against the stultifying conventions which she felt had ruined her life. She came from the privileged élite (she was a Wergeland), but was assailed by her own temerity in publishing at all, and tried to preserve her anonymity. It was only in later life that she began to speak out in her own name about the injustices perpetrated against women of her class – and others; and by then she had been joined by other educated women whose efforts were directed to practical reform. (See Chapter 2.)

The other pioneer of the women's liberation movement in Norway was an equally remarkable woman, Aasta Hansteen (1824–1908). She too came to feminism as a result of personal suffering. She was in many ways the opposite of Camilla Collett; although she also was privileged in terms of background and opportunity, she felt herself to be unattractive where Camilla was beautiful and fêted, yet she came – paradoxically – to seek public attention, whereas Camilla shunned it. She threw herself passionately into many causes.[5] She began her career in the 1850s as a painter and continued to regard herself for most of her life as first and foremost an artist. In the 1860s she took up the language cause, becoming only the third writer after Ivar Aasen and the poet Aasmund Olafsson Vinje to publish in *landsmål*; her book *Skrift og Umskrift i Landsmaalet* (Writing and Rewriting in Landsmaal, 1862) contains both her own original poetry in the language and her recasting of texts by other authors, including Wergeland, Asbjørnsen and Moe. It was not until the 1870s that she began to agitate for the rights of women;

and then she dedicated herself to that cause, giving public lectures and writing articles with a lack of moderation which made her a favourite subject for caricature. (She has also left more serious traces in men's writing, being used as a model by Ibsen for his Lona Hessel in *Samfundets støtter* (*Pillars of Society*, 1877) and by the playwright Gunnar Heiberg for the eponymous heroine of *Tante Ulrikke* (Aunt Ulrikke, 1884)). Embittered by lack of recognition, in 1880 she took refuge in America, where she remained for nine years, making contacts with women's organizations and enjoying the more liberal climate.

In Norway too, however, things were changing; in the 1880s, women became organized and the fight for liberation began in earnest. When Aasta Hansteen returned in 1889, it was to a quite different atmosphere. Both she and Camilla Collett lived long enough to hear their lone voices taken up by a chorus, and to receive recognition in their old age for their achievements.

Neither Aasta Hansteen nor Camilla Collett had a programme of practical reform; different as their methods were, they shared the view that it was a change in consciousness rather than in political and social structures that was needed. Both still saw woman's place as being within the family, but wanted to give her greater autonomy within her proper sphere. There were other influences that were making themselves felt during the 1860s and 1870s, however, which were to have profound repercussions for the status of women. Charles Darwin's *On the Origin of Species* (1859) was known and discussed in Scandinavia during the 1860s (and translated into Danish by the author J.P. Jacobsen in 1871–3); as in other European countries, it had the effect of making people question the superiority of mankind and the supremacy of the Church and the patriarchal institutions it sanctioned. More directly, John Stuart Mill's *On the Subjection of Women* (1869), which appeared in the same year in Danish in a translation by the critic Georg Brandes, provoked heated discussion about the place of women in society. In Norway, the gradual process of reforms continued, with women gaining more control over their own affairs, training for the new office work, and obtaining access to higher education – culminating in the admission of the first female student to the University of Christiania in 1882.

Political Progress and Social Realism

In the 1880s, development was rapid in many areas. In political life, the development of the dual-party system which culminated in the first Liberal administration in 1884 stimulated a reassessment of conservative institutions; the Liberals were more sympathetic towards underprivileged groups, including women, and instrumental in seeing through social and educational reform. But women too were beginning to take a more public role. 1884 also saw the formation of *Norsk kvinnesaksforening* (The Norwegian Women's Liberation Organization), the first public organization to fight for women's equality. Many of its most influential members were men. It was, however, cautious about going as far as demanding the right to vote, and in the following year a new organization, *Norsk kvinnestemmerettsforening* (The Norwegian Women's Suffrage Organization) was formed by a breakaway group. This was to be entirely a women's organization, and chose as its leader Gina Krog, a campaigner who had given up her teaching post in 1880 in order to devote the rest of her life to the cause. She was the editor of the movement's journal *Nylænde* (lit. 'newly cleared land') from its inception in 1887, and kept it going, often practically single-handed, until her death in 1916 (the journal actually survived until 1927). The group worked for political reform, stimulated by similar organizations abroad, in particular in America and England, and in 1890 a motion to give the vote to property-owning women got as far as the *Storting*. It was defeated, but had attracted considerable support; the women felt that the tide was turning in their favour.[6]

Literary figures played a major part in public debate in the 1880s too. This was the period of 'problem' literature, the so-called Modern Breakthrough, when social issues were a central concern for many writers. It was a literary direction which was fostered and focused by Georg Brandes, who in a series of lectures in Copenhagen during the 1870s on *Hovedstrømninger i det 19de Aarhundredes Litteratur* (Main Currents of Nineteenth-Century

Literature) had explained new developments in European literature to his fellow Scandinavians and urged them to write in a realistic manner about contemporary society. Preoccupation with modern social problems led many authors to focus on the position of women – and not only bourgeois women. The working class became a serious literary subject for the first time, rather than a rural idyll or a backcloth; and working-class women were perceived to be doubly disadvantaged. Sexual morality too became the subject of a furious pan-Scandinavian literary feud which lasted over decades, but reached its climax in the 1880s.

Drama had become a medium for literary debate in Norway by the 1880s. After a late start – the first Norwegian-language theatre was founded by Ole Bull in Bergen in 1850, followed by one in Christiania in 1852 – Norwegian theatre had acquired two major talents, Henrik Ibsen (1828–1906) and his equally famous contemporary Bjørnstjerne Bjørnson (1832–1910). It was in 1879 that Ibsen wrote what came to be seen as his clarion call for women's liberation, *Et Dukkehjem* (A Doll's House); this was followed by many plays in which it is the female central character who demonstrates a strength of purpose or a breadth of vision unequalled by the men (Mrs Alving in *Gengangere* [Ghosts, 1881], Rebekka West in *Rosmersholm,* 1886), or whose life has been ruined by lack of opportunity (*Hedda Gabler,* 1890) or callous exploitation (Irene in *Når vi døde vågner* [*When We Dead Awaken*, 1899]). Although Ibsen did maintain that he was a supporter not of women's liberation but of people's liberation, his strongest sympathies lie with those whose efforts in the pursuit of self-realization are most severely hampered, and in nineteenth-century Norway that category consisted largely of women.

Bjørnson played a central role in public debate throughout the second half of the century, taking up the cudgels on behalf of a breathtaking number of causes. Many of his plays and novels contain what would now be called positive role-models: strong and self-assured women whose men are not always equal to the challenge they pose. His emancipated women include Valborg in his play *En Fallit* (*A Bankrupt*, 1875), and the heroines of *Leonora* (1879) and *Paul Lange og Tora Parsberg* (1898). With Georg Brandes, August Strindberg and others he played a leading role in the sexual morality debate, which revolved around the question of the double standard: whether society should condone promiscuity in men while simultaneously demanding chastity of women; this led to questions of free love, prostitution, contraception, the right to divorce, etc. Bjørnson's main literary contribution to the debate was his play *En Hanske* (*A Gauntlet*, 1883), in which the item in question is thrown down in challenge to her fiancé by the heroine Svava, when she discovers that he has had an affair.

The other two writers who make up the 'four greats' of this period – Jonas Lie (1833–1908) and Alexander Kielland (1849–1906) – also contributed to the debate. Jonas Lie's novels from the 1880s, *Familjen paa Gilje* (The Family at Gilje, 1883) and *Kommandørens Døttre* (The Commodore's Daughters, 1886) explore the lack of opportunities for women and their fates under the tyranny of convention. The title of the latter novel is a reference to Camilla Collett's *The District Governor's Daughters*, and it is written in the same spirit. (It is noteworthy in this context that Jonas Lie's wife, Thomasine, played a major role – as he acknowledged – both in developing his ideas and in giving them artistic form; yet her name does not appear on any publications.)[7] Kielland's satirical novels and short stories expose male pretensions and self-delusion; he is also concerned about the exploitation of working-class girls and the evils of prostitution, a theme which aroused growing outrage throughout the 1880s until the *Storting* passed a law in 1887 abolishing legalized prostitution. Kielland's short story *Else* (1881), which depicts an honest working-class girl who is seduced by a cynical adventurer and forced into prostitution to stay alive, helped to raise the storm of indignation which led to a change in the law. Battle in this area was also joined by authors whose books caused such a scandal that they were banned: Christian Krohg's *Albertine* (1886), which went further than *Else* in portraying moral corruption (amongst the police) and the horrors of prostitution and enforced medical examination; and Hans Jæger's *Fra Kristiania-Bohêmen* (From the Christiania Bohemia, 1885), one of the major works of the 'Bohemian' literature which made the case for unfettered sexual indulgence for both men and women.

Thus the interweaving of literary activity, social debate and legislation was intimate during the 1880s; women's lack of autonomy was highlighted by socially concerned writers, who helped to form the climate of opinion which made changes possible. It is symptomatic of this involvement that in 1884, when the *Storting* had discussed the question of whether a married woman should have the right to own her own property and a referendum of local council members had overwhelmingly defeated the proposal, Bjørnson took the initiative to send a protest, signed by Ibsen, Kielland and Lie, pointing out the unfairness of making a woman automatically subject to her husband, and of asking only men to vote on the matter. (It was, commented Ibsen archly, 'like asking wolves to approve of increased measures of protection for a flock of sheep'.[8])

It was not only male writers on whom the burgeoning women's movement relied for support – although they were invaluable during the early stages, which is why they have been given so much space here. An increasing number of women were responding to the calls for socially committed writing. The most well-known was Amalie Skram, who made her debut in 1885 with *Constance Ring*. This is the first of many novels which investigate the consequences of the double standard, here the fate of a young girl brought up in complete ignorance of sexuality, who is married off to an older, experienced man – with catastrophic results. Both in her life and in her writing Amalie Skram was to demonstrate the classic problems of self-realization for an independent woman in a male-dominated society (see Chapter 3).

Amalie Skram's talent, like Camilla Collett's, has been to some extent recognized in traditional literary histories.[9] The same has not been true of other nineteenth-century women writers, who have been remembered – if at all – for reasons other than their writing. Magdalene Thoresen (1819–1903) is a case in point. Her main claim to fame was first as Ibsen's mother-in-law, and second as a model for various of his and Bjørnson's characters. A sensual woman, who was clearly not satisfied by her marriage to the kindly but considerably older Pastor Thoresen, she was thought to have been the model for Ellida in Ibsen's *Fruen fra havet* (*The*

Lady from the Sea, 1888). Many of Bjørnson's strong-willed female characters, like the heroine of *Fiskerjenten* (*The Fisher Girl*, 1868) and of *Leonora* (1879), probably owe much to the woman whose passionate nature at once fascinated and alarmed him. But she was herself a successful writer who was rated alongside Camilla Collett by critics like Georg Brandes. She published a book of poems, *Digte af en Dame* (Poems by a Lady), as early as 1860, becoming the first woman author in Norway to eschew anonymity.

Her poems still seem remarkably fresh and intimate; they give direct expression to female desire in an unprecedented way. Some are addressed by an older woman to a young man – a scandalous subject, but concealed in the imagery of flowers ('Resedaen taler' – 'The Mignonette Speaks') or as a regret for her own lost childhood ('En Drøm' – 'A Dream'). It is a theme which recurs in one of her best stories, 'Min Bedstemoders Fortælling' ('My Grandmother's Tale', 1867), in which a grandmother on her deathbed recounts the story of her hopeless love for a younger man – which was unexpectedly realized when his wife died, and she demonstrated the courage of her love and claimed him as her husband. (The young poet in the story bore such a strong resemblance to the young Bjørnson that no one could be in much doubt – and certainly not Bjørnson himself, who was so offended by her use of him that they were estranged for some time. Although he was happy to use her as a model, he did not wish to have the compliment returned.)

Magdalene Thoresen wrote throughout her life after being left a widow with small children in 1858, endeavouring to support herself by her pen – a battle which she gradually won, as her work became popular. She wrote mainly novels and short stories, somewhat uneven in quality, inclining towards the melodramatic and fatalistic; but in the best of them, such as the popular *Billeder fra Midnatsolens Land* (Pictures from the Land of the Midnight Sun, 1884–6), she gives finely observed portraits of life in rural Norway, and particularly of women. Her later work was popular with women readers, and with women critics as they began to appear towards the end of the century.[10]

Dramatic writing is a genre in which women writers have traditionally made less impact; and they play little part in the official history of nineteenth-century Scandinavian theatre, dominated as it is by figures like Ibsen, Bjørnson and Strindberg.[11] From the late eighteenth century onwards, however, women were involved in the dramatic societies which were formed in several Norwegian towns as private clubs with restricted membership. Their involvement was principally as actresses, and women from the leading families did not regard it as improper to take part. They also played a part behind the scenes, for example in translating foreign plays – though such work was often anonymous. As the nineteenth century progressed they began to write too – and had their works performed in progressively larger numbers. During the period 1870 to 1900, for example, the originally Danish-language Christiania Theatre performed fifty plays written by Norwegian dramatists, of which eleven were by women. Amongst the better-known women dramatists are Mathilde Schjøtt (1844–1926) and Marie Colban (1814–84). Amalie Skram wrote one major play, *Agnete* (1893), which did not do well when it was first staged in Bergen but has since become a popular part of theatrical repertoire.

In the history of the Norwegian theatre too, Magdalene Thoresen is an important but largely forgotten name. She wrote many plays, of which no fewer than four were staged (anonymously) at the Norwegian Theatre in Bergen during the 1850s – three of them whilst Henrik Ibsen was director. None did very well, but they were useful training for her later more successful dramas: *Et rigt Parti* (A Good Catch, 1870), a play about the immorality of young girls selling themselves to rich husbands, which was performed both in Copenhagen and at the Christiania Theatre; and *Inden Døre* (Behind Closed Doors, 1877), a study of generation conflict which had considerable success in both Christiania and Bergen, and was also performed abroad.

Of some importance in theatrical history is another largely forgotten name, Laura Kieler (1849–1932). Forgotten as an author, that is; for she has an assured place in literary history as the model for Ibsen's Nora in *A Doll's House*. Laura Kieler's marital history resembled Nora's, although the details reflected even less credit on her husband; Ibsen has drawn more closely from real life here than in any other of his plays. But he had known of her well before 1879; as early as 1869, when she was only twenty, she had published a novel under the pseudonym Lili called *Brands døtre* (Brand's Daughters). This was a sequel to Ibsen's *Brand*, which she maintained gave a false picture of Christianity; in the novel, Brand has survived with two grown-up daughters, and is brought to realize the error of his harsh religion and to exchange it for a milder faith. It is an immature novel, with melodramatic episodes interspersed with long passages of religious tracts; but the remarkable thing is that she dared to publish it at all. Ibsen said little about it, but followed her career from then on with interest. She had a difficult life as a writer, and her public image was not helped by Ibsen's use of her. Some time after *A Doll's House* she appealed to Ibsen because she was being accused of dishonesty by those who did not know the facts, and begged him to write and confirm that she had acted honourably; but inexplicably, Ibsen refused to do so. Like several other authors of this period, Ibsen practised his own form of double standard; though he helped through his writings to arouse public concern about the oppression of women, he was less forthcoming when it was a matter of lending a beleaguered woman his personal support.

Laura Kieler was responsible for the play which caused the most indignant public discussion in Scandinavia in the nineteenth century after Ibsen's social dramas: *Mænd af Ære* (Men of Honour), which was finished in 1888, published in 1890, and performed in Copenhagen in 1890 and in Christiania in 1891. The subject matter was daring: it was an attack on the ideals of free love, and a demonstration of its consequences for the woman, who faced public disgrace when her partner moved on to pastures new. Additional furore was caused by the fact that the play was interpreted by the critic Georg Brandes as a personal attack on himself – although it was not until a few months after it had been finished in 1888 that Brandes's rejected lover, Victoria Benedictsson (one of Sweden's leading writers), took her own life. Although the play was praised by many, including Ibsen and Bjørnson, it did not do well in performance, and was soon taken off.

Fin de siècle Stagnation and Final Victory

After the optimism of the 1880s, the 1890s were a time of frustration for the women's organizations. Politically, other issues were regarded as more important, particularly the future of the union with Sweden, which caused a governmental crisis in the mid-nineties. New political parties had been formed; the old Liberal Party had split into Moderates and Radicals in the late 1880s, and a Labour Party had been formed in 1887. There were many changes of government in the 1890s, and several minority ministries. The women's movement could no longer rely on automatic support from the Liberals, who feared – perpetuating the common myth – that women were naturally conservative, and that they would suffer if women were given a say in government.

Industrial strife was growing too. Industrialization had come late to Norway, but there had been rapid growth in the second half of the nineteenth century. In 1850 only 14,000 people were working in industry, but by 1875 there were over 95,000. The population had grown from 885,000 to over two million by 1890 – even though more than 400,000 had emigrated to America since 1814 – and was to reach 2.5 million by 1900. The urban population was expanding particularly rapidly – the population of Christiania more than doubled between 1878 and 1900. Accelerating industrialization brought industrial unrest, and demands for better working conditions. Unions had begun to form in the 1870s, but the union movement did not acquire momentum until the end of the 1880s. It was galvanized by two strikes in 1889, one of which was a protest by women matchmakers against their dangerous working conditions and low rates of pay; this achieved much public support and led to the formation of the first women's trade union, *Kvindelige Fyrstikarbeideres Forening* (The Women Matchmakers' Union) in 1890. Finally, in 1899, a trade-union federation, *Landsorganisasjonen*, was formed. Women could be members of unions, but they were mostly run by men for men; the idea of equal pay for equal work was a long time coming.

The campaign for extending the franchise to women, which had seemed to be gaining ground during the 1880s, received several setbacks during the 1890s. In 1891 the Liberals published a manifesto declaring their support for universal *manhood* suffrage – a double insult to women in that it would exclude even property-owning women whilst including all classes of men. Then in 1896 the *Storting* decided to give the vote to all taxpaying men, whilst still excluding all women. The anger caused by this led to disagreements within the Norwegian Women's Suffrage Organization between those women who were campaigning for the right to vote for all women and those who believed that a property qualification was advisable. The organization consisted entirely of middle-class women; there was no broad women's movement in Norway which succeeded in uniting women of different classes, although they had campaigned for better conditions for working-class women and engaged in social and charitable work, especially between 1888 and 1895. Working-class women had always made common cause with their class rather than with middle-class women. But the disagreement resulted in a split in the organization; when the majority voted to lower its sights and try to achieve partial voting rights, Gina Krog left, and with her fellow sympathizers formed *Landskvinnestemmerettsforeningen* (The National Women's Suffrage Organization), which took over the old slogan of 'national and local suffrage *on the same conditions as men*'. The ultimate goal of both groups was universal suffrage, but different tactics were employed.

By the end of the century, no progress had been made on the vote, although other reforms had been achieved, which improved the position of unmarried mothers and their children and introduced proper training courses in household management, cookery, etc. An important step was a change in the constitution in 1898 to allow women to be appointed to government and civil service posts. But both women's organizations were electrified when, in 1901, the Liberal Party put before the *Storting* a motion to extend voting rights to non-taxpaying men – again without including any women. Only idiots, convicts, paupers – and women would not be enfranchised. A storm of protest followed, and it became clear that support from the Conservatives, traditionally the opponents of reform, was now greater. In May 1901 came partial victory: the right to vote in local elections was extended to women of a certain income. But it was a near thing, with only one vote tipping the balance.

During the first years of the twentieth century, links with international organizations were strengthened. Moral support from women in other countries, particularly in England and America, had always been important, but until now it had been largely a matter of personal contact. In 1904 Norwegian women, on the initiative of the indefatigable Gina Krog, founded *Norske kvinners nasjonalråd* (The Norwegian Council of Women), which became affiliated to the International Council of Women. Support from abroad gave new hope; and with their recent acquisition of partial voting rights Norwegian women, who had felt for so much of the nineteenth century that they were lagging behind other Western countries, were now in the forefront of reform.

In 1905 came the decisive crisis in the union with Sweden. The growth of national feeling culminated in a demand for independence which the *Storting* decided to test by a plebiscite on 13 August. The result was overwhelmingly in favour of dissolving the union. Unfortunately, however, it was yet again decided to exclude women from voting. So they held their own poll, using their nationwide organizations, and by 22 August they were able to hand in a petition of 300,000 names in favour of dissolution. Their action impressed the *Storting* and helped to swing the tide of opinion in their direction, aided by the fact that the decision of 1901 had not been the catastrophe that some had feared; women had used their vote in local elections in increasing numbers and with responsibility.

After this, the worst struggle was over. In 1907 the *Storting* decided, by a comfortable majority, to enfranchise women of a certain income in general elections. Congratulations poured in from abroad, as although this was not total victory, it was a great step forward on an international scale. After this followed universal suffrage for local elections in 1910, and finally universal suffrage for general elections in 1913. At the final vote, not one member of the *Storting* voted against.

Norwegian literature in the 1890s was still partly dominated by the authors of the 1880s; the 'four greats' lived until the early twentieth century, and with the exception of Kielland produced important works during this last decade. Yet there is a shift of emphasis, particularly in the work of Ibsen and Lie, during the 1890s. Ibsen had moved away from social drama, and was writing symbolic explorations of guilt and retribution and of his own artistic vocation, such as *Bygmester Solness* (The Master Builder, 1892) and *When We Dead Awaken*. Jonas Lie, who had had to do violence to his fascination for the mystical and mysterious to suit the 1880s vogue for 'problem literature', now allowed his imagination freer rein in works like *Trold* (*Trolls*, 1891–2), short stories which draw on folk belief in trolls and demons to incarnate the irrational forces which can invade the daylight consciousness of the mind. A similar change can be seen in the work of another author who had made a significant contribution to the social debate – and to the linguistic debate (he adopted *landsmål* as his literary medium) – in the 1880s: Arne Garborg (1851–1924). In 1886 he had published *Mannfolk* (Menfolk), a collective portrait of male sexuality which was deemed so crass that it cost him his government post; by 1891 he had written a novel with the typical title *Trætte Mænd* (Tired Men), a study of a decadent, cynical and burnt-out man.

The new male authors of the 1890s showed a similar tendency to strike out in new directions. The most important of them, Knut Hamsun (1859–1952), gave a series of lectures in 1891 in which he declared war on 'modern literature' in the shape of Ibsen, Bjørnson, Kielland and Lie, and heralded the advent of 'psychological literature', which would investigate the finer nuances of the life of the soul. He proceeded to provide examples of this way of writing in novels such as *Sult* (*Hunger*, 1890), *Mysterier* (*Mysteries*, 1892) and *Pan* (1894), exquisite studies of tortured souls struggling with their own internal conflicts. There is a *fin-de-siècle* atmosphere about the work of many authors during this period: a sense of disillusion, a movement away from realism and rationality, and a disinclination to take up causes. The poet Sigbjørn Obstfelder (1866–1900) is in many ways a typical nineties figure, writing poems which are mood-pictures of wonder, fear and alienation, and dying appropriately of consumption at the end of the decade. Hans E. Kinck (1865–1926) began writing in the 1890s, and his short story collection *Flaggermus-vinger* (Bat-wings, 1895) investigates the obsessive and potentially destructive power of irrational and erotic forces over the human mind.

The central female figures in these works from the 1890s are typically rather different from heroines in the socially aware 1880s, who were generally either oppressed victims or articulate activists. Now the emphasis shifted back to woman as a sexual being; the interest of writers in the irrational and the subconscious involved a return to a theme which resurfaces continually in literary history and had last done so during the Romantic period earlier in the century: that of dangerous female sexuality. There are signs of it in Ibsen's plays; a major element in the destruction of Solness the master builder is his erotic fascination for the provocative Hilde, and the young sculptor Rubek from *When We Dead Awaken* was only too aware of the temptation posed by his beautiful naked model, which he had to resist in order to be able to create. Jonas Lie's *Trolls* goes further in its depiction of the demonic in woman; the story 'Jorden drar' ('The Earth Draws'), for example, depicts the battle for a man's soul between his ordinary, pretty blonde fiancée and the black-eyed, broad-shouldered, hairy troll's daughter who lures him into the mountain. The troll wins, as in most of Lie's haunting stories; everyday rationality is no match for the power of repressed desire.

Woman as an object of desire predominates in the work of the new authors of the 1890s too. Hamsun's hero in *Hunger*, starved of sex as well as food, becomes fascinated by a girl he sees in the street, whom he transforms in his dreams into Princess Ylajali, who waits longingly for him on a throne of yellow roses. Lieutenant Glahn in *Pan* makes love to real women and dream women under the midnight sun, but desires nothing so much as the one woman it seems he cannot have. Obstfelder's priest in *En Prests Dagbok* (*A Priest's Diary*, 1900) intoxicates himself with visions of the breasts and thighs of dancing women. Kinck's stories imbue the whole of nature with a seductive sensuality which has an equally powerful effect on both men and women. It is not only in literature that the threatening power of female sexuality is so central during this period; the painter Edvard Munch's various studies entitled *Vampire*, a red-haired woman enfolding and devouring a passive man, are from the first years of the decade, and his *Harpy* is from 1900.

Thus it was not only politicians who did little to advance the cause of women's equality during the 1890s; women campaigners had some reason to feel aggrieved at this literary reaction to the rationalist 1880s. Not all books fall into these categories, of course; authors do not fit neatly into decades. Bjørnson continued to write committed literature until his death in 1910, although his views became more conservative with advancing years, and Garborg's defeatism in *Tired Men* reverted to a more optimistic belief in the strength of an earthy country lass to overcome demons in the poem-cycle *Haugtussa* (1895). But there is nevertheless a marked swing of the pendulum which coincides with the 1890s' lack of interest in the idea of woman as a political animal.

The work of women writers during this period, however, does not exhibit the same dichotomy between the mood of the 1880s and that of the 1890s. Women were not tired of the ideas of equality, and did not feel that the subject of social injustice and oppression had been exhausted. Camilla Collett and Aasta Hansteen were still campaigning, and the latter continued well into the twentieth century. Amalie Skram's writing changed and developed, but not in a mystical or neo-Romantic direction. She carried on writing studies of the crippling effect of sexual ignorance on young women in novels like *Forraadt* (*Betrayed*, 1892), and later in the decade she produced semi-autobiographical accounts of the struggle of being an artist as well as a wife and mother (e.g *Professor Hieronimus*, 1895). In between her other writings she was also working on *Hellemyrsfolket* (The People of Hellemyr, 1887–98), her epic Naturalistic study of a Bergen family trapped in a Zolaesque downward spiral into despair.

Women who made their debut in the 1890s belong in general to the category of writers overlooked by literary historians. Alvilde Prydz (1846–1922) began writing in 1870 but had even more of a struggle for recognition than most women; her breakthrough did not come until the 1890s. In two linked novels, *Mennesker* (People, 1892) and *Drøm* (Dream, 1893) she depicts Helene Ørn's unsuccessful attempt to achieve a marriage based on mutual respect; and in a four-volume series of which the central novel is *Gunvor Thorsdatter til Hærø* (Gunvor Thorsdatter at Hærø, 1896) she studies different kinds of women: the young bride who is tyrannized by an older husband; the snake-like, sexually voracious woman who drains the strength from a man; and the fearless independent woman whose qualities are not recognized by the man until it is too late. She is a nineties author in the sense that her ideals are portrayed as ultimately unrealizable, and the end is often disillusion. She also wrote several plays, of which two were staged: *Han kommer* (He's Coming) at the Christiania Theatre in 1895, and *Aino* at the new National Theatre in 1901 – to a mixed reception.[12]

Dikken Zwilgmeyer (1853–1913) has a place in literary history as a writer of books for children. Her books about Inger-Johanne won lasting popularity; she is one of the best-selling children's writers. Her books for adults, however, are less well known. In 1895 came *Som kvinder er* (The Way Women Are), a collection of stories about disappointed lives. These are women who stand outside the mainstream of society as companions, spinsters and aunts, their talents unrealized and their dreams of fulfilment mocked. The sisters Olga and Malli in 'Paa egne ben' ('On Their Own Feet') are left helpless by the death of their parents, with no training for any work and no idea of how society functions; Olga ends up in a cold, lonely job in the city as an underpaid cashier, whilst Malli chooses the other evil: life as the wife of an older, petty-minded country teacher. In an introduction written in 1913, Sigrid Undset drew attention to the originality of these stories:

> In the midst of a time of neo-Romanticism they stand quite on their own, these grey stories about fine, unnoticed petty-bourgeoises. Through all the stories there vibrates the undertone of these women's desperate, unspoken longing for love and warmth and fulfilment . . .[13]

But when they were published, this volume and the subsequent novel, *Ungt Sind* (A Young Mind, 1896) met with little appreciation, and it was some time before Dikken Zwilgmeyer wrote any more books for adults.

Hulda Garborg (1862–1934), the wife of Arne Garborg, made her debut with an outspoken contribution to the sexual morality debate, *Et frit Forhold* (An Open Relationship, 1892). The novel traces the fate of a young shop assistant through seduction, pregnancy, rejection and the death of her child; it is unusual in its frankness about physical details and in the elasticity of its heroine, who refuses to be crushed by her tragedy but manages to salvage a tolerable life in the end. Her most popular success was as a playwright, with *Rationelt Fjøsstel* (Rational Farming), which was performed more than eighty times at Christiania Theatre between 1897 and 1899 – more than any other play by a woman in the nineteenth century. It can hardly be said to have struck a blow for women's rights, however, being a comedy which pokes fun at a farmer's daughter who thinks she has all the answers to modernizing the farm. Hulda Garborg, like her husband, was a staunch supporter of the *landsmål* movement, and wrote in both languages; her wide-ranging authorship, including essays, memoirs and journalism as well as novels, poems and plays, continued until her death. She always wrote from a woman's perspective, though she was not always in agreement with more radical campaigners; she laid more stress on the essential maternal nature of woman than did some of her contemporaries.

The end of the nineteenth century saw many more women taking up writing as a profession. Some of the most important authors who made their debut in the years before 1913, however, will be considered in the next chapter, as the main bulk of their writings is in the later period; Nini Roll Anker's first novel was published in 1898 and Sigrid Undset's in 1907. But there is one author who, because of the shortness of her life, both began and finished her writing in the few years between the turn of the century and 1913: Ragnhild Jølsen (1875–1908).

Ragnhild Jølsen was an isolated figure who has only recently been 'rediscovered', with new editions of her books and renewed critical attention. More than the other women writers she combines the demands for autonomy of the women's movement with the interest in the darker irrational forces of the mind expressed by the neo-Romanticists. Her central female characters in *Rikka Gan* (1904) and *Hollases krønike* (The Chronicles of Hollas, 1906) are women with their own aims in life, who challenge male domination; yet both acknowledge the power of their own sexuality and the way in which it can make them accomplices in their own defeat (see Chapter 4).

Conclusion

With the exception of Camilla Collett and Amalie Skram, the women writers of Norway's first century of independence are not well known in their own country – much less abroad. One part of the problem is that they have been overlooked by a tradition which still writes them out of history; another is that their works are often uneven in quality. When one enquires why that should be so, one finds an answer resembling the one Virginia Woolf discovered to her famous question: why is there no female Shakespeare? [14] The women of nineteenth-century Norway did not have the time, the money, or the education to write; it was a struggle with practical difficulties as much as with the Muse.

Even the life of a male author in nineteenth-century Norway was not an easy one; the reading public was small, and making a living by one's pen was a considerable challenge. Ibsen did not make a comfortable living until he was well over middle age, despite comparatively substantial sales. Alexander Kielland complained constantly to his publishers that he could not make ends meet, and Knut Hamsun nearly starved before his work was recognized. Travel grants and stipends were vital to authors, and especially important from the 1860s onwards was the *diktergasje*, a guaranteed annual stipend awarded by the *Storting* to selected authors. During the last forty years of the century this stipend was awarded to Bjørnson, Ibsen, Lie, Garborg and several minor authors – though not to Kielland, whose refusal was a *cause célèbre*. But the only woman to be awarded a stipend was Camilla Collett, who had to wait until 1876 and be content with considerably less than her male colleagues. Magdalene Thoresen applied for a grant but was told that she was not eligible since she was born Danish, although she was married to a Norwegian; Amalie Skram applied but was told that she was not eligible since, although she was born Norwegian, she was married to a Dane. All three women were bringing up children alone, and their lives were dogged by fear of destitution.

Financial assistance was not required only to maintain a decent standard of living, however; it was essential to be able to travel. For most of the nineteenth century, the capital Christiania was a cultural backwater, and the cultural centre of Norway remained Copenhagen. (Interestingly, it showed no sign of moving to Stockholm; Norwegians' feeling of greater temperamental – if not linguistic – affinity with Denmark has persisted to this day.) The largest publishing house in Scandinavia in the nineteenth century was Gyldendal in Copenhagen, and it remained the main publisher of Norwegian literature until the turn of the century. Theatrical life, too, flourished in Copenhagen as it did not in Christiania.

It was not only Denmark to which Norwegian authors felt drawn. The nineteenth century was the time of the grand tour;

and Scandinavian authors as well as English sought out the classical European centres of humanism, to partake of a culture which would enrich their provincial experience. Ibsen spent twenty-five of his most creative years in Germany and Italy; Bjørnson, Kielland, Lie, Hamsun and many others spent formative years in the cultural capitals of Paris and Rome. Artistic interchange flourished at *Zum schwarzen Ferkel* in Berlin, where Munch and Strindberg belonged to an international community. Such an interchange was difficult for female writers to experience, when their opportunities for travel were restricted by convention as well as lack of funds. Camilla Collett was desperate to travel and did so, but at the cost of breaking up her family; and for many women authors it was not an option. Small wonder, then, that the privations of the artistic life took a particular toll on women who wished to write.

2
Camilla Collett (1813–95)

Life and literary apprenticeship

> I grew up under the threefold pressure of a crushing loneliness,
> individuals of gigantic strength in my nearest family and in
> others who gained power over me, and in addition a harsh
> law of femininity, of which it is difficult nowadays to have any
> conception. (*SV* II, p. 204) [1]

This statement from the essay collection *Sidste Blade* (Last Leaves,
2nd and 3rd series, 1872) sums up the conditions under which
Camilla Collett's writing took shape. Her childhood home, Eidsvoll,
was a place already redolent of history when the family moved there
in 1817, three years after the adoption of the constitution. It was set
in beautiful wild country, which was the young Camilla Wergeland's
cherished refuge; yet it was a provincial backwater, bereft of cultured
society, and two days' uncomfortable journey from the capital
Christiania. It was the capital which offered entertainment and
the friendships – both male and female – for which the adolescent
Camilla longed; yet trips there were rare, and served most often to
highlight the gloom of the long dark winters.

The family into which she was born was a mixed blessing, dominated as it was by its temperamental male members. Her father,
the theologian Nicolai Wergeland, had been one of the Eidsvoll
representatives, and partly for that reason had applied for the living
at Eidsvoll. But the place did not live up to his expectations, and
his ambitions were frustrated. He became a disappointed man, a
gloomy father for whom Camilla felt a mixture of affection and
apprehension. Her eldest brother Henrik was the family genius,
recognized as a phenomenon from his schooldays; his fiery creative
energy, wild escapades and furious polemics were the focus of
the family's worry and admiration throughout his short life. Her
mother, who was of a warmer, more extrovert nature, played a

domestic role, and wanted the best for her two daughters: a happy marriage. It did not occur to anyone that there might be unusual talent in a daughter. It did not occur to Camilla herself, who agreed with the others that Henrik was the talented member of the family. Not until later did she realize that it was nurture, not nature, that had made their early lives so different:

> Take two similar shoots from a thriving forest plant, plant one of them in the fresh air and the earth where it belongs, and the other in a pretty plant pot in a little room in the house, and don't ask then why one of them shoots up strong and fruitfully whilst the other one droops.[2]

As if this were not enough, her bruising contact with assertive male egos was compounded by the fact that at the age of seventeen she fell in love with Henrik's arch-rival, Johan Sebastian Welhaven. It was a passion immediately conceived and never conquered; to the end of her life it remained her most vital experience. Welhaven was charmed by her graceful beauty, which several of his poems record; but he did not take the relationship seriously. The cause for which he fought was all-important to him, and it would have been damaged by an alliance with the enemy; he did not realize until much later the strength of the feelings which Camilla kept jealously hidden. The 'episode' dominated ten years of her life; when she finally became engaged to Peter Jonas Collett in 1839, her letters to him circled obsessively around this passion.[3]

Jonas Collett was the last of the four central men in her life, and quite a different character. He was a tolerant and practical man, deeply in love with Camilla but prepared to win her affection slowly. He responded to her confessions of her passion for Welhaven, which kept bursting out in her letters to him, with patient sympathy. There is no doubt that he provided a support which drew her affection and trust – although there are hints that he could never kindle her physical passion as Welhaven had done. They married in 1841, and Camilla bore him four sons during the next decade. He died of nerve fever in 1851, and Camilla Collett lived the last forty-four years of her life (more than half of it) as a widow.

There is a reason for beginning this study of Camilla Collett's writings with a detailed account of the men in her life; for it is a prerequisite for an understanding of her as an author. She was born into the most patriarchal period in Norwegian history, and was intimately connected with its leading figures. She was always conscious of the fact that her love for Welhaven and her marriage to Collett were both regarded by her family as a betrayal; they belonged to the opposition and both had attacked her father and her brother in print. She was bold enough to defy family feelings, but not thick-skinned enough to ignore them. She must have felt as if she had been singled out to be martyred by the passions of a time of ferment; she returned again and again in her later writing to the conflicts, trying to set the record straight. The last words in her collected works are addressed to her brother Henrik, dead fifty years, appealing to him to accept her choice of husband.[4]

To some extent her family circumstances were a help to her aspirations to write – she received a relatively good education, made occasional trips abroad, and came into contact with the leading men of her age, hearing discussion of the burning political and cultural issues – but increasingly they came to be felt as a cloak which made her own achievements invisible. The crassest confirmation of the way in which society saw her as an adjunct to her family came in 1876 when, after twenty years of trying to make her living as a writer, she was finally awarded a *half* author's stipend: the government declared that her merits were (a) that her father Nicolai Wergeland was one of the founders of the constitution, (b) that her brother Henrik Wergeland was one of the country's foremost poets, (c) that her husband Jonas Collett had been a distinguished employee of the university, and (d) that her literary works were of such merit that she deserved the nation's gratitude. It must have seemed a rather backhanded compliment.

After her death, literary historians perpetuated the myth. Accounts of her writings in literary histories until quite recently have devoted as much space to her men as to her writings. Her husband is given the lion's share of the credit and she becomes a medium rather than an originator; thus Kristian Elster the Younger in 1924: 'He salvaged her passion and suffering and spiritual strength for a great body of writing', and Francis Bull as late as 1960: 'Collett had succeeded in restoring his wife's courage, calming her restlessness and showing her the way to a great life's work as an author.'[5] In these accounts she becomes the object rather than the subject, a fate she shares with many other women writers.[6]

Writing was a strong drive in her from early youth, but at first it was channelled into letters and diaries rather than fiction.[7] Both tell of her family conflicts, her love of nature, her trips to Christiania; and above all of her love for Welhaven. Many letters are addressed to Emilie Diriks, her shy confidante in Christiania, who admired her greatly, and reflected back her passions like an enlarging mirror. In the letters Camilla paints various scenarios for her own life, experiments with style and language, discovers the vivid metaphors drawn from her own experience which were to become a hallmark of her mature work. She compares her own lack of purpose with the heroic actions of women from Sparta and Rome; she feels condemned to 'a nightcap-life' (*DB* II, p. 316), where she must 'sit at the spinning-wheel in an old, desolate vicarage in a desolate district of a lonely, desolate country' (ibid., p. 289). She plans a magazine, 'Forloren Skildpadde' ('Mock Turtle') with Emilie (of which a couple of handwritten issues did appear) and plays half-ironically with the idea of being an author: 'I must tell you frankly that I do think in all seriousness that Our Lord was thinking of making some such thing out of me, but that he had second thoughts halfway through, and told himself: "Oh no, there are enough in that family"' (ibid., p. 82). Yet she is entirely serious in her comments on style, striving for a natural tone and referring wryly to Paul de Kock's comment that no woman can write two lines without becoming precious. Signs of her wide reading of European literature, particularly German and French, are already apparent. She has discovered George Sand, a writer whose style she greatly admired and to whom she often turned as a model – though she had more ambivalent feelings about her lifestyle: 'I'm just reading George Sand's *Jacques*. How light and fluent these letters are, how natural and entirely free of artificiality is this Fernande – or rather her style. . . . This George Sand is marvellous. She is a blot on our sex as A. Dudevant, but as George S. she is its greatest glory' (ibid., pp. 245–6).

Towards the end of the 1830s she was beginning to write more sustained prose, encouraged by Jonas Collett, who saw in her writing a distraction from morbid dwelling on the past. Her first article, published in 1842 in the journal of Welhaven and Collett's party, *Den Constitutionelle* (The Constitutional), was

'Nogle Strikketøisbetragtninger' ('Reflections of a Knitter'), in which she took men to task for their arrogant treatment of women. Several more articles followed, all anonymous; though the anonymity was an open secret in Christiania. Asbjørnsen and Moe were frequent guests in her home, and both Colletts were interested in their work on folk literature; this led to some collaboration, with Camilla retelling stories she had heard as a child from her nurse, and actually composing some parts of Asbjørnsen's stories. (The join cannot be seen; their styles were so similar that even Jørgen Moe could be deceived and accused Asbjørnsen of being the author of one of her journal articles.) Her interest in folk tales and in the supernatural is evident from many later stories.

Despite her recognition within an inner circle, there was nothing which could have prepared her acquaintances for the appearance of the novel *The District Governor's Daughters*. When Jonas Collett died in 1851, she had made a start on the introduction; but she had got no further, and had been discouraged by him: 'Our civilized society, he maintained, was still in a stage of fermentation, and had not yet formed any foundation on which a novel could be securely built. . . . And perhaps nothing would have come of it if I had not become a widow' (*SV* III, pp. 90–91). That remark is a useful corrective to those who would give Jonas Collett the credit for her achievements. The first part of the novel was ready in 1853, but she was nervous of showing it to anyone; finally she approached the Danish author J.L. Heiberg, and was so encouraged by his positive response in the summer of 1854 that she allowed it to be published that year, and then finished the second part so quickly that it appeared in June 1855.

The District Governor's Daughters: the first swallow

We are taken into the world of the novel by means of the arrival of an outsider, Georg Kold, who has come to take up the post of private secretary to Amtmand Ramm. Through his conversation with a post-house keeper we gain our first impressions of the family:

Finally he asked whether the governor had many children.
'Of course he has children; he has a son.'
'But no daughters?'
'Oh good heavens yes, he has daughters too; there was Miss
Marie and Miss Louise, they got married, one to the clerk and
the other to the tutor who got a country living. Now there's
only Miss Amalie at home.'(*SV* I, p. 244)

This conversation reveals as much about unconscious attitudes as it
does about the situation. First, it is clear that it is the governor's
son who counts; he is immediately visible, whereas the existence
of daughters is revealed only on further probing. Yet as the title
indicates, it is the daughters who are the subject of the novel;
the son disappears to become a student in Christiania. Secondly,
it becomes apparent a few pages later that there is another level
of concealment in this exchange, for there are in fact not three
daughters but four; the fourth one, Sofie, being not only female
but also a child, is not visible at all. Yet it is this fourth daughter,
Sofie, whose fate is to be the focus of the story.

The family live on an estate two days' journey north of
Christiania, in an isolated rural area. They are the leading family
of the district, comfortably off and cultured. Yet this combination
of circumstances, which guarantees the son good prospects, is the
source of their major problem for the four daughters. They have
been educated with one aim: to make a suitable marriage; and
yet their opportunities of doing so are alarmingly restricted. They
travel infrequently, and are practically dependent on attracting the
attention of one of the more or less eligible men who come their
way. Inclination is rarely involved. This is demonstrated by the
fates of the two eldest daughters. Marie, the beauty of the family,
was still single at the age of twenty-five, and so was urged into a
marriage with Broch, a pedantic, middle-aged pietist; within three
years she had lost the desire to live, and simply died. Louise had
been forced to give up her love – because the man she loved had
not declared himself formally – and to marry the tutor Caspers,
who turned out to be a drunkard. During the time of the novel
she is eking out a wretched existence, earning enough money by
weaving to pay for her son to be brought up away from home to
escape from the pernicious influence of his father.

The fates of the two remaining daughters are not decided when Kold arrives; yet little has been learned from experience. For the same pressures under which they gave way still exist, and are embodied in the figure of their mother, fru Ramm.

Fru Ramm is the dominant figure in the parents' partnership, and – it is unequivocally stated by the omniscient narrator – the less noble nature. The governor is a rather sad figure, who wishes everyone well but lacks the energy to take any decisive action. He had married his wife without asking if she loved him, and by way of compensation her energies have been channelled into duty and propriety. In the perverse way of those who have been denied their own fulfilment, she has brought her daughters up in the same spirit, deluding herself that it is best for them:

> I married my husband without loving him passionately, and our marriage has been happy despite that. I found my happiness in resignation and in the fulfilment of my duties. My eldest daughters have not made marriages of inclination either; but they have become happy wives nevertheless . . . And my daughters . . . will one day thank me for it, thank me for teaching them that self-denial is a woman's greatest virtue. (*SV* I, pp. 395–6)

With such a capacity for self-deception, fru Ramm offers little support. Yet she is not tyrannical; she allows Amalie to marry the man she has chosen and refuse a much better match. Even this marriage, though, falls far short of the ideal; for Amalie, with her sentimentally romantic notions, has chosen a man who could not be more different from her dreams of him. Brøcher is a humourless pedant, and the poetry of their engagement culminates in a depressingly prosaic marriage.

As she matures, Sofie becomes conscious of the miserable compromises around her. The marriage of her beloved sister Louise, when Sofie was ten, left a deep fear in her mind, which becomes a fear of love itself. She is an intelligent girl, who loves to read and to think – and yet does so alone, knowing that it is not a 'feminine' activity, and torn between her growing sense of her own worth and her awareness of what life has to offer. It is an awareness which fru Ramm loses no opportunity of reinforcing with well-chosen examples such as that of Jomfru Møllerup, who was so sure of her love that she wrote a passionate letter of declaration, which her beloved repaid by circulating it amongst his friends. For the cardinal crime of declaring herself *first* she has paid with madness, and her life is now spent continually knitting and unravelling the same sock.

Sofie falls in love with Georg Kold; but the effect of her conditioning is such that she devotes all her energies to concealing her emotions. Kold is equally in love, and equally inhibited, though for different reasons. His behaviour is affected by his other friends. His mentor Müller comes to see him at the governor's home and teases him unmercifully about his propensity to fall in love; his predictions that Kold will marry one of the daughters make Kold determined to prove him wrong. He is also made uncertain by Margarethe D, an older woman who has been disappointed in love and whose courageous life inspires him with a determination to act nobly. On her death he receives her letters and diaries, in which she implores him never to force his attentions on a girl, but to wait until he is sure of her love; only then will it be a mutual bond, not an abuse of power. Georg, who is as sensitive as the other suitors in the novel are unfeeling, determines that he will wait for a sign from Sofie.

This stalemate is interrupted by the intervention of another of the novel's rich gallery of characters, Lorenz Brandt.[8] Brandt was a young man of great promise who succumbed to the temptations of the student life in Christiania and became a disreputable drunkard. He too loves Sofie, and his presence stirs Kold into action. Kold saves Sofie from him in a dramatic incident which involves carrying her across a stream; jolted out of her usual firm resolve, she admits her feelings for him, and their happiness seems secure.

A happy ending, however, would go against the whole drift of the novel – and it is not to be. Sofie's consciousness that she has acted wrongly in declaring herself first is reinforced by overhearing Kold declaring to Müller – from whom he is determined to keep his love secret – that she means nothing to him. From then on she refuses to have anything to do with him, never giving him the chance to explain; she agrees to marriage to the much older Dean Rein, who is looking for a companion and a mother for his children. She thus reinforces the pattern of the whole novel, accepting a union of mutual respect, but one where sexual fulfilment will for ever be denied.

The District Governor's Daughters was an ambitious undertaking – an attempt, as Camilla Collett put it in her preface to the third edition, to depict 'the social conditions which prevailed in our patrician Norwegian life after our political rebirth' (*SV* I, p. 239).[9] It is painted on a broad canvas, with a mixture of narrative styles. The main part is related in the third person by an omniscient narrator, who sometimes reports events without comment, but often – as in the depiction of fru Ramm – makes her opinion of characters clear. The narrative is also punctuated by first-person interpolations from several of the characters in the form of letters, diaries and memoirs. The pace of the narrative varies, and there are longueurs in the early part; yet the various threads of the story all have a bearing on the central theme, providing a background against which Sofie's dilemma is thrown into relief.

It will be evident from my summary that there are many parallels between the events in the novel and those of the author's life. Not only does she transmute her own struggle with a love which dares not speak into that of Sofie; many of the details of the novel are drawn directly from her own letters and diaries, and thus acquire a deeper resonance. Margarethe's pronouncements about woman's lot are Camilla's own; in her macabre predictions of her own death, the reference to the 'black casket' reminds the reader of the black casket in which Camilla all her life carried around her correspondence with Welhaven, and Margarethe's doctor's remark that she would probably die 'when the leaves fall from the trees' (*SV* I, p. 343) is a direct quotation from Welhaven's letter of farewell from March 1836: 'Camilla! In the summer when the leaves fall from the trees it is time to part' (*DB* I, p. 235).

The author did not deny the connections; in 1868 she characterized the novel as 'the long-repressed scream of my life' (*SV* II, p. 63), into which she had poured her despair at the fact that her life's greatest victory was over her own feelings. Yet at the same time, she maintained, it was much more: it was an account, in no way exaggerated, of the way in which women of the 'better' classes lived in mid-nineteenth-century Norway:

I have decided to let the story retain the title of *The District Governor's Daughters*; but it could perhaps much more accurately be adapted to *A Country's Daughters*. It provides, *considerably softened*, a portrait of the destinies in store for daughters of the educated classes, especially in more isolated rural areas. . . . In my long life, spent under these conditions, I have not come across anything other than tragedies in these families, nor, as far back as the stories go, heard tell of anything else. (*SV* I, p. 239)

When the novel first appeared, it occasioned considerable critical debate.[10] Intellectuals in Norway were acutely aware of the lack of an independent tradition of prose writing. Poetry had flourished since 1814, with Wergeland and Welhaven in the vanguard; but the only prose writer of any note, Maurits Hansen, was traditional and conservative, and his stories, although popular, soon became dated. This novel, with its minutely observed depiction of everyday life in a Norwegian milieu, was immediately hailed and has since been canonized as Norway's first realistic novel. To modern readers, however, it will probably be the non-realistic aspects which are more apparent; there is a tendency to idealize some of the characters and scenes which is more reminiscent of Poetic Realism than of what we would now understand as Realism proper. With historical hindsight, it is truer to say that *The District Governor's Daughters* represents a transitional stage between the Romantic tradition out of which it grows and the Realist writing which it heralds.

In its content too the novel is a transitional work. It was the first work of Norwegian literature which deserves the name of 'tendenslitteratur' (the Norwegian equivalent of 'littérature engagée'), and the first to take up for serious discussion the rights of women. However, the rights which Camilla Collett advocates are minimal compared with those demanded by activists elsewhere in Europe and in America at this time.[11] Compared with those of Mary Wollstonecraft or her admired George Sand, Camilla Collett's aims are modest indeed. The message of the novel is the need not for practical political reform, but for what she calls 'inner liberation'. Neither here nor anywhere else in her writings does Camilla Collett dispute the fact that marriage is a woman's ideal state, and that to be left an old maid is the saddest fate of all.

It is the conditions of marriage that she is trying to change; it is a woman's feelings which should be consulted rather than a man's more superficial judgement.

The boldness of Camilla Collett's stand shows up more clearly, however, if it is seen in a Scandinavian context. She was writing during a time when pietistic moralizing texts about women's duties as wives and mothers were popular reading, and before writers like Ibsen and Bjørnson challenged traditional assumptions. Her literary sisters in other Scandinavian countries hardly provided radical models. The most popular woman writer of the day, the Danish Thomasine Gyllembourg (1773–1856), was one of her favourites, and she began her novel with the intention to model it largely on the former's 'Hverdagshistorier' (Everyday Stories) from the 1830s; she soon found, however, that she could not conform to the reactionary tone of stories which presented obedient wives as models of femininity. The only comparable feminist writer of the period was Sweden's Fredrika Bremer (1801–65), whose novels from the 1830s, like *Presidentens döttrar* (The President's Daughters, 1834) and *Nina* (1835) also describe the struggles of bourgeois daughters to decide their own fates. Together with Fredrika Bremer's works, *The District Governor's Daughters* could be said to mark the beginning of the raising of public awareness in Scandinavia about the injustices in the position of women.

Camilla Collett's novel, however, is of more than purely historical interest. Though its ideas have been superseded and the social conditions out of which it grew had changed radically before the end of the nineteenth century, it has retained its popularity.[12] The drama of the doomed relationship between Sofie and Kold, the liveliness of the portrayal of family life, the accuracy of the descriptions of the Norwegian countryside – all these have retained their appeal for new generations of readers. Modern literary criticism has returned to the novel with renewed interest in aspects of it which had earlier been obscured by a concentration on its overt message. Closer attention to the novel's symbolism, and in particular to Sofie's 'grotto', reveal it to be a study of female space.[13]

The grotto is a natural formation, part cave, part overhanging cliff, surrounded by thick vegetation and not visible until you are upon it; difficult of access, it is a wild and secretive place in contrast to the gentle, cultivated contours of the estate. It is discovered by Sofie, and associated particularly with her. Her first experience of it is as a small child, on her first real voyage of discovery, when she experiences an ecstatic communion with nature. On her return, however, she is harshly punished by her mother for her dirty, torn clothes and her long absence. The shock of this punishment, which she does not understand, leaves a lasting impression on Sofie, who becomes nervous about experiencing pleasure, wondering always whether retribution will follow.

Thus the grotto becomes for Sofie a joy which must be kept hidden. It is the place where she can relax and do as she pleases. It is to the grotto that she brings her books, to study with a concentration that the world would find eccentric. It is here she plays with her favourite doll, called Louise after her sister – and here that she buries the doll on the day of her sister's wedding. Here she has her decisive meeting with the two suitors, Brandt and Kold. And here, finally, she has her last meeting with Kold just before her marriage, when he appeals to her to break off the engagement, but she has lost her courage and it is too late. Her private space takes on different functions at different stages of the novel; at first a paradise, it becomes a playroom, a school, a church, a fortress and finally a tomb. When Kold leaves her there for the last time, she is sitting with a white shawl over her head 'like a shroud' (SV I, p. 516).

Not only is the grotto a place where Sofie can find refuge, however; it is also herself. The sexual overtones of the grotto episodes suggest a Freudian interpretation, in which the grotto stands for the female sex organs – a place at first innocently associated with pleasure, rapidly overlaid by repression following her mother's reaction.[14] Sofie's upbringing does not allow free expression of her sexuality, but inhibits her so that she almost manages to conceal her passion.

In line with this interpretation, the rivals Brandt and Kold become the two sides of her personality which are struggling for control. The names are significant; Brandt (= firebrand), a man in whom wildness is dominant, represents Sofie's repressed libido, her id: whereas Kold (= cold), the correct, socially acceptable character whose passion is spiritual rather than physical, is her superego. In the clash between them in the grotto, Sofie chooses Kold; but this rejection of Brandt entails – if the symbols are thus interpreted – a rejection of her natural sexual drive, and thus makes it impossible for her to find fulfilment in a sexual union. This interpretation of the novel demonstrates that Sofie is in an impossible situation: she can never reconcile her spiritual and her physical needs. Her possibility of happiness is dashed not by a combination of chance circumstances but by her own insoluble conflicts.

A more recent interpretation has challenged the Freudian one, which interprets the novel on male premisses – reducing Sofie to a sexual object of the two males' desires and giving their rivalry a disproportionate importance.[15] Instead of seeing the plot in terms of achievement or denial of sexual fulfilment, it can be interpreted as a woman's struggle for the achievement of her own integrity. The grotto thus becomes not just a sexual symbol but, together with the countryside around it, a 'female landscape' which takes on the contours of a woman's body.[16] Such a landscape commonly expresses a woman's sense of her own private identity; it is a 'Temple of Solitude', a refuge from the demands of the Other, be they sexual or merely temporal. Sofie's private hours of studying in her grotto help her to develop her own opinions and put her in touch with her feelings. It is a temporary victory, for she must leave her grotto at the end, returning to the traditional female role; yet it is a demonstration that independence of spirit is attainable. This reading of the novel allows for a somewhat more positive conclusion than the one which sees Sofie as a passive victim.

The District Governor's Daughters is a novel which has proved fruitful in many contexts, and provoked interpretations which often go beyond the author's conscious intentions. Instead of losing its relevance as its historical moment passed, it has acquired new relevance. Indeed, one could argue that its central point about the vital importance of *inner* liberation is one that has not lost its force despite progress in practical reforms since the 1850s. That was certainly Camilla Collett's opinion in 1872 when she looked back on what her novel had achieved:

As it has been understood to be speaking out for women's liberation, the first swallow in this country, one might now be of the opinion that we have progressed far beyond it. I cannot share that opinion: we have still not reached the stage of liberation with which my story is concerned. In our current attempts to improve the situation of women we have begun *from outside* instead of beginning *from inside*. We have achieved some concrete advantages, whilst there still in the invisible internal world are a thousand abuses which go unnoticed, a thousand chains which need to be loosed. (*SV* II, p. 183)

Later writing

After *The District Governor's Daughters*, Camilla Collett wrote no more novels. Having poured her life's drama into this one work, some critics maintain, she had no more material. Yet she has created other short fictions; it is truer to say that sustained fictional writing was not the genre which came most easily to her. The novel is episodic in structure, and she preferred the short story or folk tale, in which the essence of a human fate could be captured in a cameo sketch.

Both before and after 1855 she wrote stories which were published in 1860 as *Fortællinger* (Short Stories). The collection covers a wide range of moods, from the tragic 'Kongsgaard', in which young lovers are parted and condemned to an early grave by the treachery of a brother who conceals the father's consent, to the self-mocking 'Oktober-fantasier' ('October Fantasies'), the story of four female friends who are given the gift of tongues by a passing comet, and make stirring political speeches – only to forget it all again and return to their domestic arrangements as the comet disappears. The collection also includes an early piece, 'Langs Andelven' ('By the Duck River') from 1842, written in the form of a teasing letter to Asbjørnsen about folk tales she has discovered, and including a tale of her own invention, 'Prinsesse Killinkas Veninde' ('Princess Killinka's Friend'). There is a lightness of tone in many of these stories which can be deceptive, like the sting in the tail of a casual remark about cows who wander off the path: 'Some of them, who display too great a tendency to be bold and romantic, have to have a plank tied across their eyes; then they stay up on the smooth and level path. Such a plank is a marvellous invention; it can also be used successfully on other kinds of foreheads' (*SV* I, p. 155).

I de lange Nætter (In the Long Nights, 1862), her next work, is an autobiographical account purported to be addressed by the narrator to her insomniac sisters, in order to shorten the long nights. With this typically self-deprecating introduction, the narrator embarks on a story which for much of the book is Camilla's own; an account of what it was like to grow up at Eidsvoll with Nicolai and Henrik Wergeland, of her experiences of being sent away to school and of her half-pretended dismay at suddenly finding herself an author. It has always been Camilla Collett's second most popular work, and has aroused renewed attention with the recent interest in women's autobiographical writings.[17]

In 1863 Camilla Collett published a slim pamphlet – it takes up only 12 pages in her collected works – called *En undersøisk Parlament* (An Underwater Parliament). Reminiscent of Chaucer's *The Parlement of Fowles* in its title, like the latter it portrays a debate, though this time between fish instead of birds, and with a more outspoken satirical intent. The issue is not how to be successful in love but how to make ends meet as a widow – a subject to which Camilla Collett's later writings make constant reference. In a final dark vision the flying fish sees a still, black lake in the middle of a thick forest, with an endless queue of black-clad women emptying cups into it: 'It is the lake of widows' tears – that lake which never dries up, but never, however much it is filled, spills over its banks; and the roads which lead to it are the paths of need and loneliness, through the forests of sorrow and care' (*SV* II, p. 51).

The element of documentary or polemical material had been growing in Camilla Collett's works since the mid-1850s; and after 1863 she practically abandoned fictional writing, producing collections of essays, articles, travel descriptions, or open letters, direct contributions to debate. From 1868 to 1873 she published five selections called *Sidste Blade* 1–5 (Last Leaves); then this rather melancholy title was exchanged for more challenging ones: *Fra de Stummes Leir* (From the Camp of the Mutes) came out in 1877, and two volumes entitled *Mod Strømmen* I–II (Against the Current) appeared in 1879 and 1885. (The title of *Mod Strømmen* contains a reference to a well-known folk tale, 'Kjerringa mot strømmen' ['The Old Woman against the Current'], about a man and his wife who could never agree. Finally, the man grew so exasperated at his wife's obstinacy that he picked her up and flung her in the river. But instead of being carried away downstream by the rapid current, as he expected, she floated away upstream, contrary to the last.)

Camilla Collett's writings became more outspoken as she grew older (she was sixty-six when *Mod Strømmen* I appeared). In 1873 she had begun to write under her own name. The central issue remained the same – the position of women in contemporary society – and Camilla Collett continued to insist that *inner* liberation was the first essential; but she did come to realize that practical reforms were also necessary. She was one of the few women who spoke out about the evils of prostitution, a subject which it was not considered proper for a woman to know about; she joined in the polemics of the sexual morality debate in the 1880s, protesting in an open letter from 1888 about the unfairness of the double standard of morality and its devastating consequences for women:

> It doesn't seem to upset [society's] logic in the slightest that the putting into practice of its theory of moral inequality, full freedom for him and strict chastity for her, is based on a physical impossibility. A victim for each hunter's shot, – for every acceptable moral transgression there must be an unacceptable one. Society split between forgiving and punishing! Only here it follows the opposite method from that applied to rabies epidemics: it is the victims who are struck down, the despoilers who go free. (*SV* III, p. 451)

In all Camilla Collett's contributions to contemporary debate, her knowledge of European ideas and movements is striking. She was instrumental in introducing European authors to Norway, as a recent French critic has observed:

Like Germaine de Staël, Camilla Collett was also a great cosmopolitan author. She spent long periods abroad, she learnt much in Italy, in Germany, and above all in France, and she gave the Norwegian people the benefit of her discoveries; she is largely responsible for drawing Norway out of the considerable moral isolation into which it had been plunged by National Romanticism. She introduced George Sand, Legouvé, Balzac to the writers and artists of her country, she revealed many unknown aspects of realistic and social literature. . . . For Norway she opened wide the windows on Europe.[18]

She was familiar with publications from abroad on the question of women, and quoted with approval John Stuart Mill and Ernest Legouvé's *Histoire morale des femmes* (1847), whereas the reactionary *La Femme* (1848) by Adolphe Monod came in for withering scorn, as did the repressive Napoleonic Code. She continually viewed the Norwegian struggle for women's emancipation in the context of progress in other countries, and the result never fell out in Norway's favour. Things were bad enough in Germany, where women were treated as inferior, and France, where they were set on pedestals but denied participation in public life; but in Norway they were simply not visible. England represented the ideal for Camilla Collett – the land in which *men* were working for women's equality. The humorous 'Brev fra en ung Klodebeboerske til en Korrespondentinde i Maanen' ('Letter from a Young Earth-dweller to a Penfriend on the Moon', 188-; *SV* III, pp. 265–8) describes the situation in terms of a chariot race between France, Germany, England and Norway, in which all the chariots have one large and one small wheel; England wins easily, whilst Norway is discovered to possess only one wheel, and that the big one. (If she had lived another few years, the author might have changed her mind about the winner!)

Camilla Collett's own personality is everywhere evident in her writings. She did not just read about the rest of Europe, but travelled through it continually during the second half of her life, driven by her need to escape from the sterility of Christiania despite penury and her own frailty. Undeterred by frequent accidents (she was remarkably absent-minded and accident-prone), she reports from European cities in a way which links the personal with the general and illuminates both.[19] A visit to Versailles prompts historical reminiscences which range from Napoleon to Mary Queen of Scots to Marie Antoinette ('Tre Dage i Versailles' ['Three Days in Versailles'], *SV* II, pp. 113–30); an account of Balzac's wonderful portrayal of Parisian boarding-houses in *Le Père Goriot* prefaces a tragi-comic description of her own vicissitudes in such places ('Pensioner i Paris' ['Parisian Boarding-houses'], *SV* II, pp. 97–112).

Camilla Collett often bases her judgements of works of European literature on the author's portrayal of women. The long essay 'Kvinden i Litteraturen' ('Women in Literature') in *From the Camp of the Mutes* (*SV* II, pp. 376–490) looks at the history of the novel from this unusual perspective, and takes European authors from Goethe onwards to task for the passivity of their female figures. The modern novel exhibits alarming tendencies towards sadism; a woman of any independence exists only in order to be conquered by the man – or she must die. Her analysis of contrasting female types in French novels prefigures modern studies of the Mary/Eve or angel/monster stereotypes.[20] She is aware, too, of how women writers can be influenced by popular mythology; their novels often contain female figures who are no less negative than those of their male counterparts.

Camilla Collett had decided opinions about her fellow Norwegian authors.[21] Jonas Lie was most congenial, with his descriptions of 'the awakening human dignity in women' (*SV* II, p. 438). Her relationship with Bjørnson was fraught; she admired his stance on the sexual morality question, but was suspicious of his politics and of his willingness to help her – somewhat unfairly, because although he could be quite rude about her in his letters,[22] he nevertheless did what he could to help her into print. The man himself she found alarming – to the extent of literally running away from him on one occasion.

Her attitude to Ibsen changed as his career progressed. The heroic Viking women of his early dramas filled her with enthusiasm, but Brand was a sadist in his treatment of Agnes, and Solveig in *Peer Gynt* (1867) was a depressing figure: 'In Solveig we meet this silent, self-destructive brooding over something awaited without hope and long since thrown away – thrown away through her own powerlessness to intervene and to act herself – the fate of thousands of women in our country!' (*SV* II, p. 419). The plays of his middle period, like *A Doll's House* and *Ghosts*, with their stronger female characters, not surprisingly met with her approval – and typically, she spoke out in defence of *Ghosts* in the early 1880s, defying the almost universal opprobrium which had greeted its outspokenness about venereal disease. Ibsen's plays at this time may well have been influenced by her, for he knew both her and her ideas well by the end of the 1870s, and she had told him off roundly for his self-sacrificing women. She thought she recognized herself in the figure of Ellida Wangel in *Fruen fra Havet* (*The Lady from the Sea*, 1888), and Ibsen's letter to her on that occasion, though it is somewhat elusive on that point, confirms that she was an influence on his writing:

> Yes, there are points of contact. Many, indeed. And you have seen them and felt them. I mean things which for me could only be a vague supposition. But it is now many years ago that you, by virtue of your life of spiritual endeavour, first began to play a role in my authorship in one form or another.[23]

Camilla Collett played many roles in the course of her long life: as sister, daughter, wife and mother; as model and muse; and above all as author, literary critic and polemicist. She was eternally dissatisfied, both on a personal level with lack of recognition, co-operation and money, and on behalf of her sex. Measured by more militant standards, she was seeking only limited equality; but in the context of her time and society she was radical and outspoken. Ibsen showed his usual perceptiveness when he advised her friends not to try to cure her dissatisfaction; for that was the fount from which her writing sprang.

3
Amalie Skram (1846–1905)

Early life and writings

Amalie Skram was born Berthe Amalie Alver on 22 August 1846, in Bergen, Norway's second largest town. Bergen had for centuries been Norway's main trading centre, a west-coast seaport whose prominence dated from the Middle Ages, when it had been a Hanseatic town; by the middle of the nineteenth century it was still a bustling, cosmopolitan town which was the focal point for trading along the extensive western coast and had stronger links with other European seaports than with the capital Christiania, far away over the mountains. Although the first Norwegian railway was built in 1851, it was not until 1894 that Christiania and Bergen were linked by rail; throughout the nineteenth century, the people of Bergen were regarded by those from the capital almost as a foreign race.

Amalie's family lived in the heart of Bergen, close to Fisketorget, the marketplace where the fish on which Bergen's prosperity rested were sold; her absorption in the atmosphere and her close observation of the lives of ordinary people were to bear fruit in her later writings. Her family were not well off; her father ran a small shop and her mother was a cobbler's daughter. Despite this, her mother saw to it that Amalie and her four brothers were educated at the town's best schools. It was more than the family finances could bear; her father went bankrupt when she was fifteen. He left for America to try to make money, hoping that his wife and younger children would follow; but Amalie's mother refused to go, even though he returned to collect her. The family split up, and in the 1870s it was reported that he was dead – though later evidence suggests that he changed his name and remarried, for another and final announcement of his death reached Amalie in 1898.[1]

The relationship between her parents, and between her and them, was always a difficult subject for Amalie; she left little comment in her letters and autobiographical sketches, and it was not until 1898, in a letter to Erik Skram, that she attempted any analysis.[2] She felt that her mother was most to blame, and tended to idolize her absent father. Her fictional works often portray fraught relationships between children and parents, especially between mother and daughter.

The most immediate effect of the crisis, however, was that Amalie, at the age of eighteen, married a wealthy sea captain, Bernt Ulrik August Müller. She bore him two sons, Jacob and Ludvig, in 1866 and 1868, and between 1864 and 1871 accompanied him on many voyages, later taking the children too. Thus she visited many exotic places: the West Indies, Mexico, the Mediterranean and the Black Sea – and once they sailed round the world. It was an opportunity which in any other circumstances would have been out of the question for a woman of her time and class. Life at sea suited her; she was a born sailor, healthy and energetic. In this way her marriage gave her much; in other ways it was a less ideal arrangement. Again she made little comment in her letters at the time,[3] but from later hints it is evident that her marriage as an inexperienced adolescent to an older and experienced man was a great shock. Physically their relationship was never happy, and the intellectually curious girl had little in common with the practical sailor, despite his best efforts. In 1871 they settled in Bergen, and the situation deteriorated until Amalie had a breakdown in 1877, due to family pressure on her to stay with her husband against her will. They separated in 1878.

Amalie was beautiful, a fact to which many contemporary comments as well as her portraits bear witness. This could be an advantage; no doubt it was a major factor in enabling her to make a good marriage, and facilitated her entrance into cultural circles in Bergen and later in Christiania. Yet she regarded it increasingly as a handicap; it so often meant that men would adopt an ironic, flirtatious tone with her instead of discussing a subject seriously. It also led them to expect a sensuality in her make-up which for a long time was dormant. Her first husband had failed to awaken it; she was suspected by some – and probably suspected herself – of being frigid. It was not until she met Erik Skram in 1882 that she 'understood what it was to love'.[4]

Before that, however, she had been taking her first steps as a critic. Her first review was printed in 1877, whilst she was in

Bergen, and she carried on writing reviews whilst she was living in Fredrikshald with her brother in 1878–81 and in Christiania in 1881–4. After 1884, when she was concentrating on her own fiction, she practically ceased reviewing. Her early reviews were written anonymously or with the signature -ie; but from 1883 onwards, in her articles as in her fiction, she used her own name. Despite the anonymity, however, there was no timidity in her attitude as a reviewer; she wrote with authority as one who could set what she read in a European context, and was not slow to criticize faults. In her first review, of the Danish author J.P. Jacobsen's novel *Fru Marie Grubbe*, her enthusiasm for the book did not prevent her taking the author to task for insufficient psychological motivation. Her criteria are already clear: she places great importance on psychological accuracy in character portrayal, and singles out for praise authors who have 'filled their minds and hearts with the ideas of their time'.[5]

Amalie Skram was particularly receptive to the realist writers of the 1870s and 1880s. She wrote with enthusiasm about Ibsen, Bjørnson, Collett, Kielland, Garborg; she read Dostoevsky avidly, and wrote the first Norwegian review of Tolstoy's work in 1879. She welcomed Camilla Collett's *Against the Current* as a prophetic work. Ibsen's early plays struck a sympathetic chord; in a long review of *A Doll's House* (1880), she commented on the skill with which the characters' interrelationships are explored, and underlined the message that true marriage will not occur until husbands and fathers treat their wives and daughters as equal human beings, and until women stop accepting their oppression. When the reviled *Ghosts* appeared, she courageously defended Ibsen for having demonstrated the logical consequences of a hypocritical social system; and she maintained the author's right, like a student of anatomy, to dissect the most horrible of society's corpses in order to understand and learn. (Ibsen's later works, however, were to have less appeal to her; *The Wild Duck* she dismissed as 'a miserable piece of work' and *The Master Builder* was 'boring and hysterical'.[6] When Ibsen moved away from his concentration on social issues towards a more symbolic drama, she could not follow him.)

These articles provide evidence of her growing interest in the position of women and the consequences of what she called 'the damned system of concealment [*fortielsessystem*]'[7] which kept young girls ignorant of the facts of life before committing them, totally unprepared, to marriage. From the beginning she took an active part in the debate about sexual morality which was to dominate the 1880s. Opponents of the double standard were divided into two camps: those, like Georg Brandes and the members of the Christiania Bohemia, who advocated free love for both sexes, and those, like Bjørnson, who thought on the contrary that chastity before marriage should be the ideal for both. Amalie Skram, like most of the other women who took part in the debate, rejected the idea of free love as being unworkable; it would serve only to perpetuate injustice in a society which still discriminated against unmarried mothers and 'fallen women'.[8] Her reaction to Bjørnson's *A Gauntlet*, which she reviewed on its first performance in 1883, is typical. She found it lacking as a play – it was more like a thesis – but welcomed its message and saluted Bjørnson in biblical terms as the prophet of a power 'whose kingdom is not of this world'.[9] But it was the relationship between the mother and daughter in the play which interested her most; for society relies for the perpetuation of its 'system of concealment' on the connivance of mothers in concealing the truth from their daughters, and fru Riis's acquiescence in this hypocrisy 'for her daughter's sake' made the lie possible.

Whilst she was busy as a reviewer, Amalie Skram was also beginning to make her mark as an author. She had experimented with fictional and dramatic writing, but her first published work, a short story called 'Madam Høiers Lejefolk' ('Madame Høier's Tenants') was not printed until 1882, when she was thirty-six.

The setting of the story is a Bergen back street, and it is a bleak study of the poorest of the poor. Madame Høier's tenants are a destitute family: a crippled husband who has taken to drink and an exhausted wife who has just increased her already large family by giving birth to twins. As there is no money to pay the rent, they are thrown out into the street, baby twins and all, in the middle of winter; and in an attempt to persuade the babies to sleep, the hapless mother gives them brandy, which kills them. She is imprisoned as a result, with at least the comfort, as the ironic last line informs us, that 'she would have a roof over her head for a time' (*SV* V, p. 15).[10] The central figure of the story is Madame Høier herself, a termagant who regards her lodgers as scheming parasites determined to cheat her. Devoid of pity, she is concerned only that she should not be exploited; she is indifferent to the fate of the wretched family. Similarly, the narrative itself is devoid of sentimentality; there is no romantic aura over the young family, whose children are filthy and covered in sores and whose parents are apathetic. Amalie Skram's sense for the telling detail is already in evidence; the grimy curtains with undarned runs in them and the ragged blinds which all hang crooked characterize the house itself before the characters appear. It is minutely observed and dispassionately presented, making its point without indignant rhetoric.

The story was received with interest, and its author was encouraged. But the beginning of her literary career was a time of great financial and personal struggle. She was conscious of the fact that she was starting late, and felt that she would never achieve anything worthwhile, a worry which was to continue to dog her. Newly divorced, she was trying to earn enough to keep her two sons; and her situation was a vulnerable one. She had hopes of being appointed editorial secretary of a new radical journal to be started by Bjørnson, Ernst Sars and Georg Brandes; but when her application was publicly discussed in 1881, she was terrified that the association of her name with those of such notorious men might mean that she would lose custody of her sons in an imminent court case.[11] In the event she did not get the post, and she was certain that it was because she was a woman.[12] Nearly thirty years after the publication of Camilla Collett's *The District Governor's Daughters*, it was still considered inappropriate for a woman, particularly a mother, to take part in public life.

Despite these problems, the years in Christiania in the early 1880s were exciting ones for Amalie. She became acquainted with the radical writers of the day, including Bjørnson, Garborg, Kielland and Brandes, all of whom encouraged her writing; with several of them she kept up a correspondence for many years. Her relationship with Bjørnson is worth a chapter on its own; having first approached him anonymously as a nervous acolyte in 1878, she grew in confidence through a correspondence which was to last for the whole of her life, until she was replying to his frank and often dismissive comments on her work with equal frankness and indignation.[13] She was an outspoken letter-writer, not afraid to declare roundly to her male colleagues that she loved them for their achievements, but equally not slow to denounce the same people to their faces when they displeased her.

The meeting with the Danish journalist and novelist Erik Skram in 1882 was a turning point for Amalie. As well as her lover, he became her adviser in literary matters; their common passion for literature was a part of their bond, and it seems that he recognized that her talent was greater than his and devoted himself to nurturing it. In 1884 they married and Amalie moved to Copenhagen, where she was to live, with brief interruptions, for the rest of her life.

1884–94: Novels of marriage and *The People of Hellemyr*

The next decade was one of great productivity for Amalie: she published six novels and a play, as well as several short stories, some of which were almost novel length. The main body of her production during this period can be divided broadly into two categories, the larger of which is her novels and stories of marriage; the main titles in this category are *Constance Ring* (1885), 'Knut Tandberg' (1886), *Lucie* (1888), 'Fru Ines' (1891), *Forraadt* (*Betrayed*, 1892) and the play *Agnete* (1893). In between these works she wrote the series of four novels which have the common title *Hellemyrsfolket* (The People of Hellemyr): *Sjur Gabriel* (1887), *To venner* (Two Friends, 1887), *S.G. Myre* (1890) and *Avkom* (Descendants, not published until 1898).

Constance Ring faces squarely the problem of social hypocrisy in sexual matters. The eponymous heroine is a naive girl, who discovers that society is totally different from what her upbringing and religion have taught her to expect. She is married at the start of the novel to a merchant sixteen years older, a well-meaning man who loves her passionately but awakens only repulsion in her. His jovial bonhomie she finds vulgar, and physical contact she tolerates but cannot enjoy; nothing has prepared her for this. He takes comfort in an affair with their maid, who becomes pregnant; when Constance discovers this she demands a divorce, only to discover with horror that her best friend, her priest and her family unite in their efforts to dissuade her. After all, it is no more than most wives have to endure, as her aunt explains: 'The world is organized in such a way that women have to get married; they are unhappy, for a while at least; but an unmarried woman – well, her fate is far more miserable' (*SV* I, p. 124).

Constance returns, cowed, to her husband. Shortly afterwards he dies in a shipwreck, and she drifts into apathy, from which she is rescued by Lorck, a man of the world who had earlier tried to seduce her but had been so chastened by her refusal that he had changed his way of life. For a while their marriage is happy, and he even overcomes her frigidity so that she discovers physical rapture; but their relationship is destroyed by her discovery that he too had a mistress from the lower orders, who bore him a child whilst he was supposedly languishing with unrequited love for Constance. This time her anguish is not just for herself but on behalf of the whole class of women exploited by cynical seducers:

> That poor woman with her child! Why had she been repudiated? With what right did men behave like that? They enjoyed the youth of these women, their health, their love, as if they had been created for that purpose alone, they enjoyed until they were gorged. If they saw something more attractive, they tossed them aside and abandoned them to the fate which men's brutal egoism had prepared for them. (*SV* I, pp. 237–8)

After this second shock, Constance thinks she has no illusions left; yet she is drawn again to a totally different man, the timid Meier, who has worshipped her from afar. Here at last she thinks she has found an exception; yet she cannot take the step of committing adultery until she has discovered Lorck again making love to the girl who was his mistress. In her fury she gives herself to Meier, only to discover from a photograph in his wallet that he too has a mistress – Constance's own seamstress. She returns home and poisons herself.

The novel has been compared with Flaubert's *Madame Bovary* (1856–7).[14] It was a novel Amalie Skram knew; she read French easily, and was well acquainted with contemporary literature. Lorck even asks Constance early in the novel if she has read *Madame Bovary*, to which she replies: 'I'm so tired of all these frivolous women' (p. 43). Similarities of plot between the two novels are evident: the inexperienced heroine, to whom marriage is a disappointment, seeks fulfilment in relationships to two other men, the cynical man of the world followed by the sensitive artist, and finally, after they have all disappointed her, takes her own life. The realism of the two novels is similar too: in both, the cracked façade of respectable bourgeois life is mercilessly exposed, and no veil is drawn over the physical repulsiveness of death by poisoning. Yet to lay too much emphasis on the similarity of the novels obscures important differences between them. *Madame Bovary* is a study of an individual, a woman whose exaggerated aspirations are bound to be frustrated. Constance also cherishes illusory aspirations; yet this novel broadens into an indictment of a social organization which condones hypocrisy, which rears girls like Constance as unsuspecting victims of men who, as Lorck says, 'do not live chastely; they *cannot*, they *should* not do so' (p. 253).

The disastrous consequences of an alliance between a fresh young girl and an older man with a jaded palate is a theme to which Amalie Skram returns with crusading zeal. Fru Ines in the story of that name has been married as a girl to a world-weary diplomat who, it is suggested, has unnatural sexual appetites and whom she will not allow near her; she has become a renowned coquette, who beneath the façade of sensuality fears that she is frigid. She takes a young lover, only to be confirmed in her belief that sexual ecstasy is something she will never know. Ory in *Betrayed* has been kept in ignorance of the facts of life by a mother who expostulates on the day of her wedding to sea-captain Riber: 'Why should I sully your imagination before it was necessary?' (*SV* V, p. 41). The impression that sex is dirty is one Ory never overcomes, and her sexual curiosity, denied a healthy outlet, is channelled into an obsessive desire to know every detail of her husband's former sexual adventures. Both stories are permeated with grotesque fantasies and dreams, and both end in violent death; fru Ines's lover commits suicide after she has rejected him, and she dies of a haemorrhage after aborting their child; whereas in *Betrayed* it is Captain Riber who leaps into the sea, hounded to death by his wife's morbid probing into his sexuality whilst she denies him any outlet for his desire.

Of particular interest in the context of the sexual morality debate is the novel from 1888, *Lucie*. At the time when she was writing it, Amalie Skram was also making a public stand about the matter: in 1887 she published an article in defence of

Christian Krohg's novel *Albertine* (1886), the story of a poor girl raped by a policeman and forced into a life of prostitution, which had just been banned for immorality. In the article she praised the style of the novel, which had obviously been observed with the eye of a painter, and drew attention to the plight of prostitutes, with whom she had previously been disinclined to sympathize. She underlined the operation of the double standard which branded prostitutes whilst men went scot-free. Why should women be ruined by such behaviour any more than men? 'There are examples of so-called women of ill repute becoming good, loyal, efficient and self-sacrificing wives.'[15]

The heroine of *Lucie* is precisely such a 'woman of ill repute', not a prostitute, but almost equally reprehensible – a Tivoli dancer who has had an illegitimate child. She is the mistress of the respectable lawyer Theodor Gerner, who marries her in order to keep her. Physical sex comes as no shock to this sensuous young woman, who is as experienced as her husband; yet the match proves no less disastrous than those in the texts I have just discussed, for different reasons. Despite his resolution to start afresh, Gerner cannot help dwelling on his wife's past, and her sensuality, which at first attracted him to her, becomes a constant painful reminder of her origins. He watches her every move with consuming jealousy, and criticizes her easy manners until she hardly dares move for fear of offending him. The faults are not entirely on his side, however. The subtle psychological portrayal of Lucie demonstrates how she has been irrevocably marked by her past; she delights in narcissistic self-contemplation (she frequently admires herself in a mirror) and cannot adapt to the refined drawing-room behaviour of a bourgeois wife. She is not monogamous, any more than the experienced men of Amalie Skram's novels usually are; she cannot help but respond sexually to a sexual advance. Finally her bitterness at Theodor's cruelty prompts her to run off; she lies down exhausted in a field to dream of making love to a young lieutenant with whom she has danced, and is raped by an ugly stranger. Returning to Theodor, she finds herself pregnant, and takes to religion in an effort to ward off the possibility that the child might be the rapist's. When it is born, however, she sees from a birthmark on its face that her prayers have failed, and loses the will to live, dying of childbed fever.

Around the fate of Lucie are woven discussions of the burning issues of the day, which are relevant to her situation. There is talk of Bjørnson's *A Gauntlet*, Krohg's *Albertine*, Jonas Lie's *The Commodore's Daughters*. It is the women in the novel who support the new radical ideas, whereas the men prefer the status quo. Lucie is befriended by fru Reinertson, a freethinker who – in contrast to most members of the circle – has no prejudices about her past and believes it is an advantage if women enter marriage with some experience. She helps the amazed Lucie to realize: 'So she was just as good as Theodor, and didn't need to be ashamed because she'd been like that' (*SV* IV, p. 99). But in the last resort she is no help; Lucie is not in a strong enough position to challenge the social mores.

It is remarkable how often Amalie Skram's novels of marriage end in death; at least one of the partners, more often the woman, is literally destroyed. Constance Ring is compared to 'a sickly plant' at the beginning of the novel, and seems to be waiting to die from the start; 'Fru Ines' and *Betrayed* are filled with portents of death and destruction. Sex is often inextricably linked to violent death, as if the two are associated in the author's consciousness. There are exceptions to this, however; there are some women in Amalie Skram's works who defy the destructive potential of their relationships. Birgit Tandberg in the story 'Knut Tandberg' proves to be stronger than her weak and selfish husband; when she discovers he has fallen in love with a younger woman, she releases him from their marriage, because where there is no love, there should be no tie. The heroine of the play *Agnete* places all her hopes on love; when the man she has secretly loved declares his love for her, she tells him she wants no secrets from him: 'For the only thing I have craved and yearned for is to strip myself spiritually naked for the man I love on this earth, so that he should see me just as I am, and if possible love me despite the fact that he knows me fully' (*SV* V, p. 206). Her hopes are shattered when he has to tell her his love is not strong enough to bear the truth – that she has been lying and stealing from friends in order to keep up appearances, when actually she is destitute. Yet disappointment does not destroy her; though happiness eludes her, she quietly accepts her only alternative, which is to become a housekeeper for her widowed brother. For women like this, failure in love can be borne; but for those who have early on 'been blighted' (a phrase Amalie Skram uses several times about herself in her letters), there seems no hope of recovery. Yet the author possessed the spiritual strength to draw on her own sufferings as a source for art; she contained both kinds of woman within herself.

In between her novels of marriage, Amalie Skram was working on the tetralogy *The People of Hellemyr*. These novels are set not in the middle classes but at the lowest level of society, where no façade can conceal the grey hopelessness of poverty; it is a return to the setting of 'Madame Høier's Tenants', of which characters in her other works catch the occasional horror-stricken glimpse. The four novels trace the lives of a working-class family through four generations.

The first volume, *Sjur Gabriel* (1887), introduces a fisherman's family in the Bergen district. Sjur Gabriel and his wife Oline, with their many children, are miserably poor; their lives are passed in grey toil, and starvation constantly threatens. As in 'Madame Høier', there is no suggestion of the 'nobility of labour' or of redemption through self-sacrifice; Oline, worn out by childbirth, has taken to drink to forget her misery, and her embittered husband beats her senseless when he finds her drunk. The one lighter point in the story comes with the birth of the youngest child, Vesle-Gabriel, whom his father has to care for as Oline is ill after the birth; with him he forms a bond which gives his life a purpose – but then the child falls ill and dies despite his father's desperate attempts to save him, and Sjur Gabriel takes to drink himself.

The second volume, *To Venner* (Two Friends) was published in the same year; once Amalie Skram had begun writing, it progressed swiftly. This novel and the next take as their central character the grandson of Sjur Gabriel and Oline, Sivert. *Two Friends* is the name of the ship on which he is a cabin boy, and the novel follows his adventures at sea. After struggling to adjust to the ferocity of the sea and the brutality of some of the crew, he learns to cope; yet he carries within him his own downfall in the shape of an irresistible urge to steal and to lie. In his letters home to his parents he tells tall stories of how he saved the ship single-handed. He even steals money from two passengers who have befriended him; despite his good qualities and his earnest desire to 'get on in the world', his nature is against him.

Sivert's feeling that his efforts to make something of himself will always be blocked grow stronger in the next novel, *S.G. Myre* (1890). Here he has returned to Bergen and found work as a shop assistant; he is optimistic, yet every time he has worked himself into a position of trust, he has to do something to ruin his chances. He spends more than he earns on impressing his friends and on risky speculations, lies and drinks and steals from the till – and is inevitably discovered. He feels persecuted through most of the novel by the mocking finger of fate in the form of his grandmother Oline, now a public drunkard and a figure of fun in the town, who seems to pop up whenever he feels that he might break with the past in order to remind him of his origins. Finally he can bear it no more, and one day, when he meets her on a lonely stretch of coast, he hits her and accidentally kills her.

As well as following the fate of Sivert, this novel also tells the story of his wife Petra. She was a housekeeper for the rich consul Smith and his invalid wife, and has pretensions to better herself – which lead only to her becoming Smith's mistress. When he rejects her, she marries Sivert because 'She had to marry somebody some time, and it was all the same to her who it was' (*SV* II, p. 429). Sivert has been in love with the unattainable Lydia Munthe, and though he is determined to love Petra, he feels that it is unlikely to be a successful marriage.

The course of this marriage and the fates of its children are the focus of the final novel *Avkom* (Descendants), which I shall consider here although it was not published until 1898. The marriage turns out as disastrously as one might have foreseen; the inadequate Sivert cannot provide for his family and turns to crime, ending up in prison, and Petra is selfish and unloving. As a mother she becomes a monster, Amalie Skram's fullest portrait of 'the wicked mother'; she denies her children any affection – and even enough food, although she always has something extra for herself. There is no escape for the children, Severin and Fie. Severin becomes a poverty-stricken student who resorts to stealing from a friend – and, when he is found out, hangs himself in shame. Fie is pressurized into marrying a rich older man whom she does not even like in an unsuccessful attempt to rescue her father from financial ruin. The only ray of hope at the end of the novel is Fie's letter to her mother in which she accuses her of lack of love and declares that she will love her *own* daughter, whatever she has to put up with in her marriage. So the chain may be broken for the next generation.

There is a shift in perspective as the tetralogy proceeds. The last two novels, both set in Bergen, broaden out to become a study of a whole society, a panorama containing a range of figures from all social levels. The picture which emerges is not a rosy one: most people's lives are a struggle to put a good face on things, if they have not given up altogether, and with few exceptions, marriages are unhappy unions between incompatible people. The women are generally worse off; in this society as in Camilla Collett's, marriage is still a woman's only respectable career, and few of them are granted the luxury of marrying for love. A pattern that repeats itself is that of a lower-class girl seduced by a rich man with whom she falls in love; but marriage is impossible and her experience serves only to make her realize what happiness she must forgo.

The Hellemyr novels cost Amalie Skram much; there are many harrowing scenes of pain and despair, and the view of humanity which informs them is a gloomy one. The final novel took so many years because of its toll on her; she had to give up the attempt to write it more than once. But even the earlier novels have a history of struggle; she is no dispassion-ate observer, as she commented in 1888 in a letter to the painter Georg Achen about *Sjur Gabriel*: 'I wrote most of that book in streams of tears. I have felt and lived and suffered with Sjur Gabriel.'[16] Her exchange of letters with Bjørnson about the series is illuminating as regards the temperaments and literary ambitions of both. Bjørnson the social reformer urged her to let the series end happily(!) with the family rising from its miserable start to prosperity. She explained that the series originated in the experiences of a brother and sister she had known as a child, whose fates were identical to those of Severin and Fie; the whole point of the narrative was in leading up to that ending. In any case, her constitution was such that she must see the sordidness which he seemed able to shrug off:

So people suffer and are upset by reading my book – well let them! What is life about? When I was in Christiania recently there were men who were raping children, boys and girls. Maimed for life, bloody, one murdered, ripped apart on the ground. And when I walk through the streets here [Copenhagen], I hardly ever get home without having seen sights of misery and destitution which rend my heart. *I* cannot overlook all this. Happy the man who is raised so high that he can.[17]

The 'Hellemyr' series was well received, despite complaints in the conservative press about the lack of delicacy exhibited by the author. Radical critics appreciated the books. The influential left-wing Danish critic Edvard Brandes (brother of Georg), who reviewed practically all Amalie's books, was critical of the passivity of her female figures in the novels of marriage – missing the point that it was precisely this passivity which had been instilled in them through their upbringing. Yet he praised the boldness and accuracy of the Hellemyr novels – perhaps because they were not written from 'a woman's viewpoint', which most male critics, despite their theoretical support for women's rights, found it hard to adjust to.[18] Edvard Brandes found that the works resembled Naturalist paintings; and there is a consensus that *The People of Hellemyr* is the greatest achievement of Norwegian Naturalist writing. From her earliest days as a critic Amalie Skram had admired the works of Naturalist authors such as Arne Garborg and the Danes J.P. Jacobsen and Herman Bang, with whom she felt an affinity; in 1881 she defended Jacobsen's *Niels Lyhne* when its author was accused of defeatism, and declared that the misery of the world would not be reduced by writing romantic songs to love and regarding existence through rose-coloured spectacles:

There is a different kind of love, which brings with it no intoxication, any more than dreams of pleasure and happiness, and it is that which is born from the pain of pity in the hearts of those who understand and have eyes for human suffering, and it urges us before all else to work, work to ease the suffering.[19]

The People of Hellemyr is often compared to the novels of Emile Zola, which it resembles in its precise descriptions of the effects of poverty, and its studies of individuals caught in a downward spiral. With her familiarity with contemporary French literature, Amalie Skram would certainly have known of Zola's work, and though there is no evidence that she had read him, she may well have been influenced by his ideas. Yet Amalie Skram's Naturalist studies differ from Emile Zola's in that she is not concerned simply to dissect with clinical exactitude 'une tranche de vie', but – as the quotation above implies – is inspired by the wish to do something about it, so that the hopeless may be given hope. In this sense her intentions are closer to those of Realist authors like Bjørnson than he was always prepared to accept.

By the end of her first decade in Denmark, Amalie Skram had won recognition as an author, although she often felt that critics missed the point of her portrayals of women. It had not, however, been an easy decade; as well as struggling to the point of exhaustion with her literary material, she found that her second marriage too brought conflict, and by 1894 her life had again reached a crisis.

1894–1905: Novels of insanity and final years

Even before Amalie and Erik Skram were married, it was clear that there were differences between them – most markedly in the area of sexual morals, an issue on which Amalie was so sensitive. With unusual honesty, he told her that he had a relationship with a young girl whom he intended to keep seeing as long as Amalie was not living with him. He must have been surprised by the violence of her reaction, coming from a woman who had shown herself ready to discuss such matters openly; but as she told him, her knowledge that such things happened did not make her any less vulnerable: 'And yet – I experience it again and again – my knowledge has not got beneath my skin. I must be covered in a layer of oil, for everything which is foreign and repulsive to my nature slides off me again, even if you were to plunge me into it from head to foot.'[20] It is a strikingly physical image of revulsion.

Marriage did not end the problems. Amalie was jealous; whether she had cause to be is unclear. Erik denies in letters that he is unfaithful, yet his answers to direct questions are often evasive.

Whatever the truth was, Amalie's suspicions caused her great pain. Added to this were problems with her work; she needed to earn money – the marriage was based on the premiss that both would contribute financially – and felt increasingly in the early 1890s that she was unable to produce what she wanted and needed to. Work on the last volume of *The People of Hellemyr* depressed her. The birth of her daughter Johanne in 1889 (when she was forty-three) increased the tension; she wanted to spend time with her daughter, but also wanted time to write. When she salvaged a little time for herself, she spent it worrying about her daughter. Finally she was on the point of breakdown, and agreed to be admitted as a patient to the psychiatric ward of Copenhagen Municipal Hospital in February 1894, for a 'rest cure'.

Her experiences at the hospital came as an overwhelming shock; she found she had no rights, no contact with anyone outside, and was at the mercy of a doctor who told her straight out that he thought she was mad. She found herself fighting for her sanity, and as soon as she was released from the hospital and her subsequent compulsory stay at a mental asylum, she set about writing about her experiences in two strongly auto-biographical novels, *Professor Hieronimus* and *På St Jørgen*, both published in 1895 (and translated together as *Under Observation*).

The heroine of the novels, Else Kant, is a painter; this is the third time Amalie Skram has used a female artist as a character, after Birgit Tandberg in 'Knut Tandberg' and Sara Wulf in *Agnete*. For each of these women, the fact of possessing meaningful work of their own is a source of strength; but for Else Kant, for the first time, it is also a major source of her problems. She has reached a crisis in her work, and cannot finish the painting she is working on; she is in a typical double bind situation where her family distracts her from her work and her work from her family. Ill and sleepless, she begins to hallucinate, and agrees with her husband that she should go into hospital and put herself in the hands of Professor Hieronimus, a man of whose professional skill both have heard much. When the hospital doors close behind her, however, she is plunged into a living nightmare; she is locked in a cell and deprived of possessions, expected to obey a strict regime without question, and tormented day and night by the shrieking and banging all around. Told that she is mad, she suspects that she may well be driven mad by the treatment. Professor Hieronimus turns out to be a petty-minded authoritarian who cannot tolerate criticism and demands that she should accept discipline. Added to her misery is the fact that her husband Knut neither writes nor visits; it is not until much later that she discovers that Hieronimus had prevented him doing so. What saves her from despair is the kindness of the nurses, who provide the only humanity in a situation where the male doctors seem inhumane, and her sympathy for the other female patients. *Professor Hieronimus* ends with her being removed against her will to St Jørgen, a mental asylum where she may be held indefinitely.

At St Jørgen takes up the story of her stay at the asylum, where she discovers to her surprise that her treatment is more humane than it was in the hospital. The doctor there is suspicious at first – after all, she has been transferred as being insane, and he interprets her rage at Professor Hieronimus and her refusal to see her husband as a sign of that madness. What in a 'normal' person might seem healthy anger is seen in a 'mad' one as a dangerous obsession. However, her behaviour soon convinces him that she is not disturbed, and she is allowed to leave the asylum two months after being locked away – not to return to her husband, who she feels has been unforgivably weak, if not heartless, but to a convalescent home.

These two novels could be labelled Naturalist in the sense that they present a thoroughly researched study of the ugly and depressing aspects of human existence. Else is surrounded in both institutions by women in various stages of dementia or despair, and their behaviour is described minutely, with no glossing over the grotesqueness of physical detail, as in the scene where Else watches the dying agony of a woman who has drunk bleach. Yet out of the horror rises pity for these women for whom life has no more use, women who nearly all, like Else, spend much of their time grieving for their children – either real children or imaginary ones, like the paper children Mrs Hamilton has cut out and stood on her table, and who make her cry constantly because they must freeze so. There is an inescapable feeling that there is an element of punishment for the fact of being women in the treatment of many of the inmates – that the asylum is simply an extreme form of male control over women's lives. In this sense these novels can be linked to other studies of madness as a specifically 'female malady'; Mary

Wollstonecraft's *Maria; or the Wrongs of Women* (1798) is the first of many works suggesting that female madness may be directly caused by patriarchal society.[21]

Even more than with her other novels, Amalie Skram wrote *Professor Hieronimus* and *At St Jørgen* not merely in order to describe suffering but to get something done about it. Her zeal was fuelled by personal indignation against Professor Knud Pontoppidan, the real-life Hieronimus who treated her in a way most people would find incredible, as she admits in a letter to Bjørnson: 'I can see you shaking your dear, handsome head with a sceptical expression, and I can well understand it, for who can willingly agree to believe that anything so medieval as what happened to me can take place in Royal Copenhagen in 1894.'[22] Her novels led to a public debate, and Pontoppidan defended himself, stating that a woman whose mind had been disturbed could hardly be expected to be a reliable witness. But there had been other complaints about him, and about the treatment of the mentally ill in Denmark in general; although Norway had a law since 1848 guaranteeing the mentally ill some minimal rights, there was no such law in Denmark – and one was not to be passed until 1938. Although Amalie Skram's novels may not have led directly to improvements in the treatment of the mentally ill, however, they did raise public awareness about it.

Life after her experiences in the mental ward was no easier for Amalie. She recovered enough to travel – to Russia in the summer of 1894 and to Paris for some weeks in 1895–6. And the work of transforming her 'medieval' experiences into the two novels had a therapeutic effect. Her writer's block about the *Hellemyr* series was released, and she was subsequently able to complete *Descendants*. Yet she was to be dogged for the rest of her life by financial and health problems, often being forced to take to her sickbed. Her relationship with Erik Skram deteriorated after 1894 – partly as a result of his behaviour in connection with her mental treatment, but largely because of his promiscuity – until they divorced in 1899. (Her letters to Viggo Hørup, a leading left-wing Danish intellectual and editor of the newspaper *Politiken*, whom she sought out as a friend and confidant during the years 1896–1900, document her anguish at the state of her marriage during this period.[23]) Her struggles were not just those of a disappointed wife, however, but those of an artist for adequate conditions for her work. Like many female writers in the nineteenth century, she felt that there was no *room* for her work; her creativity was physically squeezed out, as she complained to Viggo Hørup:

> At home I have only *half* a room, that is to say my and the little one's bedroom, whilst Erik has two at his disposal, a bedroom and a study, which no one may enter whilst he is busy with his writing . . . 'You can write in the living room,' Erik has so often said. In the living room! A room that everyone uses, and where I must flee as soon as anyone comes, with my papers and my housecoat.[24]

One is irresistibly reminded of Jane Austen writing in the drawing room, and of Virginia Woolf's insistence on the need for physical as well as emotional space.

In 1898 Amalie Skram did finally achieve a room of her own, renting a small room in the apartments where the family lived. It was an important step in enabling her to complete the *Hellemyr* series that year. After the divorce, she lived mostly in the flat with Johanne. Two more complete works were to follow: a volume of short stories entitled *Sommer* (Summer, 1899) and a novel, *Julehelg* (Christmas Holiday, 1900). Neither of them suggests any more optimistic a view of the human condition. Most of the stories in *Summer* are concerned with the failure of love. *Christmas Holiday* has a male central character, Arne Hoff, a sensitive soul on whom life seems determined to force all that is ugly. He becomes engaged to his brother's rejected fiancée out of pity, only to discover that she is physically and spiritually repugnant to him. (In Amalie Skram's writing, moral and physical ugliness go hand in hand, especially in women; her innocent young brides are always beautiful, and her evil mothers and morally ignoble women almost deformed in their ugliness.) Arne is rescued from his despondency by becoming the lodger of a family filled with the love he never had; he falls half-Platonically in love with the young mother, who becomes the 'good mother' he has been searching for. He moves away to work, but longs always to return; and the love which cannot be of this earth finds its apotheosis as he falls ill and dies with a vision of wandering with his beloved 'into the red and golden clouds of the evening sky' (*SV* VI, p. 338).

During the last few years of her life, Amalie Skram was engaged in writing the novel *Mennesker* (People), which progressed with extreme slowness and was published in instalments during the years 1902 to 1905; it was unfinished when she died.[25] It is a collective novel which follows the fortunes of a group of people in a country vicarage, and particularly their erotic relationships. Madness is again a theme, and several of the characters exhibit abnormal or grotesque behaviour; the author's emphasis on the bestial aspects of human sexuality has grown stronger. Her ambivalence about physical sexuality has given way to revulsion, as the only love which appears unsullied is a purely spiritual one.

Amalie Skram's relationship with her native country became strained towards the end of her life. That she is a Norwegian author is indisputable; she wrote in Norwegian, sometimes (like much of the Hellemyr series) in dialect, and the majority of her works were set in Norway. Her concern for documentary accuracy meant that she spent many periods in Norway after 1884, especially in Bergen. Yet she felt rejected by the countrymen who had refused her a grant, been grudging in their recognition of her (Bjørnson was a case in point) and unutterably provincial in their attitudes. The radical milieu of Copenhagen had welcomed her in quite a different way. In 1901 she published a pamphlet called *Landsforrædere* (Traitors), in which she explained why she wished to be regarded as a *Danish* author; it was Danish criticism she had to thank for 'that scrap of understanding, that scrap of recognition, which give a person courage to work on . . . . Not for nothing have Georg Brandes and Edvard Brandes lived and worked down here for nearly a generation.'[26]

Danish public opinion had recognized Amalie Skram as a serious author. Not that her books were received on her own premisses; like those of other women authors, they were praised when they approximated most closely to the interests of the male critics – when they were perceived as most 'masculine'. The greatest praise that Erik Skram could find in his enthusiasm for 'Madame Høier's Tenants' was that it was 'not at all womanish',[27] and Edvard Brandes crowned his praise of the 'Hellemyr' series by calling it 'a highly gifted woman's most manly work'.[28] For this reason too, Amalie Skram's Hellemyr novels were long considered her major works; not until recently, with the advent of modern feminist criticism in Norway, have her novels about women's lives received close attention and taken their rightful place alongside the social and psychological studies of other 'greats' of her time.[29]

As one of the most prominent female writers during the ferment of the Scandinavian modern breakthrough, however, Amalie Skram helped to ensure that the discussion of social and moral issues was not conducted wholly on male terms. She did not wish to compete with men in all fields; she had no ambitions to be a public figure, and had conventional views on the upbringing of her daughter: 'Any influence I have over my daughter I have used to persuade her not to take her exams and become a student . . . No, she is to learn domestic management, cookery and handiwork. And of course carry on with her language studies and her music lessons.'[30] But even if she did not envisage a complete break with traditional roles, her works provide striking evidence of the damaging effects of treating women as the second sex.

4
Ragnhild Jølsen (1875–1908)

Tradition and rebellion

If Ragnhild Jølsen had waited as long as Camilla Collett and Amalie Skram to make her debut as a writer, she would be unknown to literary history. *The District Governor's Daughters* was published when Camilla Collett was forty-one, Amalie Skram's first story was published when she was thirty-six; Ragnhild Jølsen's first novel was published when she was twenty-eight and she died shortly before her thirty-third birthday. This fact alone makes her remarkable in a period when most women writers, because of convention or domestic circumstances, began publishing relatively late; they then frequently continued to be productive into their old age.[1]

Its brevity, however, was not the only way in which Ragnhild Jølsen's life was remarkable; like the lives of other writers who have died young, it was a turbulent one. She was a strange mixture of deep-rootedness in tradition, and rebellion. Like Camilla Collett, she grew up in the country on an estate not far from Christiania, yet far enough in terms of the travel arrangements of the day to make the capital both alluring and difficult of access. Unlike Camilla Collett, however, she was born into a family which had lived on that same estate for generations. Ekeberg farm at Enebakk had belonged to her ancestors since 1634; both her mother Pauline Holmsen and her father Holm Jølsen were descended from Holm Hanssøn, the original owner. Ragnhild was by several years the youngest of a family of five; she grew up with a deep attachment to her home, and a feeling that she was the last scion of an exhausted family tree.

She was to witness the end of an era. Her father, an energetic entrepreneur, had decided to transform the poverty-stricken rural settlement into a model industrial community by building a matchmaking factory in 1866. For a while the factory flourished, the standard of living rose and the future looked bright. It was not long, however, before things went wrong, owing to a combination of bad luck and bad management: the buildings burnt down several times without being sufficiently insured, investments and natural resources were overstretched, and miscalculations about the building of the railway, which was not after all routed close to the estate, made transport costs prohibitive. By 1889 Holm Jølsen was ruined, the estate was mortgaged and the family moved to a flat in Christiania. Although they moved back to Enebakk in 1896, it was only a temporary measure until the estate was sold in 1904 and the family moved to Solbakken, the engineer's house built along with the factory, which was to be Ragnhild's home from then until her death.

The collapse of the family finances and virtual loss of the estate when Ragnhild was fourteen left an impression on her which is evident in much of her work. The next seven years in Christiania were to be of great significance too; it was here that her rebellious spirit began to show itself in earnest. In theory she was finishing her schooling; in fact she was much more attracted by the cafés frequented by the Bohemian artistic circles of *fin-de-siècle* Christiania. These were dubious acquaintances for a girl, yet she persisted despite parental opposition and minor scandals. She became engaged to a writer, Thomas Krag – an engagement she broke off after a few months – and had an affair, the first of several, with the much older Halvor Wiborg.[2] The meeting with Wiborg was fateful; he was – or became in her imagination – a cynical seducer, who stirred a passionate and slightly masochistic sexuality which was heightened by the illicit nature of the affair. Sexual fulfilment and domestic security became irreconcilable elements for Ragnhild Jølsen after that experience, as they are for the heroines of her novels.

At her parents' insistence, she moved back with them to Enebakk in 1896; her rebelliousness did not extend to breaking with her family. Indeed she never really left home; she remained the 'daughter in the house' with only short periods of a few months at a time away: in Cologne in 1896, in Copenhagen in 1904, in Florence and Rome in 1906–7. She nursed her mother on her deathbed in 1903, her father on his in 1906, and wrote all her books at Enebakk.

Writing had early been a favourite pastime, growing out of her own fantasies and tales told by her mother, who passed on to her both fairy tales and family anecdotes. She had most of her time to herself, and would roam around the estate inventing stories. She wrote letters to her cats, her closest friends. A story about a kitten's death, torn violently to pieces by a hunting dog, is her earliest preserved work, written when she was about sixteen; it ends with the gloomy prophecy which is to find an echo in much of her later work: 'When I grow fond of anything, God takes it from me' (*RF*, p. 643).[3] She published little before her first novel, *Ve's mor* (Ve's Mother), in 1903; after that she wrote as if she knew she had little time, publishing four books in four years: *Rikka Gan* (1904); *Fernanda Mona* (1905), *Hollases krønike* (The Chronicles of Hollas, 1906) and *Brukshistorier* (Tales of an Industrial Community, 1907).

With Ragnhild Jølsen's novels we enter a world far removed from the bourgeois drawing-rooms where Camilla Collett's or Amalie Skram's novels of marriage are played out; here the battle of the sexes is more naked and violent. In her first three novels the setting is a family estate, which is more than just a background to the story:

> The sun rose and the sun set over the grey farm with its neglected land, where grass grew on the heaps of manure, which had once, years ago, been dumped but never spread. And the gleaming brown horses, which were useless for pulling loads. And the metre-high thistles, and the weather-beaten hop-vine which clung to the walls, from which the windows peered like the surly eyes of an old bachelor. (*RF*, p. 9)

In this first paragraph of *Ve's Mother*, decay and neglect are evident in every aspect of the estate; days and years pass over untended fields and buildings. Nature is taking over, as grass and thistles flourish in rank profusion, and there is a hint of lazy voluptuousness in the gleaming coats of the useless horses. Even a suggestion of sexual enmity is evident in the personification of the windows of the old house.

It is to this unwelcoming farm that the middle-aged Gerhard Winkel brings his young bride Paula. The tensions prefigured here are soon manifested, not only with Winkel's family but between the couple themselves; Winkel is captivated by his beautiful bride, but her feelings are more ambiguous. She calls him '*bjørnefar*', 'father bear', indicating that she has been both caught by a wild animal and lured into a quasi-incestuous relationship. At the same time her senses are in thrall to a young hunter – of game and of women – Ove Munk, who arrives at the farm one summer night. She rejects him then, and soon after bears a son, Dag (Day), who absorbs her so that she forgets both husband and lover. But she must lose what she loves: Dag is killed by a threshing machine, and in her despair she turns to Ove to fill her emptiness. She bears his son Ve (Woe), a deformed and sickly child and the opposite of her healthy Dag – 'A cripple for a cherub' (p. 65). When her taunting of Winkel becomes so blatant that he finally loses his temper and hits her, the barrier between them is broken and she turns away from Ove and to him – only to see him sicken and die shortly afterwards. She is left with nothing, and turns to morphine to deaden her pain – until one day her son Ve appeals to her, and she realizes that in caring for him she can build up some purpose in life again.

The natural surroundings from which we are led into the human conflict provide a continual commentary on the action. Animal imagery is rife, often stressing the dangerous aspects of sexuality: Ove is like a snake; Paula fights like a wild cat as Winkel takes her by force, and later her mind shrinks from the memory of their fight as from a beast of prey. Not all the references, however, are so elevated. The coarse antics of the farm workers in a drunken brawl provide a grotesque parody of Paula's sexual exploits, and the locals make pointed remarks to her about the effects of spring on less noble creatures: 'Now the snakes are sunning theirselves on the hillside, and if you poke around in an anthill they'll send up a stream of juice fit to make a body sneeze. There's not a crawling creature but the sap isn't running in it, thick and sticky . . .'(*RF*, p. 16). On this farm there is something rank even about spring. Autumn is no better; as she goes out to meet Ove after Dag's death, it is flaming over Gruvang farm 'in sick, infected colours' (p. 54).

Paula is not allowed to be a romantic heroine; her escape with her 'dream lover' is tainted from the start. Although he can satisfy her sensual demands, and make her briefly forget, she is confronted at every turn by grotesque mimicry or reminders of decadence and decay. In this infected place, no healthy love can grow. In the end, she accepts what seems to be her fate; the farm has won. The only hope for the future is a sickly changeling, and it is difficult to believe that he will be strong enough to bring an ultimate resolution of the conflict on the estate.

The estate is the central character in *Rikka Gan* (1904).[4] Here again, it is the first thing we see, and the impression is forbidding:

> Black lay Gan farmhouse with its sleepy echo, and the tree roots shivered down in the garden.
>
> The sun came sparkling in summertime, clear and strong as only summer sun can sparkle. It was unable to sparkle in anything at Gan: not in one tile on the roof. Not in a single window. – It might almost be seen as a symbol, that, of how Gan farm by the lake no longer belonged to the daytime now, – as it closed itself in, stubborn and set, and slept in its fallen greatness. (*RF*, p. 103)

The novel was written in the year in which Ekeberg was sold out of Ragnhild Jølsen's family.

Rikka Gan is the descendant of a long line of strong women and weak men, whose fates are intertwined with the estate which once belonged to the family. She and her sister-in-law Fernanda are determined to move back to the farm, by persuading the new owner Mattias Aga to employ her brother Jon Torsen as a tenant farmer. The price, however, is that Rikka should take Mattias Aga into her bed. It is a price she pays not altogether unwillingly; for she is a woman of strong passions who responds to this forceful entrepreneur. Yet it is a position which demands sacrifices: of her peace of mind, of her dreams of love, and – most horribly – of her own children, who are murdered one by one as they are born.

The situation becomes intolerable for Rikka, watching her sister's children growing up whilst tormented by grief for her own; she hallucinates that all the little dead children, naked and blue with cold, are calling out to her to warm them and kiss them and give them milk. Half deranged with grief, she meets the beautiful young people from Herby farm across the water, 'the love farm', and brings about the death of the girl who is engaged to the young man she desires. It seems she is entirely taken over by evil; yet one thing can still reach her: the affection of her niece, little Fernanda.

When she realizes that little Fernanda is being prepared to take over her place in Mattias Aga's bed, with the connivance of her mother, Rikka determines to save her. By threatening to reveal the murder of the children, she persuades Mattias to sign the farm over to Jon Torsen during his lifetime and to commit a deed of gift to little Fernanda, making her independent of him. In return she promises to go away and never return; but as she and her sister-in-law try to row across the lake during a storm, they fight over which way to go and lose control of the boat, and both are drowned.

Like *Ve's Mother*, this novel is a story of erotic – almost demonic – possession. Rikka, like Paula, inspires and experiences violent passion, only in this case it is literally murderous. Rikka kills from frustrated desire, and she and Aga have a love–hate relationship in which she nearly stabs him to death. She too has a dream lover, who exists in fantasy only: Vilde Vaa, who visits her in the forest with a flying bird carved on his naked breast. It is into his arms she sinks as she vanishes beneath the waters of the lake.

Love of another kind is available to Rikka, though it is not a love to which she can respond. The district bailiff, a kindly and philosophical man, keeps a fatherly eye on her throughout. His feelings are indeed more than fatherly, but he is not a passionate man, and she sees him only as an ally to whom she can turn for practical help. To him it is left to note her death in the local records; but he does so in words unusual in such accounts:

> And never did this girl have anyone with whom she could talk quietly and calmly. Never understanding without complaints. Never confidences without grief. And never had love touched her. – Yes, of her it can in truth be said – and so say I, the bailiff from Haug: 'The Lord God filled her with bitter fruit. He made her drunk with wormwood.' (p. 184)

The archaic, quasi-biblical tone of this statement is typical of the style of this novel, giving it an aura of myth.[5] It is not difficult to believe that the dead walk again, and that a malevolent spirit inhabits the very walls of this ancient building with the resonant name. Gan gård was the name of a real farm, but Ragnhild Jølsen was no doubt attracted to it partly because of its linguistic associations; the verb 'å gande' means to practise sorcery, and it is used of the Lapp shamans ('gandfinn') believed by many

Scandinavians to have black magic powers. The farm is imbued with the spirit of Rikka's ancestress fru Brynhilda; she invokes her aid to kill her rival. Her visions are as real to Rikka as the people around her; she sees a strange procession which becomes a macabre dance of death, and in the end she meets her fate in the shape of a serpent:

> Rikka Torsen looked out over the black surging surface of the lake. And as she looked, there arose from the depths the body of a fearful serpent whose fin-covered curves rose up until they filled the area between earth and sky. It moved lazily in the heavy grey air. But the waters rose up and foamed. (pp. 164–5)

When she visits the old bailiff for the last time, he notices that her white face with the black, wet locks around it resembles that of the Medusa.

The stylized, rhythmical, almost ritualistic descriptions of this novel are reminiscent of the pictorial style of the *Art Nouveau* or *Jugendstil* movement:

> the distinguishing feature of *Jugendstil* was the curving line, which in natural surroundings turns into plants and other growths, froth-topped waves or birds with long necks. The motifs convey an atmosphere of intimacy, unreality and myth, and have a tendency to touch on matters which are taboo in social and private life.[6]

The drawings of Aubrey Beardsley are a classical example of the style, and one can see parallels in them to Ragnhild Jølsen's writing – in its insistence on destructive sexuality and its powerful appeal to the senses, and in its approach to visual description. The farm, the landscape, the lake and the sky combine into swirling patterns which are a mood-picture as much as a framework for the story. The description of the serpent above is a particularly striking example of the combination of landscape and atmosphere into a tangible symbol of demonic possession.

The *Art Nouveau* movement was flourishing in the 1890s, when Ragnhild Jølsen frequented artistic circles in Christiania. She had always been interested in the plastic arts, particularly in sculpture. She has left quite a few sculpted figures, though as time went on she turned increasingly to sculpting in relief. She spent some months in

Copenhagen studying sculpture in the autumn of 1904, just after *Rikka Gan* had been sent to the publisher. In all her writings there is a plasticity of line which makes buildings, plants and people stand out as clear outlines in just a few strokes, rather than a detailed naturalistic description.

Fernanda Mona (1905) takes up the story of Gan estate after Rikka's death. The eponymous heroine of this novel is Rikka's niece Fernanda, whom she had hoped to rescue from the same fate as herself. Her efforts are backed up by the old bailiff, benevolent as ever towards the women of Gan, who persuades Fernanda to move to his house. He arranges for her to be invited to parties at the festive Herby across the water, where she falls in love with the young master, Daniel Falbe. But despite his efforts, Fernanda is doomed; her lover abandons her, and she returns sick at heart. She makes one last effort to escape, and to respond to the old bailiff's patient love in an active choice to come to him; but even as she does so, he dies of a heart attack, and she sees no way out but suicide.

Around Fernanda Mona's story are woven those of the others whose fates are linked to the estate. Her sickly father Jon Torsen grows ever weaker in mind and body, and exploitative of all who come near; and her younger sisters, 'the Gan lynxes', are more like wild animals than adolescents. In them the wildness of the Gan women has degenerated into bestiality, as they roam around the farm unkempt and dirty, dreaming of a lover who is black or red and turns into 'a big shaggy animal' (p. 219). Mattias Aga cannot stay away from Gan either, but returns on a tour of inspection – only to break his leg because the girls frighten his horses. After that he can no longer leave the farm, but stays there bedridden as his leg festers, haunted by the ghosts of past crimes.

Sexuality takes even more extreme forms in this novel. At the one extreme is the old bailiff's selfless devotion, happy to offer Fernanda the joys of love with someone else. At the other there is a frequent emphasis on perverted or bestial forms of sexuality, as with the 'Gan lynxes'. Jon Torsen is desperate for a woman after his wife's death, and tries to entice his daughter Fernanda into his bed by telling her the story of Little Red Riding Hood, and the wolf with his long arms – until she begins to see him as the wolf, with dreadful glinting eyes. When she refuses him, he takes to engaging housekeepers who do not object to a hand up their skirts. He falls for a farm hand, Kaie, a woman who subdues bulls with her bare hands – and is fatally injured by a bull as he tries to get to her. Mattias Aga, having also failed to seduce Fernanda, in whom he can see the features of the woman who still obsesses him, turns into a Peeping Tom at the Gan lynxes' naked bathing sessions in the lake.

Between these two extremes lies the possibility of an equal relationship when Fernanda Mona falls in love with Daniel Falbe. But the ideal turns out to be a chimera, for Daniel Falbe is another version of the 'dream lover' whose prototype we saw earlier in Ove Vang and Vilde Vaa: a physically gorgeous but eternally faithless seducer. In Ragnhild Jølsen's fictional world ecstasy is short-lived and dearly bought; there seems no way of combining the delirium of the senses with any kind of trust or commitment.

Plant metaphors provide a commentary on characters in this novel, too, and are particularly associated with Fernanda. She tends the bailiff's garden, and he sees her mind and senses growing in strength as the garden flourishes; but when the storm comes, the only way she can protect the roses is by picking them – that is, killing them. He realizes that she is a plant which has been grown in the shade and which he has attempted to transplant into the sunlight. The change has been too abrupt:

> What happens to the flower of shade when it comes into the sunlight? For a moment it flames up – perhaps its petals take on forms which are especially fecund and wild, and it outshines the flowers of the sun, because it resembles them not at all, and the flowers of the sun, those cultivated and confident ones, prepare reluctantly to make room for their new companion. But they don't need to, because soon the flower of the shade curls up and withers. Annihilation overtakes it because it cannot endure the light. (p. 296)

When Fernanda was lost in dreams of love, she associated it with an unknown plant which shot up in the garden, which in her imagination would be a poppy, red as running blood and flaming like autumn leaves; but when it flowered, it turned out to be a fragile white lily, 'that pale flower of coldness and mourning wreaths' (p. 283). From that moment she felt her summer threatened by winter frosts. And when she chooses to join the bailiff in death, her final words are a confirmation of the failure of his attempt to uproot her: 'When the shoot is torn away from the trunk, it dies' (p. 328).

Chronicles and stories

With *Fernanda Mona*, Ragnhild Jølsen's books about the power of family homes over their inhabitants come to an end, as if she had exorcized her grief at her own family's loss. Her next book, *The Chronicles of Hollas* (1906), is more episodic in its intertwining of several stories into a loosely knit whole. It is also a book in which her sense of humour, which had previously shown itself only in glimpses, comes to the fore.

The chronicles, as the title suggests, are historical tales; but the historical period in which they are set, although loosely the eighteenth century, is impossible to pinpoint, as there are inconsistencies in the internal evidence. The aim was not to provide historically accurate episodes from Norwegian rural life but to establish a framework of beliefs and traditions against which human passions can be highlighted. It is a setting in which peasant shrewdness and earthiness are mingled with a religion which is still half superstition, and the supernatural is a dangerous force. The central character around whom the stories are woven is Hollas, often with the epithet 'the evil one'; he is in league with the powers of darkness, and at some points even seems to become the Devil himself. He tries to cheat his neighbours out of their land, forges his own coins, cripples a child who sees him stripping lead off the church roof, inseminates his black mare – which then produces a foal with a human face – buys the church and preaches the Devil's word in it, and deliberately infects the whole village with cholera. He is not invincible; he finally catches cholera himself, and dies of it. Yet he can never be quite eradicated; his last words are 'Hollas lives for ever!' (p. 471), and after death his ghost can be seen in the churchyard, fighting with his neighbour about disputed boundaries.

Hollas's main opponent is the priest's sister, Angelica. She is an artist who dreams of painting the image of Christ; she is also a woman who dreams of earthly love. Hollas has designs on her, but she will have none of him; she desires the handsome son of a local landowner, Otto Kefas. Otto becomes dangerously ill, and she pleads with God to let him live, ruthlessly offering up the life of the crippled child instead. Her wish is granted, and she takes Otto Kefas as her lover; their passion is consummated on a summer's night as she leads him into a field of ripe corn which becomes an image of realized passion. The morning sun rises on her triumphant love; but it is short-lived. Even more than with earlier 'dream lovers', the narrator – who in this book often exhibits an ironic distance to her characters – makes it clear that Otto is a man whose exterior raises expectations that he cannot fulfil:

> Otto Kefas was the god of manhood – man himself – Adam – just as he left the hand of the creator and in the image of the creator, handsome and strong – just such a man as we women would gladly give the apple to eat, and who naively and without wisdom accepts the red fruit and confidently bites into it. . . . To hell with longings, to hell with dreams, to hell with anything other than just what we have – don't let your eyes get inflamed, Otto Kefas. – No, rest assured: Otto Kefas and his like never ask too much of life. (p. 393)

Angelica determines to paint the picture of Christ, which will hang in the church, with Otto's features. But Hollas's influence corrupts her work, and when the picture is unveiled, it is a portrait of Hollas. Trying to paint Christ, she has painted the Devil: an indication not just of Otto's weakness but also of the power of the darkness over her mind. Looked at in another light, the episode suggests that sexuality is not just summer nights, pastel colours and blue-eyed young gods; it has a darker side too, which Angelica must acknowledge in order to render herself less vulnerable to its attacks and to be able to portray the truth in her paintings. This interpretation is indicated by the conclusion to her story: she is not destroyed by her defeat, but wipes out her work – painting it out in black – and leaves the village to seek better conditions for her work elsewhere. As she leaves she makes a final prayer to God that the future will allow women to realize their love more actively, freed from both stifling convention and romantic delusion:

Let us women, oh Lord, have greater rights for our love – that it is not exposed against the clouds as so pale and fragile a creation, that is so easily stained by splashes of earth!

Let our love on this earth, oh Lord, receive the eternal seal of this earth, the humus, strong and rich as the life from which it springs – so that it does not need to be hidden away in the dark . . .

Lord God, you have in your world a wondrous creature, wild and free in the great forests. It may have a spotted skin; but the spots are simply the marks of its race – and who could deny the leopard its beauty? I beg you: Let me be like the leopard, Lord God! (pp. 436–7)

It is an attractive vision, but one that is never realized in Ragnhild Jølsen's works. Although Angelica reaches a more positive conclusion than her earlier women, she leaves the fictional world at this point, and we hear no more of her.

Surrounding these central characters is a whole community of figures, all individualized and many of them comic; the language in which they are described, in contrast to the incantatory speech used about and by Angelica, is earthy and forthright. Ragnhild Jølsen's canvas is broader here than in her earlier works, and she paints the antics of humanity with relish. The style ranges from a mock-heroic 'saga-style' which exposes the self-importance of local bigwigs to a racy, even coarse, dialect. More than one critic has pointed to the similarities in theme and treatment with Boccaccio's *Decameron*.[7]

Penury and family commitments restricted Ragnhild Jølsen's opportunities to travel; her applications for grants had been unsuccessful, and her concern for her failing parents made her want to be close at hand. In 1906, however, her father died, and in the same year she was finally awarded a small travel stipend (400 kroner). She wanted to visit Italy, and in November 1906 she travelled to Florence. She was disappointed; Italian classical art did not appeal to her, and the warm South turned out to be cold and lonely. She made a brief trip to Rome, which she found more congenial; she stayed there for six months. However, it was not the Rome of classical architecture and sculpture which attracted her, but the café life of the circle of Scandinavian émigré artists and writers to which she gained access. Her taste for a Bohemian lifestyle was reawakened, and she would drink and talk late into the night, with little regard for her poor health. She also finally met Hans Kinck, who lived in Rome. She had been aware of the affinity between their literary styles from the start, and had written to ask his opinion of her first novel before it was published; he had encouraged her with positive criticism, and she felt she owed him a great debt.

Whilst she was in Italy, she tried to get down to serious work on a project she had long cherished: a novel to be called 'Den røde Høst' ('Red Autumn'), which was to sum up the experiences of a woman looking back at the end of her long life. Perhaps here she would have portrayed a woman who had realized a life of which her earlier heroines can only dream. But she could not concentrate on the task in Italy, and it kept getting pushed aside by other work, until, finally, it was too late. In Rome, she managed only short pieces: a few stories and travel epistles for the newspapers back home. She had to return to Enebakk in order to settle down to writing again.

Her travels abroad did not so much provide Ragnhild Jølsen with new material as help her to focus more clearly on the material she already had. It is as if distance enabled her to get into perspective the events through which she had lived and to see how they could be transmuted into art. When she arrived home in Enebakk in June 1907 she at once set to work, and at great speed produced a volume of tales about her own valley, *Brukshistorier* (Tales of an Industrial Community, 1907).

Her father's industrial experiments are the background to these stories, and part of the motive for them is to provide a tribute to her father's memory; he appears in several of the tales lightly disguised as Helle Holm, a benevolent patriarch who has realized his childhood dream of bringing prosperity to his valley. There is no undercurrent of criticism of his actions; he is in charge not only by virtue of inherited wealth but also because of his superior understanding. The conflicts in the tales are between one worker and another, not between worker and boss.

The focus of the stories, however, is the community itself, and its members are sympathetically and humorously described. From being a sleepy rural community, unchanged for generations, the valley is precipitated in a single movement into the modern age; the Middle Ages are brought face to face with the Industrial Revolution. And the peasants bring with them into the factory the habits of mind of former ages. This is an account not of industrial strife and unionization, but of the meeting between the superstitious medieval mind and unfamiliar forces. Jens Vaktmand, the night-watchman who appears in several of the stories, is a man with the ability to communicate with spirits; he sees factory wheels driven by potentially malevolent sprites. When he foresees an accident, it happens; and when the factory is burnt down, the cause is revealed to him in a vision. This is a people still in tune with mysterious natural powers.

Much has been made of the fact that this collection of stories appeared in 1907, the year in which 'neo-Realism' made its breakthrough in Norwegian literature.[8] It can only in part be subsumed under that heading; it is not a realistic depiction of working lives so much as a study of the way in which folk beliefs are an active force in the community. Seen in this way, it is less of a break with Ragnhild Jølsen's earlier writings; irrational forces still hold sway over people's minds. The strength of religious feeling in the community is exploited by the new generation of travelling preachers, the only group depicted with little sympathy in the tales; they are hypocrites and parasites, preaching hellfire to a terrified audience whilst living comfortably and not very morally themselves.

The undercurrent of eroticism, never very far from the surface in Ragnhild Jølsen's writings, is in evidence in many of these tales too. The attraction of forbidden sexuality is as potent as ever, and can haunt people beyond all reason or sense. In 'Hanna Valmoen', a village girl is in love with a student who she knows will leave her for a 'fine lady', but when she hears his whistle on the night air she cannot help herself, but must go to him. A lone fiddler playing dance tunes in his isolated hut in 'Felelåten i engen' ('Fiddle Music in the Meadow') entices women into his hut to make love. In some of the stories it seems as if all of nature is possessed by a demonic eroticism, reminiscent of Kinck's stories in *Flaggermus-vinger* (Bat-wings, 1895), which Ragnhild Jølsen knew well. Grotesqueness and violence are frequently linked with sexuality too, as in 'Mørkredd' ('Afraid of the Dark'), in which a girl is practically raped on her way home through the forest by an lecherous old man, and 'En Don Juan' ('A Don Juan'), in which an eighty-year old man sets out to find himself a woman, and encounters only coarse ridicule.

Despite its darker sides, however, the collection conveys a sense of a closely knit community. There is no ironic distance here between the narrator and the events recorded, as there was in *The Chronicles of Hollas*; there is a feeling of solidarity between the author and the people of whom she writes.

It was to be a short-lived harmony. Ragnhild Jølsen's health was broken; she was overworking, sitting up all night to write whilst smoking cigars and drinking coffee. She was taking other stimulants too; her account of taking morphine in *Ve's Mother* was based on her own knowledge, and by this time she was living on a mixture of stimulants and sleeping drugs. Living at home in Enebakk had not stopped her taking lovers, and there is strong evidence – from the man himself – that by the end of 1907 she was pregnant by her latest lover, the artist Karl Dørnberger. It may not have been her first child.[9] She died suddenly on 28 January 1908, after taking what was probably an overdose of sleeping drugs. Whether her death was suicide or a result of ill-health compounded by an accidental overdose, no one will ever know. Her doctor (who was also a former lover) decided not to do an autopsy, so the facts about her death – and her supposed pregnancy – were never established. She was under great stress when she died; but she was also working furiously and at the height of her creative powers.

Conclusion

Jens Bjørneboe, a radical author and iconoclast, wrote a documentary novel in 1964 about Ragnhild Jølsen, *Drømmen og hjulet* (The Dream and the Wheel). It is a very personal account, but it is based on research (he was living at Enebakk at the time), and brings her eccentricity and passions vividly to life. He puts his finger on some of the tensions out of which her writing springs:

Between these two extremes Ragnhild Jølsen grew up until she was fourteen years old: on the one hand an ancient family and family estate, with endless dark forests, legends and fairy tales – and on the other hand the industrial community, the bankruptcy, the slum. This produced two worlds in her; an ecstatic romanticism and a sharp, almost raw realism alongside it. It left its mark on her writing by making her into a dreamer and an observer at one and the same time. And she was just as homeless in the past as in the present.[10]

She read little contemporary literature; her reading at home consisted mainly of ancient tomes of medieval literature or history, and folk tales such as those by P.Chr. Asbjørnsen. At the same time she was a child of the 1890s, and her writings share much of the same *fin-de-siècle* atmosphere as those of Sigbjørn Obstfelder and Hans Kinck: a sense of alienation and rejection of the practicalities of everyday life as well as an aversion for 'causes', and a fascination for the irrational, the morbid and the taboo.

Ragnhild Jølsen was the only woman writer of this kind of literature, and this caused her many problems. Not only did she live in a way which was hardly respectable for a woman, she also wrote in a way which was hardly respectable for a woman. Some critics had difficulty in accepting that this was in fact a woman writing, and the similarity between her style and Hans Kinck's led some to believe that he was the author of her first book. *Ve's Mother* was described as 'a genuinely masculine piece of work', and 'in some parts positively shaggy and bestial'.[11] Even when she was well established, her books were thought unfeminine; and as in the case of Amalie Skram, critics seemed to think that it was a compliment to her to deny her sex. A review of *Tales of an Industrial Community* declared unequivocally: 'There is a man's will and hardness in her naturalistic mysticism . . .'[12]

A greater openness about sexual desire in both sexes is in evidence in other turn-of-the-century writers; Knut Hamsun's novels of the 1890s, for example, describe secret meetings between lovers in the forest, where the women respond delightedly to the men. The passage in *Pan* (1894) where Lieutenant Glahn summons up his 'dream lover' Iselin in the forest is similar in language and atmosphere to Ragnhild Jølsen's depictions of sexual bliss. Yet in

Hamsun's novels the man is the hunter, and the observer; we see the beauty of the woman mirrored in his eyes. In Ragnhild Jølsen's descriptions the woman is at least an equal partner and frequently takes the initiative, and her handsome young men are described with a sensuous enjoyment of their nakedness which had previously been reserved for women. No wonder some critics found it hard to take.

Ragnhild Jølsen lacked moderation; she took the commandments of the Bohemians more seriously than many of them did themselves, even down to the final one of taking her own life. In her fascination with the morbid and the exotic, she had no desire for the calm happiness of married love. The link between love and death which is evident in Amalie Skram's work is even stronger here, as ecstasy can only be fleeting and any promise of lasting love seems bound to be cut short by death. In her short life, Ragnhild Jølsen was obsessed by death; she courted it and wrote about it, often in violent forms. In her favourite flower, the poppy, she saw all the glory of love in its blazing colours, the attraction of danger in its associations with opium, and the ephemeral nature of life in its brief flowering.

Compared with Camilla Collett and Amalie Skram, Ragnhild Jølsen was no activist for women's liberation. Although she did not lack social awareness – she writes about society's cruelty to its stepchildren in *The Chronicles of Hollas*, for example, and is aware of the problems of the underprivileged in her industrial tales – she did not put her energies into working for social or political reform. Only once did she publish an article about women's rights – 'Dødvekten i leiren' ('The Dead Weight in the Camp'), in *Urd* in 1906. The title is a reference to Camilla Collett's *From the Camp of the Mutes*, and the article takes to task those women who oppose the struggle for independence, like slaves who are afraid of freedom; they are as much of a hindrance to progress as men: 'When we women win ourselves, we shall win the world' (*RF*, p. 733). Although she was a sympathizer, she was a passive one. Yet in a different way, through her portraits of passionate women and through her own unconventional lifestyle, she helped to break down the old barriers. She did not protest about women's rights; her life was her protest.

PART II
1913–1960

5
On the Back Burner

International and domestic issues

During the twentieth century, Norway was drawn more fully into the international arena; she was to be embroiled in the convulsions which shook the rest of Europe. Yet at the beginning of the century there were few signs of this involvement. As a newly independent country in 1905, Norway was very much aware of her own nationhood, and principally concerned with internal affairs; national pride was to the fore as it had been in the early years of the nineteenth century, and in cultural as well as political life there was a concentration on building up native traditions.

During the First World War Norway, like the other Scandinavian countries, declared her intention to remain neutral, and succeeded in doing so. The resources of her substantial shipping fleet were made available to both sides, and the early years of the war were boom years for the Norwegian economy. Shipowners and speculators made fortunes overnight on freight earnings and shares, whilst many Norwegian ships were lost on hazardous enterprises. It is a time on which many Norwegians later looked back with unease.[1] And it was short-lived: fortunes were lost as quickly as they were won.

The Liberal government remained in power until 1920. The Labour Party was growing more powerful, but did not take over the government for some time. They were seen as too extremist; they were the only socialist party outside the Russian empire to join the Communist Third International in 1919, although unwillingness to take direct orders from Moscow meant that the affiliation lasted only four years. The next fifteen years were characterized by an unstable political situation, with twelve changes of government between 1920 and 1935. The world economic crisis of the end of the 1920s and the early 1930s affected Norway too, with over 40 per cent unemployment during the worst months of 1932. Yet there was a gradual recovery during the thirties, and by the end of the decade Norway was considerably more prosperous than she had been in the early twenties.

The increasing political instability in Europe was felt in Norway during the 1930s. She had joined the League of Nations in 1920 to help promote world peace, and had begun to make her presence felt internationally – thanks largely to the efforts of one man, the explorer Fridtjof Nansen, who became a kind of ambassador for world peace.[2] The rise of National Socialism in Germany was viewed with increasing concern, as was its offshoot in Norway, Nasjonal Samling, with its vociferous leader Vidkun Quisling. A stable Labour government was finally elected in 1935, but the country was in a very weak position; little money had been spent on defence for a long time, and in 1938 Norway left the League of Nations in protest at the lack of a common will to stand firm against German frontier violations.

The country was ill prepared to resist the German invasion on 9 April 1940. Most of the south of the country was overrun almost at once, although pockets of heroic resistance meant that the king and government were able to escape to the north and later across to England, and fighting continued with Allied assistance for a couple of months around Narvik. The occupation of Norway and Denmark, originally intended by the Nazis as model protectorates, became increasingly harsh as the war progressed. Relations with Sweden were yet again strained; the better-defended neighbour was left to be 'neutral', while the Germans demanded concessions which amounted to infringements of neutrality. Sweden became a safe haven for Norwegians and Danes on the run, and provided help in many ways, including harbouring all the Danish Jews and as many of the Norwegian ones as made it across the border; yet her readiness to grant concessions to the Germans and her relative prosperity revived the latent ill feeling towards 'big brother' which was a legacy of earlier history.

Although Norway was for most practical purposes out of the war after the summer of 1940, her ships in international waters again played an important role. The end of the occupation in 1945 was relatively peaceful; only in the far north did the Germans destroy villages, in order to delay the Russians on their heels. As in most of the war-affected countries, Norway's wartime shortages continued after the end of hostilities. Yet the return to prosperity was relatively fast; by the end of 1947 the pre-war standard of living had been restored, and it continued to improve during the 1950s. The caretaker government which oversaw the return to normal conditions gave way in October 1945 to an elected Labour government, which was to stay in power, with a single month's interruption, for twenty years.

After the war, Norway wanted to assert both her Scandinavian and her European identity. She joined the United Nations in 1946 (providing it with its first secretary-general, Trygve Lie), and the North Atlantic Treaty Organization in 1949; in 1952 she agreed with Denmark, Sweden, Finland and Iceland on the setting up of the Nordic Council, a forum for discussion of inter-Scandinavian matters. Norway had found her place in both the international and the Scandinavian community.

If one examines the role played by women in the social and political development of Norway during this time, one finds that they are less visible than in the years immediately preceding 1913. The vigorous campaigning on the suffrage issue was succeeded by a period of relative stagnation. In terms of political representation, for example, women were slow to avail themselves of the opportunity to elect their own representatives. The first woman MP was not elected until 1924, and numbers remained small; in 1937 it was down to one again. The first woman Cabinet Minister, Kirsten Hansteen, was not appointed until 1945 – and she was largely a token figure, without her own department. Numbers of women on all national and local elected bodies remained extremely small until the late 1960s.

The standard Norwegian history, *Norges historie*, devotes a chapter in Volume 12 (1884–1920) to the women's movement and universal suffrage; Volume 13 (1920–45) makes no mention of the women's movement, except for a brief reference to Katti Anker Møller; and in Volume 14, nothing is said on the subject until the chapter 'The New Women's Movement', dealing with the period from 1960 onwards.[3] According to this account, then, practically nothing happened as far as women were concerned in the forty years between 1920 and 1960. T.K. Derry concurs in his *A History of Modern Norway 1814–1972*; between 1914 and

1965, no woman is recorded as historically present except Sigrid Undset.

These accounts, of course, are 'men's history', in the sense that they concentrate on governments, wars, kings, treaties – the areas of public life in which women are less likely to figure prominently. Yet a similar picture emerges in women-centred accounts of the period. Anna Caspari Agerholt, in *Den norske kvinnebevegelses historie* (The History of the Norwegian Women's Movement), noted that in 1937, when the book was written, there were very few women in top jobs, and Kari Skjønsberg's introduction to the new edition of 1973 states: 'The introduction of universal suffrage in 1913 resulted in the struggle for women's rights losing impetus. There was no longer a great cause to unite them, and the great majority lost interest.'[4] Irene Iversen's essay on this topic in *Norsk kvinnelitteraturhistorie* (A History of Norwegian Women's Writing) refers to the fragmentation that followed after 1913.[5]

The loss of impetus immediately after winning the vote was not unique to Norway. In *The Feminists* Richard Evans suggests that 1920 marks the end of the era of feminism internationally, and that the women's movements in many countries had become less radical even before enfranchisement was achieved – a fact which helped women to attain the vote but ensured that it did not advance the cause of women's rights as they had hoped.[6] In *Sexual Politics*, Kate Millett labels the period 1930–60 'Counterrevolution'; she stresses the fact that the underlying social order, based on marriage and the family, was unaltered by the seeming victory of enfranchisement, and that the dominant political ideologies of the interwar period – Stalinism and Nazism – shared a common belief in patriarchal values. Freudian psychoanalysis was also based on the premiss that woman's rightful place was subordinate, and diverted women's attention from social injustice to individual sexual fulfilment.[7]

The lower level of activity of Norwegian women's movements in the years after 1913 is perhaps partly due to exhaustion after the long struggle; but there are other causes too. The vote was won in a period of relative political stability, which was immediately followed by violent upheaval. The First World War gave the countries of Europe other things to think about. The economic recession of the early thirties was a setback as far as women were concerned; married women were the first to be made redundant as unemployment surged, and it became politically expedient for a woman's place to be once again regarded as the home. The early decades of this century were also characterized by internal disagreement amongst different women's interest groups in Norway, which slowed the pace of reform. Divisions of opinion between middle-class and working-class women remained. There was particular disagreement about employment laws, as to whether there should be special rules to protect women from heavy work, unsocial hours etc.; working-class women often favoured rules which would protect them from exploitation, whereas middle-class women were more in favour of absolute equality. It was not possible to organize working-class and middle-class women into one organization until 1945, when the *Norske kvinners samarbeidsnemnd* (Norwegian Women's Co-operative Organization) was established; but that lasted only until 1950, when it split over abortion.

Yet there were some energetic activists during this period, and progress was made both in legislation and in general attitudes towards equality. Katti Anker Møller (1868–1945), one of the younger members of the women's liberation movement (and declared by Aasta Hansteen to be her 'spiritual daughter'), had been working to improve the lot of unmarried mothers and their children since the beginning of the century. Despite vigorous opposition – including opposition from many middle-class women – her efforts were successful when the 'Castberg child legislation' (called after the Minister of Justice Johan Castberg) was passed by the *Storting* in 1915. These far-sighted laws not only made it obligatory for the mother of an illegitimate child to name the father and for the father to maintain his child, but also conferred on the child the right to its father's name and equal rights of inheritance with legitimate children.

Katti Anker Møller was a woman before her time: she spoke of illegal abortion and sexually transmitted diseases in an era when middle-class women were supposed to be ignorant of such matters, and defended women's right to knowledge of their own biology and ownership of their own bodies, also within marriage. She championed the availability of contraception, and was instrumental in setting up the first family planning clinic in 1924; from then on, contraception quickly became more widely available (although there was much moral indignation, until the more liberal sixties, at the idea of providing contraception for unmarried women).

Feminists like Margarete Bonnevie, Mimi Sverdrup Lunden and Åse Grude Skard pointed to the double work of women outside and inside the home, and the need to reassess not just woman's role but also man's.[8] The socialist and critic Fernanda Nissen agitated for improvement in conditions for working-class women. Laws were passed which gave married women more control of their own property, and more opportunities for a career. In 1938, all barriers to women entering professions except the clergy were dropped; in 1956 even that barrier fell, and the first woman vicar was appointed in 1961. The Commission for Equal Pay was set up in 1959.

The one area in which Norway fell markedly behind the other Scandinavian countries was in the matter of abortion, over which there was a protracted struggle. Denmark passed a law making abortion legal in certain circumstances in 1937, Sweden in 1938; but the contemporary Norwegian proposals were so radical that the *Storting* could not agree, and the 1902 law, making abortion under any circumstances illegal remained theoretically in force – although in practice the legal system turned a blind eye to the fact that it was a law which was often transgressed.[9] It was not until 1960 that a law was passed allowing abortion on certain restricted grounds, and in 1978 a liberal law allowing abortion on demand came into force.

Literature between the wars

The reduced visibility of women in public life does not apply to literature; during the period covered by this chapter many more women became successful authors than ever before, and the numbers increased as time went on. Yet few of them are remembered and republished today as the male authors are, and hardly any are known outside Norway. Sigrid Undset is the major exception, and apart from her only Cora Sandel has achieved a relative success in the English-speaking world.

The First World War had little impact on Scandinavian literature; since the countries had not been involved in hostilities, there is no Scandinavian equivalent to the literature of the trenches such as flourished in England and France. The literary response to the war is more muted; it was seen as a watershed, the end of an era of social stability, to which later generations looked back with nostalgia (e.g. Johan Borgen's *Lillelord* [1955]). Inasmuch as one can speak of a dominant direction in Norwegian literature between 1910 and 1930, it is the 'new Realism' which dates from about 1907. There was a swing away from the neo-Romantic *fin-de-siècle* writing to a renewed interest in social issues in a realistically observed Norwegian community. Even Knut Hamsun, who began as an avowed opponent of the realist tradition, moved in that direction with his novels *Børn av Tiden* (Children of Their Time, 1913) and *Segelfoss by* (The Town of Segelfoss, 1915), which describe life in a small Norwegian coastal town moving into the age of modern capitalism. Sigrid Undset's early novels and stories provide portrayals of modern young women engaged, as she herself was, in working for a living, or faced with a crisis when career plans conflict with the traditional female role. Nini Roll Anker also places her female characters in the problematic environment of a rapidly developing modern society.

The early twentieth century is characterized by a tendency towards multivolume works, which frequently have a historical setting, or trace the development of a community from earlier centuries until modern times. Well-known contributions to this genre by male writers are Johan Falkberget's *Christianus Sextus* (1927–35), about an eighteenth-century mining community; Kristofer Uppdal's *Dansen gjenom skuggeheimen* (The Dance through the Land of Shadows, 1911–24), which traces the growth of the travelling labourer class over thirty years from 1890; and Olav Duun's *Juvikfolke* (The People of Juvik, 1918–23), which follows the fortunes of the Juvik family and the development of Norwegian rural society over four hundred years.

The multivolume study of a family or a community proved to be an especially fruitful genre for women writers. Gro Holm (1898–1949) wrote her trilogy *Løstølsfolket* (The People of Løstøl, 1932–4) about the harsh lives of subsistence farmers in Hardanger in the nineteenth century, whose womenfolk are exhausted by poverty and incessant child-bearing. Ingeborg Refling Hagen (1895–1989) set the trilogy *Tre døgn i Storskogen* (Three Days in Storskogen, 1937–9) in the present, in the experiences of a young teacher's first three days in a village; but interwoven with current events are the tales he hears from the village folk, redolent with tradition and superstition. Gisken Wildenvey's (1895–1985) 'Andrine' books (1929–39) and Magnhild Haalke's (1885–1984) *Grys Saga* (1936–41) are examples of trilogies which constitute *Entwicklungsromane*, following the growth of a woman from childhood to maturity. The extended scope of a multivolume study also appealed to more well-known writers, such as Hulda Garborg, Sigrid Undset, Nini Roll Anker and Cora Sandel.

Hulda Garborg continued to write both literary works and polemical articles well into the twentieth century. She was better known as a controversial public figure than as a writer, with her agitation for traditional folk culture, for the New Norwegian language and for a Norwegian theatre. Her views about the women's movement were somewhat ambivalent; her novel *Kvinden skabt av Manden* (Woman Made of Man, 1904) portrayed woman as an irrational being on the basis of biological determinism, and provoked refutation by several radicals, Gina Krog amongst them. Yet her own career belied her political opinions, and her fictional women grew more independent in the course of time. Her four-volume 'Hedemark' series (1920–25) focuses on a woman, both strong-willed and strongly sexed, who refuses to let herself be determined by her sex, and succeeds in running the family farm on her own as well as playing a role in local and national affairs.

Sigrid Undset (1882–1949) brought a detailed study of the minutiae of everyday life both to her contemporary and to her historical works. She wrote two multivolume historical series, *Kristin Lavransdatter* (1920–22) and the 'Olav Audunssøn' series (1925–7), which set the ethical and religious struggles of passionate individuals against a well-researched medieval background. She too was a polemicist who took up 'the woman question' in articles and speeches; and as with Hulda Garborg, what she said was not always welcome to feminists, since she had a more traditional view of the uxorial and particularly the maternal role of woman. This was unfortunate as her statements had a unique authority, coming as they did from a Nobel Prize winner and all-time best-seller (see Chapter 6).

Nini Roll Anker (1873–1942) was a close friend of Sigrid Undset; there are those who think that if it had not been for the award of the Nobel Prize, her reputation would have been as great. She came from a privileged background, being married early to a rich estate owner; but she soon decided that her sympathies lay with the working class, whose cause she espoused in her novels and in her public statements – so much so that she was declared 'a traitor to her class'.[10] She attacked women's liberationists for being elitist in their lack of understanding of the burdens of working-class women, and for denying women's sexuality in their efforts to become the equals of men.

Nini Roll Anker's first major novel, *Det svake Kjøn* (The Weaker Sex, 1915), borrows its title from the Swedish author Ellen Key (1849–1926), who was campaigning around the turn of the century for a recognition of the *differences* between men and women and a reassessment of the 'feminine values' related to motherhood, which society did not prize enough. The novel follows the life of a young girl from adolescent conflict connected to the problems of emancipation, through love and sensual obsession, disillusionment and death. It has no clear message, but points out the dangers as well as the rewards of trying to live 'authentically', in accordance with one's own nature.

Anker's historical 'Stampe' trilogy was published in the twenties, as *Huset i Søgaten* (The House in Søgaten, 1923), *I Amtmandsgaarden* (In the District Governor's House, 1925) and *Under Skraataket* (Under the Sloping Roof, 1927). It follows the Stampe family through five generations, with the focus moving from the provincial 'official' class of mid-nineteenth-century Norway to the upheavals caused by the parliamentary crisis of 1884, and finally to Christiania during the First World War, with stock-exchange gambling, modern luxury and wavering moral standards. The alternative to moral decay is the revolutionary Labour movement, with its roots in the working class and its inspiration from the Russian Revolution.

The novels were immensely popular; *Huset i Søgaten* went through five editions in the first year of publication. And they have stood the test of time – they were reprinted in the 1970s, as were two of her other novels. *Den som henger i en tråd* (Hanging by a Thread, 1935) is set in a small town where the main employer is a clothing manufacturer. The novel follows a group of female workers, and the first stirrings of protest at economic and sexual exploitation. The protagonist, Karna, organizes an abortive strike;

at the end she is left isolated but unshaken in her belief that organization is the only answer. *Kvinnen og den svarte fuglen* (The Woman and the Black Bird, published posthumously in 1945) is an anti-war novel, written from the point of view of a woman who sees her sons go off to die. Amongst Nini Roll Anker's many other novels were three light-hearted parodies under a male pseudonym, Kåre P.; the first one, *Liv, livet og jeg* (Liv, Life and I, 1927), published when she was an established author of fifty-four, so thoroughly deceived the critics that it was praised as 'A talented and witty little book, written by a real man with healthy instincts'.[11]

Cora Sandel (1880–1974) was a contemporary of Sigrid Undset and Nini Roll Anker, but began publishing so late that she seems to belong to a different generation. The first volume of her 'Alberte' trilogy, *Alberte og Jakob* (*Alberta and Jacob*), appeared in 1926, and it took her thirteen years to complete the series with *Alberte og friheten* (*Alberta and Freedom*, 1931) and *Bare Alberte* (*Alberta Alone*, 1939). It is a female *Entwicklungsroman*, following Alberte's struggle – against society, and against her own internal blocks – to establish herself as an artist. Cora Sandel was a pseudonym; her real name was Sara Fabricius. She took little part in public debate; her novels and stories were produced painstakingly by a consummate stylist, as aware of the significance of what is not said as of what lies on the surface (see Chapter 7).

The 1930s were a time of intellectual ferment in Norway, comparable to the 1880s in their radical questioning of accepted attitudes. It was a decade of *causes célèbres*, with furious arguments – and not infrequently court cases – raging over most matters on which personal conviction ran deep: political and religious beliefs, sexual morality and the family, the upbringing and education of children.[12] New systems of knowledge or belief were popularized, in particular Marxism and Freudianism. In these debates, women's voices are muted.[13]

Cultural debate in the 1930s was dominated by the 'radical trio': the novelist Sigurd Hoel, the poet Arnulf Øverland and the dramatist Helge Krog. They all served their apprenticeship in the twenties in the 'Mot Dag' movement, in the circle of intellectuals around the magazine of that name, roughly translated as 'Towards the Dawn'. In this time of *rapprochement* between the political left in Norway and the Communist Party in Russia, many of Norway's radical intellectuals were Communists or sympathizers. Sigurd Hoel's novels from the 1930s are influenced by Freud – and as time goes on, also by Wilhelm Reich, with his insistence on the importance of liberated sexuality for harmonious individual development. Arnulf Øverland, a declared Communist, published withering attacks on Christianity – which earned him a trial for blasphemy in 1933. Helge Krog's plays and polemics campaign for the liberty of the individual, and especially for women's rights; in plays like *Konkylien* (The Conch Shell, 1929) and *Opbrudd* (Breakaway, 1936) he portrays strong female characters with the courage to leave relationships which are no longer satisfactory. The son of Norway's first female student, Cecilie Thoresen, Krog followed Ibsen in identifying women as being still the oppressed group in Norwegian society.

Although women were not prominent in public discussion, their literary works often commented on ideologies and their consequences particularly for the lives of women. Nini Roll Anker's descriptions of female sexual desire were thought unseemly for a woman, and she depicts the consequences of the sexual revolution in the form of more widespread contraception, illegal abortions and the persistent double standard which castigates women who live out their desires in a way which has traditionally been allowed to men. Religion and sexuality clash frequently in the works of Sigrid Undset, and Cora Sandel demonstrates in many of her short stories how little effect all the new liberal ideas have had on the lives of women trapped in the grey sameness of a loveless marriage.

Conservative critics naturally objected to the iconoclastic literature of the radical generation, and nowhere more strongly than in the area of sexuality. In a notorious article from 1931, the critic Fredrik Ramm started a debate on the sexually explicit writings of contemporary authors ('A filthy stream is flowing across the land . . .'). Most of the 'filthy' works were by male authors like Sigurd Hoel, but included in the attack was one by a woman, *Sår som ennu blør* (Wounds Which Still Bleed, 1931), by Karo Espeseth (born 1903). The novel is an extraordinary account of a sadomasochistic relationship between a German man, psychologically damaged by his war experiences, and a Norwegian woman student. With its intimate descriptions of sadistic sexuality, based on psychological analysis of the man's past experiences, it shocked critics. It was also unconventional in form, being more like a long prose poem than an ordinary novel. It was an isolated phenomenon; Karo Espeseth wrote no more novels – whether as a result of the critical reaction is not known – and literary histories record little of her.

Lesbian sexuality makes its first appearance in Norwegian literature during this period too – later than in Denmark, where Martha Grüner was the pioneer in 1890 with *Vildsomme veje* (Wild Ways).[14] Edith Øberg (1895–1968) portrayed sexual attraction between women in her novels *Skum* (Froth, 1921) and *Boblen* (The Bubble, 1922). In 1935 Borghild Krane (born 1906) published *Følelsers forvirring* (Emotional Confusion), which describes a fully realized lesbian relationship and the women's struggles to gain public acceptance for their love – with tragic results. These novels were not the subject of public debate; as so often, this kind of 'deviation' was greeted with uniform silence.

The first decades of the twentieth century saw the growth of the light entertainment industry in Norway. Films became widely available in 1905–10, and even the smallest villages soon boasted a cinema; there were regular radio broadcasts from 1925, and *Norsk rikskringkasting* (the Norwegian Broadcasting Corporation) was formed in 1933. Women's magazines became a powerful force; several had been started well before 1900. They provided an outlet for women writers of romantic fiction, as well as for others. The division between 'trivial' and 'serious' literature was not so absolute as it later became, and serious authors were also published through these channels; though increasingly it was light entertainment which dominated. The magazine *Urd* (which took its name from one of the three Norns) was an exception; from its beginnings in 1897 until it ceased publication in 1958, it concentrated on 'quality' articles aimed at an élite readership. In time it lost readers because of its elitism and its traditional stance; it insisted that the private sphere was woman's natural domain.[15]

Narrative prose was the preferred medium for women authors in this period, as in the earlier one. The theatre was not very welcoming to women dramatists, except in the area of plays for children; few were performed, and runs were short. Even those who were relatively successful were often badly served by miscasting or by interpretations which distorted the message, as was Nini Roll Anker. She had five plays performed at the National Theatre between 1911 and 1934, but in the case of *Kirken* (The Church, 1920) at least, had to suffer a producer who cut vital lines which explain the central character's motivation.[16] With the possible exception of Hulda Garborg, who was the most performed of female dramatists before 1935, drama was not the major genre of any of the well-known women writers during this period.

Women poets are thin on the ground in the interwar years too. When Halldis Moren Vesaas (born 1907) published her first collection of poetry, *Harpe og dolk* (Harp and Dagger), in 1929, she was 'the first new woman poet in almost a generation'.[17] Her *nynorsk* poetry focuses on the 'feminine' subjects of love, nurture and nature; but it is borne by a strong current of sensuality where the physical sense of female experience is given a new weight. Her first collection was followed by another three before 1939, and three more after the war (see Chapter 8). Shortly after her followed Ingeborg Refling Hagen, already known as a novelist, with *Jeg vil hem att* (I Want to Go Home, 1932). She was to become only the third woman to be awarded an author's stipend – in 1936, after Camilla Collett and then Sigrid Undset in 1922.

The other major woman poet writing between the wars was Aslaug Vaa (1889–1964), who made a late debut with *Nord i leite* (Looking Northwards, 1934). Her poetry, written in her native Telemark dialect, unites impulses from Norwegian folk tradition and European Modernism. She lived abroad for many years, particularly in Paris after the First World War, where she was fascinated by the explosion of artistic experimentation which developed into Dadaism and Cubism; but also in London, Berlin and (in 1937) in Africa. Her poetry reflects the experiences of these years – and also of older European influences, for example in her use of the sonnet form and her affinities with William Blake. Yet she never forgot her roots in Telemark traditions, and echoes of ballads and folk songs are apparent in all her seven collections of poems. The central theme of her poetry is love, but love between two independent people rather than a male subject and a female object.

The Norwegian Authors' Association, *Den norske forfatterforening*, which on its foundation in 1893 had been rather like a gentlemen's club, became a cultural and political force during the 1930s, campaigning for better working conditions for authors and defending intellectual freedom; it issued a sharp reprimand to Knut Hamsun in 1935 when he attacked the imprisoned German pacifist Carl von Ossietzky. Women came to play a central role in the organization, including Nini Roll Anker (deputy chairman from 1916), the critic Eugenia Kielland, and Sigrid Undset (chairman 1935–40). The author Nils Johan Rud even went so far as to call the interwar period in the Authors' Association 'an era dominated by women': an exaggeration, no doubt, but significant in that it reveals that women were becoming distinctly more visible in that arena at least.

The Second World War and its aftermath

The German occupation put a stop to independent literary production in Norway; the Germans were aware of the power of propaganda, and seized control of the publishing outlets at once. Only innocuous or Nazified texts were allowed into print. Many authors responded by ceasing to write, or at least to publish, until after the war; some were published abroad, usually in Sweden. Some disguised their criticism in seemingly innocent books or newspaper articles, like Johan Borgen's gossipy *Mumle Gåsegg* series in the daily paper *Dagbladet*. The remaining alternative, as the occupation progressed, was to make use of the illegal printing presses of the Resistance movement to print and distribute direct appeals.[18] Short texts were particularly well suited to this form of distribution, and apart from illegal newspapers, it was poetry which proved the best vehicle for opposition through the printed word. It is a trio of male poets whose names are best remembered in this connection, and whose patriotic poems were passed secretly from hand to hand: Arnulf Øverland, Nordahl Grieg, and Gunnar Reiss-Andersen.

But women wrote Resistance poetry too; among the best-remembered are Inger Hagerup and Halldis Moren Vesaas.[19] Inger Hagerup (1905–85) published her first collection of poetry, *Jeg gikk meg vill i skogene* (I Lost My Way in the Forests), in 1939 – a combination of poems about a woman's experience of seeing herself as an object in men's eyes, and about the threatening situation in Europe. Her next collection, *Flukten til Amerika* (The Flight to America, 1942), was published in Norway during the occupation, and contains personal love poetry rather than political poetry. But at the same time she was writing poems about the occupation, which could not be published legally in Norway; like those of Grieg and Øverland, they were passed round anonymously from hand to hand. These poems are included in the collection *Videre* (Onwards), which was published in Sweden in 1944, after she had taken refuge there. They include the famous poem written in March 1941 about the German reprisals after a bombing raid on Lofoten, 'Aust-Vågøy':

They burnt our farms.
They killed our men.
Let our hearts repeat it
Again and again.

Let our hearts throb
In a hard, harsh way:
They burnt our farms.
They did it today.

They burnt our farms.
They killed our men.
Behind each one who died
Are thousands more again.

A thousand others stand
Defiant and uncowed.
Listen, dead comrades,
Our heads will not be bowed.

It is a typical Resistance poem, with short, emotionally charged lines, regular rhythms and rhymes and a defiant message, easy to memorize at a time when it was best not to possess incriminating documents. One might call it a 'masculine' war poem – it could as well have been written by Grieg or Øverland. Halldis Moren Vesaas's war poetry has a different flavour, and differs less from her other writing; the dominant mood is not defiant, but grief-stricken at the waste of it all and sympathetic to the human suffering on both sides. In 'Regnet og krigen' (The Rain and the War), written in

June 1940, she welcomes the rain falling on the thirsty earth to give new life, and wishes it could grow to a flood to wash away the blood and the hatred.

When the floodgates opened in 1945 after the lifting of German control, a vast amount of literature poured out – not all of it equally good. After their first experience of occupation by an enemy power the Norwegians had to come to terms with what had happened, and the literary repercussions lasted a considerable time; they have still not quite died away. Some war novels took the predictable form of thrillers about patriotic Norwegians pitted against evil Germans; the more interesting ones took a more balanced view. Several established authors produced psychological novels which concentrate on the ambivalent attitudes of 'good' Norwegians, and portray Nazism as a threat from within rather than a purely German phenomenon (e.g. Sigurd Hoel: *Møte ved milepelen* [The Meeting at the Milestone, 1947]; Johan Borgen: *Vi har ham nå* [We Have Him Now, 1957]; Tarjei Vesaas: *Bleikeplassen* [The Bleaching Yard, 1946]).

Amongst women prose writers, the war years brought about a generation shift. Nini Roll Anker died in 1942, and Sigrid Undset wrote no more fiction after the war. Cora Sandel did continue to write for some time, although the war is not a major theme of her novels. In some of her short stories, however, she studies its impact on the lives of individuals, particularly women and children. The story 'Berit', for example, describes the German invasion in April 1940 from the viewpoint of a small child.[20] Of the large number of new writers in the immediate post-war years, a considerable number were women. Amongst those who began their literary careers in 1945 were two whose first works sprang directly out of wartime experiences: Torborg Nedreaas (1906–87) and Ebba Haslund (born 1917).

Torborg Nedreaas's collection of short stories, *Bak skapet står øksen* (The Axe Stands Behind the Cupboard, 1945), depicts the German occupation as experienced by the occupants of a Norwegian village, where the enemy was not a monolithic force but a number of ordinary people with ordinary virtues and failings, with whom a human relationship inevitably arose. Most of her later works concentrate on women's fates in a repressive environment; *Av måneskinn gror det ingenting* (*Nothing Grows by Moonlight*, 1947), for example, is the story of a teenager who is seduced by her teacher, a weak man who can neither marry her nor leave her, and continues to be her lover when she is married to someone else. In despair at the degrading way she is treated, she has a one-night stand with a stranger – then discovers she is pregnant, without knowing who the father is. She performs an abortion on herself, in an episode of sickening physical detail.

The work by which Torborg Nedreaas will probably be best remembered is her series of novels about Herdis, *Trylleglasset* (The Magic Glass, 1950); *Musikk fra en blå brønn* (Music from a Blue Well, 1960); and *Ved neste nymåne* (At the Next New Moon, 1971). Like Cora Sandel's 'Alberte' trilogy – and taking even longer in its gestation – this series follows the development from childhood to adulthood of a girl with artistic gifts, who has to struggle against her surroundings and her own conditioning. Herdis is an outsider, both by virtue of her own 'otherness' and because of her background; belonging neither to the feckless poor nor to the solid middle classes, she feels ostracized by both, and is driven back upon her own resources and her 'magic glass', which transforms the world viewed through it. As she grows and develops her musical talents, she becomes more able to articulate her awareness of the social divide and materialistic capitalism which oppresses the inhabitants of Bergen around the time of the First World War. Herdis's point of view is maintained throughout the trilogy, with the author suggesting behind her naive view of events a more sophisticated interpretation of motive and social pressure.

Ebba Haslund's first book was also a collection of short stories – a genre which has been consistently popular in Scandinavian literature since the time of the sagas. *Også vi . . .* (We Too . . . , 1945) is set in the solid middle classes, and conveys glimpses of life under occupation as it was experienced by respectable people who suddenly found the even tenor of life disrupted in the most unexpected ways. Her novel *Det hendte ingenting* (Nothing Happened, 1948) was practically ignored by critics, although it could well be said to rank alongside other more highly acclaimed post-war novels about the effects of repressive conditioning on personal development, such as Sigurd

Hoel's *The Meeting at the Milestone*.[21] Most of her fiction centres on women living 'ordinary' lives. Her novels from the
1950s were received with moderate interest – although they
were found to yield more when they were reread from a
consciously feminist critical standpoint in the 1970s. But she did
not make a breakthrough as a popular author until the 1960s,
and her most important novel about the war, *Syndebukkens krets*
(The Sign of the Scapegoat), did not appear until 1968. This
novel depicts the conflict of Resistance heroes versus inform-
ers during the occupation in the light of the biblical image
of the scapegoat; people's need to project their own weak-
nesses on to someone else is the motivation that brands them
as traitors.

Another prose writer to make her debut during the 1940s was
Solveig Christov (born 1918). Her most successful novels, from
the 1950s, were allegories of the Cold War and its threat to
humanity's continued existence. *Torso* (1952) is a story about a
community living on a narrow cliff ledge, unable to move from
where they are without plummeting to their deaths. *Demningen*
(The Dam, 1957) tells of a society's reaction to a catastrophe
caused by the bursting of a dam by floodwater: they build a bigger
dam which, if breached, will lead to incalculable destruction.

A greater proportion of poetry during the 1950s was published
by women than had been the case earlier. In 1946–50, 19 out of
the 216 collections of poetry published were written by women (=
8.8 per cent); in 1956–60, the number was 35 out of 182 (= 19.2
per cent).[22] Their voices were growing more confident in a genre
which had previously been much more of a male preserve.

Gunvor Hofmo (born 1921) made her literary debut in 1946
with *Jeg vil hjem til menneskene* (I Want to Go Home to Mankind). There are some war poems in this collection, like 'Møte'
('Meeting'), which imagines a reunion with a Jewish friend, long
since incinerated in concentration camp; but most of them
are mood-pictures, embodying what one might call a post-war
mood of emptiness and meaninglessness. Nature is as beautiful as ever, but now it is an indifferent framework around
unfulfillable longing rather than a background to a possible
romance:

One day when the grasshopper's playing
in night-wet fields and scrub,
and hay-racks are breathing bitterly
out in the paleness of night
my friend will return
the one I have never had![23]

Gunvor Hofmo's poetry became freer in its form but also more private in its reference in the three collections she published in the 1950s; and after *Testamente til en evighet* (Testament to an Eternity) in 1955, she suddenly stopped publishing. Her next poetry collection did not appear until 1971.

Amongst the other women poets who made their mark in the 1940s and 1950s one could mention Astrid Tollefsen (1897–1973), Astrid Hjertenæs Andersen (1915–85), Magli Elster (born 1912) and Marie Takvam (born 1926); the two latter with outspokenly erotic poetry of a kind not previously written by women poets in Norway. Inger Hagerup continued to write poetry after the war, as did Halldis Moren Vesaas.

The increasing number and importance of women writers in the immediate post-war period is a reflection of their growing confidence in the public arena. They were gradually taking an increasing part in public life, demonstrating their commitment to politics, peace work, family planning, journalism (especially in the magazine *Kvinnefronten* [The Women's Front], which became *Kvinnen og Tiden* [Women and Time, 1945–55]), and the arts.[24] Educational and career opportunities were improving in the reconstruction work after the war, and earlier changes in legislation were slowly acquiring practical consequences for women's lives.

6
Sigrid Undset (1882–1949)

The struggle to write (1882–1909)

In her autobiographical account of her early years, *Elleve år* (*The Longest Years*, 1934), Sigrid Undset recounts her own earliest memory through the medium of her central character:

> The first thing Ingvild remembered was that she had just crawled off the lawn across to a strip of bare earth in front of a wall of green bushes.
>
> The soil is brown and crumbly and sun-warmed, lovely to fill her hands with. The child trickles it through her fingers down on to her bare legs and white socks, turning them grey. She pours and pours, giddy with delight, hurrying because she knows that when they come they will pick her up, brush the earth off her and carry her away . . .
>
> The still, baking summer heat and the warm breeze make the little child feel that she is a part of everything that is living in the garden. The child senses it with a kind of orgiastic joy; she shuffles out a hollow, like a chicken taking a soil bath, and stirs with her hands – happy in the knowledge that she should not be doing this.
>
> Then someone does come –. Who it was Ingvild could not remember, but it must have been one of her aunts, her mother's young sisters. Because it was a light girlish voice which chirruped a greeting, and she was not scooped up from her hollow and brushed clean. Instead the newcomer crouched down and pushed something into her arms.
>
> It is a doll with a shiny, hard porcelain head, coal black on one side and shiny white on the other, with a face made of thin black stripes and pink blotches. It is wearing some stiff mustard-yellow material – it feels unpleasant in Ingvild's hands, and it is trimmed with lace and shiny ribbons, so stiff that they

scratch. Ingvild does not at all like this thing they want her to hold.

Nevertheless she makes an attempt with it. She brings the doll's head to her mouth, but it won't go in − it's too big, and hard and shiny and cold − feels nasty on her teeth when she tries to bite it. She doesn't want it. So she throws it over on to the lawn.[1]

This passage announces many of the themes which were to preoccupy the mature writer. The most immediate impression is of the sensuality of the experience; the tactile sensations of soil, sun and breeze combine to reach a peak of intensity. Although the narrator interprets the feelings in words not available to a child ('a kind of orgiastic joy . . .'), she conveys vividly the sense of surrender to physical ecstasy which is a child's premonition of orgasm.

Following instantaneously upon this feeling, however, is the child's awareness that it is forbidden, and that she will be stopped. Yet she is happy in this knowledge, as if the experience is heightened by a sense of doing something of which those in authority will disapprove. In her earliest experience, a link is thus established between a sense of ecstasy and a sense of transgression; the vividness of the emotion is intensified by the feeling that it is a forbidden delight. The incident can be interpreted in terms of Christian mythology − a memory of the Garden of Eden and the forbidden fruit − and also as a female discovery of a sexuality which is disapproved of by the mother. The latter theme recurs in fiction by other women writers, such as Camilla Collett; but there can be few who have been so conscious of it before the age of two.[2]

There is a striking contrast between the natural surroundings and the intrusion of the artificial in the shape of the doll which is thrust into Ingvild's arms. Everything about the doll is unpleasant: it is stiff and scratchy, cold and slippery, and its garish colours clash with the softer shades of nature. There is nothing she can do with it; it is not responsive to her touch like the sun-warmed soil. Her instinctive reaction is one of rejection; yet already she has been civilized enough to give it her polite attention before discarding it. This passage anticipates the conflict between nature and culture, and the emphasis on 'natural' values, which are in evidence particularly in Sigrid Undset's early work.

The ambiguous feelings aroused by this first episode are under-lined later, when Ingvild again feels a glorious communion with nature whilst sitting next to a beehive, watching the pretty creatures crawling on her dress and arms, only to be told that she could have been stung to death. The shock of this discovery reinforces the lesson that joy is linked to danger or sin. After this episode the garden becomes 'a foreign country' to her; as in *The District Governor's Daughters*, the lesson has been learnt that independent activity, particularly sexual activity, is dangerous for a woman. But Sigrid Undset lived in a more equal society than Camilla Collett, and in her writing, as in her life, the will to self-determination and the current of sensuality are so strong that they are not easily dammed by repression. As a result, conflict and ambiguity are everywhere in evidence in her work, and especially in her female characters.

In her biography of Sigrid Undset, Gidske Anderson draws a parallel between these early memories and those of Virginia Woolf, who, incidentally, was born in the same year.[3] Virginia's memory of lying in her cradle listening to the sound of the waves outside was a sensual experience on which she felt that much of the rhythm and mood of her writing was based. Different as their prose styles are, both writers convey sense impressions with an immediacy which communicates itself directly to the reader.

It is tempting to draw a further parallel between the early lives of the two authors. Virginia felt that hers had been lived under the shadow of a domineering father; if he had not died, she would never have become an author, as she wrote in 1928:

> Father's birthday. He would have been 96, 96, yes, today; and could have been 96, like other people one has known; but mercifully was not. His life would have entirely ended mine. What would have happened? No writing, no books; – inconceivable.[4]

Sigrid Undset's father was a gentler man; yet there is no doubt that he was the dominant figure of her early life. He was an archaeologist, and inordinately proud of his intelligent oldest daughter, who would, he hoped, follow in his footsteps; she was interested, but did not share his passion for research, though she did not have the heart to let him know. Perhaps she might have become a historical scholar rather than an author, if he had not died when she was only eleven years old.

Sigrid Undset was born on 20 May 1882, in Kalundborg in Denmark. Her mother, Charlotte Gyth, was Danish; her father, Ingvald Undset, came from Trondheim in Norway. As a child she spent many holidays with grandparents, and developed a deep attachment to both Denmark and Trøndelag; though when she was two, the family moved to Christiania, where she was to grow up. As well as by her father's scholarship, her childhood was dominated by his progressive illness; he had syphilis of the spine, and although he struggled to continue the research trips and publications which had brought him early recognition, he slowly became a semi-invalid. Charlotte had to take on the running of family affairs, as well as acting as his secretary; she was energetic and capable. Sigrid was too young to do much beyond read to her father; but she shied away from his illness, and would rather be out exploring. They moved several times, to houses which became less spacious as the family income shrank. When Ingvald died in 1893, at the age of forty, Charlotte was left with three daughters and a very limited income.

The girls had been attending a fee-paying school opened in 1885 by Ragna Nielsen, one of the founders of the Norwegian women's liberation movement, who had advanced ideas on women's education. It was the first school in Norway to have mixed classes, and to use female teachers at high-school level. Surprisingly, Sigrid's reaction to this school was one of opposition. Forward-looking as it was, it was still a school based on 'children's books', which Sigrid – educated at home until the age of eight, and largely on adult books – had outgrown. And after being taught by her father that history was largely speculation, she was now expected to accept it as fact. For much of her time at school she was bored. She also reacted against the optimistic belief in progress which characterized the school and its headmistress; already at this age her views on the potential development of human nature were pessimistic. Her scepticism about the aims and methods of the women's liberation movement was founded during her schooldays.

When Ingvald Undset died, Ragna Nielsen declared that the three girls could have free places until they sat their university entrance examinations. The two younger ones took advantage of this, but Sigrid stayed only until she completed her basic schooling at the age of fifteen, and then left to do a secretarial course. There were a number of reasons for this; she had not enjoyed her schooling, and although she was deeply interested in certain areas of study, she was indifferent to others. She was a selective rather than a systematic scholar. In addition, she wished to ease her mother's burden and contribute to the family economy.

In 1899, Sigrid Undset began work in the office of Wisbech, the Norwegian representatives of the German company AEG; she was to remain there for ten years. Although she valued her financial independence, she found office work tedious. The greyness of life in poorly paid drudgery and in her restricted family circle was to provide her with material for her stories of contemporary women's lives. Initially, though, her literary imagination was drawn to the more colourful medieval period of her early reading as an escape from present drabness. She had been writing since childhood, scribbling page after page and tearing it up the next morning. When in 1904 she finished a manuscript called 'Aage Nielssøn of Ulvholm', and submitted it to the Danish publisher Gyldendal, it was refused – with the advice, ironical in retrospect, that historical novels were not her genre, and she would do better to write about her own times.

Much of what we know of her feelings at this time comes from her correspondence with her Swedish 'pen friend', Andrea Hedberg; she had no close friend to talk to, but told Dea of her literary plans, and of the frustrations of her life as an 'office rat' with no outlet for her passions: 'I only want to love and be loved as a sinful child of this earth loves and is loved.'[5] Angered by Gyldendal's refusal, she nevertheless took the publisher's advice and turned to a modern subject, with the result that her first novel, *Fru Marta Oulie* (Mrs Martha Oulie), was published in 1907.

Some time after the book's appearance, Sigrid Undset wrote to Dea Hedberg: 'You ask me why I am interested in marriage problems – I can't say that any "problems" interest me, just people, and it is most often marriage which is a person's fate, or a woman's at least.'[6] Women's fates are at the centre of most of her writing, and she had ample opportunity to observe them in her fellow workers and in the streets of Christiania. Marta Oulie's story is written in the form of a diary confession, and starts with the oft-quoted sentence: 'I have been unfaithful to my husband' (*RFN* I, p. 7).[7] Although seemingly happily married, Marta has found that her kind husband Otto is neither sensitive enough to understand her feelings nor passionate enough to satisfy her sexual hunger – whereas his best friend Henrik is both: '*I* wanted to have *him*, to swallow him whole. It was a natural instinct which welled up in me, raw and insatiable, and I, a well-behaved little merchant's wife, going about so quietly and looking after my house, became in reality a dangerous and evil beast of prey' (p. 52). In her version of the tale, she has cast herself in the role of the wolf. When the trusting Otto develops consumption, her passion for Henrik turns to hatred; her life has been ruined. This short novel announces a theme which is to be played out more fully in *Jenny* – of a life in which making the wrong choice is not a redeemable fault, but a fatal error. It is as if there is only one chance, for a woman, to get it right.

Once her first book had been published, Sigrid Undset worked furiously, often writing at night, finishing a book almost every year right up until 1940. The stories in *Den lykkelige alder* (The Happy Age, 1908) take place in a modern urban setting which, as she points out to Dea, is practically unique in being based on her own experience:

> Christiania has as yet hardly ever been described by anyone other than people from out of town, who have poured out the bitterness of their wrath over our poor little provincial town – and over all the youth who are struggling and battling alone in here – and really not by anyone who has been personally involved in the struggle. (*Kjære Dea*, p. 412)

The volume is mostly taken up by two long stories which centre on a woman's choice of partner and its fateful consequences. 'En Fremmed' ('A Stranger') depicts a working girl, Edele, living a bed-sit existence in Christiania; her office job is mundane, and in her loneliness she is persuaded to become engaged to Alf Aagaard. She soon realizes that he is a petty man with whom she has nothing in common; yet she feels she must stick by her choice, and unwillingly becomes his lover. Finally she finds the courage to break with him; but she feels that she is finished with life, that her wrong choice has marked her as forever unworthy. She is helped by her lifelong friend Per Dryssen, and their relationship grows into love – yet she cannot rid herself of the feeling that she is worthless, and it is not until after a failed suicide attempt that Per finally manages to reach her. It has nearly cost her her life.

Work is a central theme in the story – the contrast between men's work and women's work. Edele feels that women's work is most often trivial, a way of passing the time before love comes along; whereas men's work is central to their lives, and gives them a strength which carries them through disappointments: 'They had something which could never be dragged down – a chaste love of their work, they were of those for whom life has days, light and cool and busy ones. Therefore they could live how they wanted – for them there was a meaning to life' (*RFN* I, p. 141). Although in theory women in the early twentieth century had more choice than they did in Camilla Collett's day – they could choose to work, they could choose their own partners – it takes more than half a century to achieve real equality of opportunity. Marriage was still the goal for most women, and their happiness hinged on making a success of it, whereas it was only a part of a man's life.

Conflict between marriage and work is the theme of the other long story, 'Den lykkelige alder' ('The Happy Age'). Uni Hirsch in torn between her ambition to be an actress and her love for Kristian Hjelde. She breaks with him for a time and goes on the stage; yet work is not enough for her, and she is plagued by nagging doubts about her own talent – can she really be a great actress, or is she sacrificing her happiness and his for a selfish whim? Finally she gives up the struggle and leaves the stage. She has chosen to live as a wife and mother with a loving but unartistic man – and does not delude herself about her sacrifice: 'There was something in her which would always long to be elsewhere, something of her innermost being which there would never be any use for in Kristian Hjelde's home' (p. 257). Fulfilment in both work and marriage is not an option, and choosing either involves a compromise.

Compared with other characters in the story, however, Uni's chance of making her own choice is a luxury; she is surrounded by women whose lives offer no escape from hopelessness. Her friend

Birgit loses her one chance of happiness when her fiancé breaks off their engagement: 'Birgit's little fate was sealed when Lieutenant Gustav had broken off. Life would come to her no more' (*RFN* I, p. 249). Her other friend, Charlotte, is an intelligent woman who longs to do something with her life – to travel, to see the world, to struggle to make her way – but she is condemned to stay at home in a routine job because her mother and younger sisters are dependent on her income. There are parallels to Sigrid Undset's own situation in Charlotte's despairing words about her cramped existence – an existence to which Sigrid Undset vicariously puts a violent end, as Charlotte shoots herself in Nordmarka outside Christiania.

Suicide as a cathartic resolution of transferred problems,which allows their author to cope with them more positively – it is a device used by Amalie Skram and Ragnhild Jølsen, as well as many other women authors. And this volume also provided a practical solution for its author; after its publication she was awarded a travel grant which gave her the financial independence she needed to leave her detested office job and set off in the summer of 1909 for southern Europe.

Exploration and consolidation (1909–19)

The next ten years were to be full ones for Sigrid Undset, bringing all that she had longed for: travel, passion, motherhood – and always writing, writing. Her trip southwards took her through Denmark and Germany, but it was Italy that was her goal; and like Ragnhild Jølsen only three years earlier, she found Florence lonely and cold, but Rome immediately congenial, with its lively circle of Scandinavian writers and artists. It was in Rome in 1909 that she met the painter Anders Svarstad, who was to become her husband.

By all accounts, they fell instantaneously in love – and it was to be the only love of Sigrid Undset's life; as for so many of her female characters, it was to be once and for all. It was not straightforward; Svarstad already had a wife and children, and had to get divorced before they could marry. But they lived as lovers from the start, first in Rome and then in Paris in 1910, before returning to Norway. They finally married in June 1912, leaving straight away for six months in London. Seven months after the marriage, their first son Anders was born in Rome; but he became ill, and in May 1913 Sigrid returned alone to Norway with him – for good, as it turned out. They began to drift apart – although two more children were born, Maren (1915) and Hans (1919). In 1919 Sigrid moved to Lillehammer, to what was to become Bjerkebæk, her home for the rest of her life, whilst Svarstad stayed in Christiania. Her early sense of the power and the transience of passion had been confirmed; it was to bear fruit in her mature works *Jenny* and *Kristin Lavransdatter*.[8]

Throughout this turbulent period, Sigrid Undset's creative energy was undiminished; in fact she felt that she worked in a more concentrated fashion when she was under pressure. On the way to Italy she had finished the manuscript of her first 'medieval' novel, *Fortællingen om Viga-Ljot og Vigdis* (*Gunnar's Daughter*, 1909), and from then on she produced a mixture of contemporary and historical works in rapid succession. It is her studies of contemporary life which are her most important works during this period: the collections of stories *Fattige skjæbner* (Miserable Fates, 1912) and *De kloge jomfruer* (The Wise Virgins, 1918), and the novel which marked her major breakthrough, *Jenny* (1911).

Sigrid Undset began work on *Jenny* in Rome, and it is there that much of the action takes place. Jenny is a member of the Scandinavian circle of young painters and sculptors struggling to make a name for themselves. Yet although she is extremely serious about her painting, it is her fulfilment as a woman which she feels will be decisive. At the start of the novel she is waiting for the passion which will shape her destiny; but like Edele in 'A Stranger' she surrenders to the wrong man. Helge Gram, an immature historian, becomes her fiancé, but fails to awaken her passion; and in the vulnerable state of a woman whose senses are half-aroused, she travels back to Norway and meets his father Gert, a failed painter but a passionate enthusiast, who becomes her lover. She becomes pregnant, breaks off her engagement and travels abroad to have her child alone. When her son is born she experiences a brief happiness, which releases her creative talents once more; but after only a few weeks the child dies, and Jenny returns grief-stricken to Rome. Here she meets her comrade and fellow artist Gunnar Heggen; and both realize that their friendship could have been the foundation for love. Gunnar insists that it is not too late, but Jenny feels that she has lost control of her own destiny, and can only wait passively. Whilst Gunnar hesitates, it is Helge who comes to her; determined to win her back, he rapes her, and when he goes, she slashes her wrists. Gunnar returns to find her dead.

It is an unusual facet of this novel that Sigrid Undset describes Jenny in part through the eyes of the men who love her. The story opens with Helge Gram's arrival in Rome, and the first section is seen through his eyes – though the narrator adds the occasional correction. We meet Jenny as he meets her, and see what he sees in her. It is only later in the novel, when the narrative stance has become that of an omniscient third person, that we realize how much his point of view is conditioned by what he wants to see. 'His' Jenny is a cool, motherly woman – which is what he is searching for; he does not see her vulnerability, or the strength of her passions, to which he is unable to respond.

The last chapter of the novel is similarly subjective; this time it is Gunnar Heggen who is thinking of Jenny and mourning their wasted opportunities. His account is more convincing than Helge's, largely because we know that this is the man who could have been her true partner. His summary of her tragedy rings true:

> He had thought that she could grow as a tree grows, and he had not understood that she could only grow like a flower, a fragile and sap-filled stalk, which strains upwards to reach the sun and burst into blossom with all its heavy, yearning buds. She had only been a little girl, after all. And it would be his eternal grief that he had not seen that until it was too late. For she could not straighten up again, when she had once been broken. She was like a lily plant, and they cannot grow again from the root if the first stalk has been broken off. (*RFN* II, pp. 297–8)

Yet this is not the entire truth; Gunnar also sees what he wants to see in Jenny. His final words about her are heavy with flower metaphors, and he raises her life almost to the status of myth; there is an undertone of sentimentality in his grief. He sees her death as an act of nature, which it was not; and that releases him from the guilt of feeling that he might have prevented it. He senses that in time his grief for her will become the basis of his artistic inspiration: her life will become his art. Although he mourns her sincerely, he too will use the part of her that is most adapted to his own needs. The real woman will have become the muse.

Another important figure for Jenny is her friend Fransiska. The two girls are very different, as is evident from Helge Gram's first observation of them. Fransiska is dark, vivacious, and sexually attractive; she has a complicated love life and is unable to conceal either her pleasure or her pain. Jenny is blonde and pale-complexioned, with an almost boyish figure; her colours are grey and blue, and her behaviour is restrained, her feelings are hidden. The two women can be seen as representatives of opposing types which recur with slight variations in many of Sigrid Undset's works, and correspond to the bad woman/good woman dichotomy analyzed by Sandra M. Gilbert and Susan Gubar in *The Madwoman in the Attic*.[9]

Gilbert and Gubar demonstrate how the tendency of male writing and mythology to divide women into two kinds, the 'bad' (monster, witch, whore) and the 'good' (angel, princess, Madonna) has been perpetuated by women writers such as Jane Austen and Charlotte Brontë. Sigrid Undset could be added to the list. The dark Fransiska has many of the 'bad woman' qualities; men perceive her as both enticing and threatening, the cause of rivalry. The fair Jenny is seen as a more asexual figure, a companion rather than a potential mistress. In this sense her final incarnation as a muse is entirely appropriate. The opposition between these two types is often further expressed by Sigrid Undset in terms of 'motherliness', which is not necessarily the same as motherhood. In this novel it is Jenny who possesses true motherliness, although ironically her baby dies; whilst Fransiska, who is not a natural mother, is the one who bears children who live.

Similar contrasting female figures can be found in several of the stories in *Miserable Fates* and *The Wise Virgins*. (The title of the latter collection is a reminder that Christian mythology also recognizes two kinds of women.) It is rare for active female sexuality and motherliness to be combined in the same person in Sigrid Undset's writings; the two traits are often mutually exclusive. In the short story 'Gunvald og Emma' ('Gunvald and Emma'), this is expressed categorically in the unmarried schoolteacher's reactions to a pupil's objectionable mother: 'The schoolmistress was one of those women who feel their sexuality as a desire to live for someone else, and Klara was one of those who feel their sexuality as a right to live off someone else' (*RFN* V, p. 82).

Klara is Gunvald's feckless wife; she does not care for their house or their children properly, and he never feels quite sure that she will not simply disappear. But she possesses him sexually in a way that makes him heedless of anything else, and when she dies he feels a sense of loss that never leaves him. He marries again, and his second wife Emma is the motherly woman who brings order to the household and love and care to him and the children; but she can never rekindle the excitement which he lost with Klara, and their marriage is based on friendship rather than passion. When they make love, he feels a sense of sadness rather than release. Emma must seek in her newborn baby the physical intimacy she cannot experience with her husband.

The story 'Thjodolf' contains a similar pairing of opposite kinds of women. Helene Johansen is the 'good mother' of the story; although she is unable to bear children, she fosters the weak little Thjodolf and he thrives in her care. The boy's real mother, Fanny, although she is fond of him, is incapable of caring for him; her life is a succession of short-lived affairs, from which she never seems to learn anything. Helene even becomes a kind of mother to Fanny – who repays her by taking the child away when she goes to live with another man, and neglects him so that he becomes seriously ill. She returns Thjodolf to Helene too late to save his life; and in the midst of her grief at the little boy's death, Helene becomes aware that her own husband has had an affair with Fanny, who is again pregnant.

The two women present an extreme physical contrast. Helene is pale and grey-eyed, dressed in a sober fashion which makes her seem older than she is – though she blossoms when Thjodolf comes into the house. Fanny is first glimpsed as a 'gleaming bright red silk parasol' (*RFN* V, p. 44); she wears flamboyant clothes which are not substantial enough to keep her warm, and her shoes are too small, her skirts too short, her blouses too transparent. The difference is also expressed in terms of a nature/culture split: Fanny is a town person, unsuitably dressed for being out of doors at all, and incapable of fending for herself. She will always need to be looked after by someone. Helene lives in the country, in a cottage which is always shining; she is often described working in the garden, and can provide the wholesome environment the child needs. She represents the positive values in the story; yet she cannot compete with to the seductiveness of a woman like Fanny. The good woman has the reader's sympathy; the bad woman gets the man.

The sadness of the woman who can be a mother-substitute but never a mother is the theme of two of the stories from *Miserable Fates*, 'Selma Brøter' and 'Frøken Smith-Tellefsen'. Selma Brøter is an efficient secretary whose unrequited love is not even noticed by its object; her most rewarding experience is looking after her sister's illegitimate baby, which she will inevitably lose sooner or later. Frøken Smith-Tellefsen has devoted her life to looking after the family of the widowed engineer Biørn, hoping that he will marry her one day. She is a good mother to the children; but she is ugly, and must watch as Biørn falls in love with another woman who is obviously an unsuitable mother. She has to leave and find another situation; and ends as the companion of an elderly religious widow, who treats her as a servant. On the one occasion when the widow has a soirée and frøken Smith-Tellefsen dresses up and has an interesting conversation with a theologian, she is sent into the kitchen to wash up and told sternly that her red blouse is too worldly and she must change back into a black one.

Miserable fates lie in store for many of the characters in Sigrid Undset's stories of this period. Contemporary life offers few opportunities for heroism, and even those who possess talent and inspiration, like the dressmaker Miss Granum in 'Omkring sædelighetsballet' ('The Charity Ball'), cannot spread their wings. She should live in a world where her creations can become works of art – but reality is an endless round of toil and penny-pinching to pay the rent. Sigrid Undset does not gloss over the degrading effects of poverty on both grown-ups and children in these stories; there is a harsh realism in her descriptions.

There was much in *Jenny* that offended contemporary morality: free love, a relationship with both father and son, and a frank acknowledgement of female desire. The author was not surprised by the upset it caused, and does not seem to have been disturbed by it. She began to take more part in public debate after her travels abroad, which she used for serious study of European art and literature. Early in her life she had discovered a taste for English literature, both for older writers who provided links with her medieval and post-medieval studies such as Chaucer and Shakespeare, and for more modern authors: Jane Austen, the Brontë sisters, Shelley, Keats, D.H. Lawrence. English culture was congenial to her, whereas German was not – a temperamental preference which was strengthened by the events of the two World Wars.

During these years she wrote essays and articles on women writers and women's position in society, which she collected under the title *Et kvinde-synspunkt* (A Woman's Point of View) in 1919. In her Afterword to the volume she freely admitted to being reactionary in her views; although she admired the early pioneers who fought for a woman's right to independence, she felt that more recent campaigns had been misguided. In her view it was of the utmost importance that the *difference* between men's and women's nature should be recognized, and that women, instead of pursuing the appearance of equality, should fight for recognition of their special needs and qualities. Women, she maintained, have confused demands for their rights with the attainment of esteem for their duties; and it is a woman's highest and most satisfying duty to care for her family.

A woman's function as a mother is her essential one, according to Sigrid Undset; and here again she understands the word in a spiritual sense – childless women are often the best mothers. To be a mother is not just work, but life itself. In the essay 'Begrepsforvirring' ('Confused Ideas', 1919) this view brought her into opposition with Katti Anker Møller's proposals for legislation about the rights of children – a position which surprised many women, including Katti Anker Møller herself. Sigrid Undset complained that these proposals would make motherhood into a paid job. She saw Katti Anker Møller as an upper-class woman with no understanding of what life was like outside her own circle, and argued that whilst her legislation might help unmarried mothers, it would disadvantage married ones, who often had a harder struggle in working-class families.

Sigrid Undset's attitude in these essays puzzled many critics.

With her background and her experience – as an independent wage-earner, a cohabitee of a married man, a single parent combining family with a career as a writer – one would expect her to protest as loudly as anyone against the burden of double work and the discrimination of the double standard. Yet her essays contain many categorical statements which even at that time must have seemed hair-raisingly discriminatory, for example: 'No unconfused woman . . . would deny a man's superiority in certain areas, amongst others in what one normally calls intelligence, that is in rationality'; 'Because of the character of a natural sexual relationship and because of the nature of men and women, he is the master in that relationship and her body is a thing he owns – even if he owns no more of her.'[10] The contrast between her statements and her life is extraordinary. Gidske Anderson is driven to the conclusion that 'she is against everybody else's "women's liberation" – whilst she herself is a whole "women's liberation" all on her own.'[11] Her fiction shows considerably more understanding of the effects of inequality in contemporary life than her polemical writings suggest.

In her Afterword to the essays, written in October 1919, she compares the depiction of women in modern and medieval literature, and concludes that 'medieval literature was chivalrous, in the sense that it was full of feeling and sympathy for woman as the one whom nature has placed in peculiarly difficult circumstances' (p. 92). Wives are viewed with respect in medieval literature, she maintains, because of a wife's paradoxical position: 'she was according to the laws of nature intended to be another person's property, and yet she was a freeborn soul with the same responsibility for her own damnation or salvation as any man' (p. 93). Whilst she was writing these words, Sigrid Undset was deep in the preparation of her own 'medieval' trilogy, *Kristin Lavransdatter*.

Kristin Lavransdatter (1920–22)

The *Kristin Lavransdatter* trilogy is Sigrid Undset's major contribution to the multivolume historical novel which was so popular during this period. It was the climax to a long study of medieval history and myth, which had produced several manuscripts during her early career. When she settled at Bjerkebæk, she was able to devote concentrated attention to the creation of her most complex heroine, Kristin Lavransdatter.

The first volume, *Kransen* (*The Bridal Wreath*, 1920), tells of Kristin's childhood and adolescence at her parents' farm Jørundgård in Gudbrandsdal during the early years of the fourteenth century. Idolized by her parents and particularly attached to her father Lavrans, she has a happy childhood in which turbulent historical events and her parents' grief at the loss of siblings impinge only marginally on her consciousness. When her father decides to marry her to the dependable Simon Darre, she agrees as a dutiful daughter should. Then by chance she meets the dashing Erlend Nikulaussøn, who rides in, in true romantic fashion, to save her from attack in the forest – and they conceive a passion for each other which is so forceful that it disregards all obstacles, human or divine. Erlend has a mistress and two children, from whom he severs himself – at the cost of being implicated in his mistress's violent death; Kristin ignores all that she has learnt of obedience and chastity, meets Erlend for secret lovemaking in barn and byre, breaks off her engagement and defies her father. Bitterly though Lavrans is opposed to the match, he is worn down by Kristin's misery and gives her to Erlend, unaware that she is four months pregnant.

The second volume, *Husfrue* (*The Wife*, 1921), continues the story of Kristin and Erlend's married life, which is as eventful as their courtship. Their strong wills clash as their temperamental differences emerge. Erlend is quick to flare up but equally quick to regret his anger, loving show and action, careless with money and imprudent in his choice of friends; Kristin is the careful planner, concerned above all for her children's wellbeing – but with a determination beneath her mild demeanour which is no less strong than Erlend's. After fifteen years and seven sons, their passion is as strong as ever, as the unhappy Simon, still in love with Kristin, is forced to see: 'That man had liberated her – for Erlend's sake she would gladly walk over glowing stones – and she had trodden over him as if she didn't know he was any more than a cold stone – .'[12]

Erlend's imprudence has landed him on the wrong side in history, in the battles for power in Norway in the time of the boy king Magnus. He forfeits his land, and in *Korset* (*The Cross*, 1922) the family moves to Kristin's inheritance, Jørundgård. She becomes the dominant partner – although that makes neither of them happy – and eventually turns Erlend out. Her last son she names Erlend, as if to confirm that his father is dead. One last time Erlend rides to the farm, to save her honour as on the first time they met, but this time he is fatally wounded. After his death Kristin leaves the farm to her grown sons; the Black Death has come to Norway, and she goes to a convent to tend the sick. Finally succumbing to the plague herself, she has only two possessions as she lies dying, her wedding ring and her father's cross – and it is the wedding ring she gives away to buy Masses for the soul of a dead woman, dying with the cross in her hands.

Love is the mainspring of the trilogy. Kristin's passion for Erlend, like his for her, is an erotic obsession which seems like a force of nature. Its earthy sensuality is heightened by the sense that this is a forbidden love; as in Sigrid Undset's autobiographical writings, there is a link between ecstasy and transgression. Once she is married, Kristin never again gives herself with the same abandon. Yet the passion remains; Kristin is one of the few women in Sigrid Undset's writings to combine active sexuality with motherliness, although there is a certain conflict between the two functions, and they dominate at different times in her life. She embodies both the 'good woman' and the 'bad woman' qualities, being obedient and defiant, chaste and passionate; never does she look more sweetly virginal than when she comes to her rendezvous with Erlend in a brothel.

The erotic complications of the novels are broadened by their implications for the more tightly knit society of that time, where illegitimacy or adultery was a matter for the whole community, not just the individual; and by the strongly religious framework. Christianity was central to the life of fourteenth-century Norway; all important events were marked by prayers and offerings to the Church, and monks and priests had an unquestioned authority. Kristin feels that God's eye is upon her continually, and her sense of transgression against society's rules, embodied in her father, is bound up with a sense of sinning against God. When their own St Olav's Church is struck by lightning, she fears that this may be a judgement on the child she is carrying beneath her heart, conceived in sin.

Yet it is not long since this devout society was pagan, and traces of an earlier religion are everywhere apparent. Local deities must still be appeased by sacrifices, unnatural beings walk the earth in lonely places, and runes are a potent force. There is something both subversive and feminine in the old religion, which sets itself up against the patriarchal order of Church and state. It is associated with illicit sexuality for Kristin; the first time she meets its temptations is when she wanders away from her father in the forest and sees the elfin queen beckoning her with a crown of gold – an image which recurs to her years later when she mirrors herself, wearing her bridal crown, but with the fruit of forbidden love in her belly. The clearest representative of the old pagan spirit is fru Åshild, a wise woman/witch who has also stepped over corpses to get the man she wanted, and who kindles in Kristin the spark of rebellion against the accepted order. Women in pre-Christian and early Christian societies were freer than they were when the Church and the state became more centralized – a process which was well under way by the fourteenth century.[13]

Kristin comes bitterly to regret her transgressions against her father and her Church, who in many ways are one for her. Lavrans is an exceptionally pious man – perhaps rather too pious, as he has never been able to respond to his wife's passion. Yet Kristin's worst sin is not that she has defied social and religious taboos, nor even that she has placed lust above all else; this Catholic society is generous in its acceptance of human appetites. Her fault is that she can never forget or forgive what Erlend has done to win her; she reproaches him in word and deed for the impetuousness which first attracted her. She cannot accept him for the kind of man he is; in the end even her father takes her to task for it, and Simon notices too: 'It seemed to him that Kristin was the most to blame. Erlend lost his temper easily – but she often spoke as if she bore a deep and hidden grudge' (*The Wife*, p. 276). Not until after Erlend's death does she realize that for all his faults, his generosity of spirit was greater than hers.

Erlend is larger than life, never happier than when he is out commanding his men on his ships, or defending his life, sword in hand. He is not cut out to be a farmer. His tragedy, as Lavrans observes, is to be a hero in an unheroic age; he does not find the great leader whom he could serve, but pours all his energies into fruitless intrigues and doomed causes. Already in the fourteenth century, Norway's heroic age was past; it was a demoralized society which had little use for its best men. Lavrans too was born to be a leader of men, but spent his life in quiet resignation on his farm.

Historical events impinge on the action of the novels at every moment; the central characters are invented, but historical characters are always on the periphery.[14] Painstaking historical research lies behind every detail of people's houses, clothes, weapons, utensils and customs. As in Sigrid Undset's contemporary novels, the emphasis is on the visual; the clothes people wear and the objects with which they surround themselves indicate the kind of people they are. The language is in keeping, as the author has attempted to recapture the thought processes of a vanished age; in both dialogue and narrative she has avoided expressions which would have been unfamiliar to a fourteenth-century ear. As a historical study it is a *tour de force*.

Kristin Lavransdatter does more than just bring history to life, however. Earlier in her career Sigrid Undset had maintained: 'One can write novels only about one's own time';[15] and the trilogy expresses her feelings about the twentieth century as much as about the fourteenth. The demoralization and 'confusion of ideas' which were apparent in Norwegian society in the first half of the fourteenth century, and were shortly to lead to the religious crisis of the Reformation, are paralleled by the searching for moral absolutes of the early twentieth century.[16] And Kristin's conflict between a wilful struggle for independence and her ardent desire to find a man who is truly her master echoes that of many of Sigrid Undset's contemporary heroines.

Contemporary readers found the trilogy of more than just historical interest; it was a huge popular success, and the print run had reached 138,000 copies by 1925. It was also an international success, translated into many languages. Not only did it assure its author's financial independence, it also transformed her into something of a national institution.

Later years

Sigrid Undset's interest in Catholicism was not only a historical one; in 1924 she asked to be admitted to the Catholic Church, at the same time as her marriage was annulled. Her conversion to Catholicism is another of her actions which has puzzled critics; how could such an independent, agnostic and – despite everything – feminist writer become a member of such a restrictive and patriarchal institution? One can find clues in her works – her affinity for the world-view of the Middle Ages, her aversion to the modern tendency to make man the measure of all things, her concern for the preservation of the family and of woman's traditional nurturing role – but it remains ultimately a private decision, which she never fully explained. She was reticent about her private life by this stage; even her open-hearted letters to Dea Hedberg tailed off after 1914. Nini Roll Anker, perhaps her closest friend during these years, never understood her decision.

She took an increasingly public role in Norwegian cultural life after 1920. In 1922 she was awarded a state author's stipend, and in 1928 she won the Nobel Prize for literature – only the third woman ever to do so. She played an active part in the Authors' Association, and became its chairman during the turbulent years 1935–40, when Nazification was threatening, particularly in connection with the Ossietzky affair. When Knut Hamsun published an article attacking the award of the Nobel Prize for literature to the German pacifist Carl von Ossietzky, who was in a concentration camp, Sigrid Undset led a large group of fellow authors in an immediate protest, which caused sharp divisions in the Association. In articles and lectures she expressed her dismay at developments in Germany, and at the outbreak of war in 1939 no one could be in any doubt where her sympathies lay.

During these years she was also bringing up her family at Bjerkebæk, and writing energetically. More than half of her production, in bulk, was published after 1924. From a literary point of view, however, most of it is of less interest than the works from the first half of her career; several of the books are hagiography, essays or autobiography. But she did continue to write both modern and medieval novels during the interwar period,which continue and develop the themes of her earlier ones.

Shortly after the publication of *Kristin Lavransdatter* came her other medieval novel series, the two-volume *Olav Audunssøn i Hestviken* (1925) and *Olav Audunssøn og hans børn* (1927), published in English as *The Master of Hestviken*. Here it is a man who is the central character; yet Olav Audunssøn's tragedy, like Kristin's, is set in motion by a passionate love which ignores social and religious taboos. Olav becomes a double murderer before he wins his Ingunn, but in so doing destroys his own peace of mind. The tension between passionate earthly love and the Catholic Christian teaching on which the society bases its laws is as strong here as in *Kristin Lavransdatter*, and although in both series it is Christianity which has the last word, it is the voice of passion which remains longest in the mind.

The imperatives and problems of sexual love are a constant theme of Sigrid Undset's contemporary novels from this period. To take one example: *Ida Elisabeth* (1932) is the story of a woman who passively accepts, like Edele and like Jenny, a man who is unworthy of her; only in this case the mismatch is even more extreme, as Fridtjof is an eternal child. She is forced not only to take care of her house and children but also to earn the money for them all to live on, until her husband, through sheer carelessness, causes the death of her daughter, and she walks out. She makes a new life for herself with her two sons, living contentedly as a seamstress, and is hardly aware of anything missing until she meets Tryggve Toksvold. This man is her true match; they fall in love and get engaged. Yet there is a tension between him and her children; sincere though his efforts are, Ida Elisabeth realizes that he will never understand them. She feels compelled to choose between them, and then there is no choice – she must send him away and remain with her children.

In this novel it seems – unusually – that the children have the power to destroy passion; that is the conclusion Ida Elisabeth comes to, and since the whole story is told through her eyes, that is the conclusion of the novel too. Yet there is more to it than this; there is something in Ida herself which withdraws from full commitment. As she sees it, their relationship is weakened by the fact that Tryggve has never made love to her; his control over his feelings renders her more vulnerable. *Not* to be overwhelmed by passion, it seems, is as fatal as to be so. Yet in this relationship, as in her earlier one, Ida remains passive; she longs to be taken, but cannot reach out for the man herself. Her only decisive act in either relationship is a negative one: to end it. The novel posits a choice between passion and duty; but it is not an active choice on the woman's part, rather a withdrawal from challenge into resignation.

Resignation becomes a more dominant note in Sigrid Undset's later works, often coloured by religious feeling; a monogamous Christian marriage is the ideal, though the difficulties of achieving it are not underestimated, either in 'modern' works such as *Den trofaste hustru* (*The Faithful Wife*, 1936) or in historical ones such as *Madame Dorthea* (*Madame Dorothea*, 1939). These works aroused less interest; although Sigrid Undset could by now rely on a faithful public, she was less in touch than before with contemporary feelings.

However, she was a well-known public figure; and when the Germans invaded Norway in April 1940, she was at once advised to flee, as she would no doubt be a target. In a dramatic series of events she travelled across the border to Sweden, and thence to the United States, arriving in New York in August 1940 by way of Moscow and Japan. Once in America, she devoted herself to the Norwegian cause, writing and talking, participating in the conflict to the best of her ability. It cost her much; in 1939 she had published *Madame Dorthea*, the first volume of a new series, but when she returned to Norway in 1945 her career as a creative writer was at an end.[17] Although she lived until 1949, she produced only non-fiction after April 1940, mostly memoirs and articles. Her family was reduced to one son: Maren died in 1939 and Anders was shot by the Germans in 1940. Although she was only sixty-seven when she died, and was universally honoured and respected, she felt she had little left to live for.

Interest in Sigrid Undset's works has not abated since her death. She has been translated into more languages than any other Norwegian woman writer, and the volume of critical studies about her writing is unequalled.[18] Her works, like those of other women writers, attracted renewed critical attention with the advent of feminist literary criticism in the 1970s; and as in the case of Amalie Skram, the focus of interest has shifted somewhat to her contemporary 'novels of marriage' and away from the historical novels which had earlier been so much more thoroughly investigated. She is an ambiguous, sometimes self-contradictory, sometimes irritating author; yet the best of her fiction transcends polemics.

7
Cora Sandel (1880–1974)

The lonely road to literature

Cora Sandel was born Sara Fabricius on 20 December 1880 in Christiania. She is almost unique amongst Norwegian authors in being referred to even today exclusively by her nom de plume.[1] This fact indicates her lifelong attitude to her public; she was a private person who rarely gave interviews, and in a period of intense public debate she took no part in the polemics. Her intellectual isolation was deepened by the fact that she lived most of her adult life outside Norway; like Amalie Skram, she raised the question of whether she should really be considered a Norwegian author.[2] She preferred to let her writings speak for themselves, and regarded as an impertinence the frequent attempts to invade her private sphere in the provincial duckpond of Norwegian cultural life:

> It is a peculiarly Norwegian phenomenon that an author, as well as writing as well as he can, must also perform outside the circus tent, display his person and comment on himself . . . I know countries where people do not go sniffing after one's private life in everything one writes. It sounds incredible, but it is true . . . That is yet another reason to join with Wergeland in pitying an author 'who in a little land is born'. He is not treated fairly – in many ways.[3]

Less documentary evidence is left about Cora Sandel's life and writings than about that of most authors; she did not keep manuscripts of her books or copies of her letters. Yet from her occasional interviews, from letters to friends and from other sources, it is possible to reconstruct the background on which she drew for her fiction.[4]

Sara Fabricius was born into an upper-middle-class family with a long tradition of service to the state. Her father, a sea captain, was away a great deal. He was eighteen years older than her mother, who had lost a daughter before Sara was born, and was very protective of her next child. Sara grew up in an atmosphere of fussiness, surrounded by women: 'attractive, elegant, extremely nervous women, mother, grandmother and many aunts, real aunts and aunts once removed . . . I was early conscious of the fact that it was men whose company one should seek in this world.'⁵ Her need to rebel against this regime and seek greater freedom – especially physical freedom: walking, running, riding horses – was strong from an early age.

Her early childhood had been a time of affluence, with long summer holidays in the country and a wide circle of acquaintances – amongst them Nini Roll Anker, who lived nearby and became a lifelong friend. But in 1892 the family moved to the far north, to Tromsø and a very different lifestyle. Tromsø was a small town in 1890, with only 7,000 inhabitants; it was in the Arctic Circle, with two months' darkness each year and no electric lights. The journey was difficult, taking several days even from Trondheim. Since the early nineteenth century the far north had been seen as a place of exile, where ambitious young civil servants spent a few years before obtaining more prestigious posts down south, or older officials took refuge from failure or economic difficulties. The latter was the case with the Fabricius family; Sara's father was in debt, and wages were higher up north. The family moved with a sense of being *déclassé* into a town where they were one of a small number of leading families; freedom of action became even more circumscribed for the young Sara.

From early in her life, Sara wanted to be a painter. In 1899, when she was nineteen, she was at last allowed to spend some months in Christiania studying with Harriet Backer, a well-known artist who set up an art school which ran from 1899 to 1912.⁶ She had also begun to write; some of her stories about animals were published in the magazine *Dyrenes Ven* (The Animals' Friend) under the pseudonyms Sven Bro and Helge Andersen. She sought grants in vain, and it was 1905 before she could return to Christiania to carry on her painting studies. From there in 1906 she travelled to Paris, where she stayed for fifteen years, studying painting and scraping a living, desperately poor but determined not to give in and go home. She painted under her own name, and her Naturalistic pictures were often unfinished. One way of making ends meet was by writing accounts of the artistic life in Paris for the conservative Norwegian newspaper *Morgenbladet*, which she regarded as almost prostitution. She moved in the Scandinavian circle of artists and writers in Paris – in which Sigrid Undset also figured in 1910, though there is no record of the two meeting. But then Sara Fabricius was not only unusually shy but also completely unknown.

In 1913, after the death of both her parents (her mother in 1903, her father in 1910), she married a Swedish sculptor, Anders Jönsson. They spent some time in Florence on a travel scholarship (his), and in 1917 their son Erik was born. It was around this time that Sara began to write in earnest; it was an easier thing to combine with caring for a small baby than paints and wet canvases, though frustration at her lack of progress as an artist may have contributed. One of her most important literary influences was Colette, whose *La Vagabonde* (1910) was a revelation to her. Both the central character Renée Nérée and the author herself demonstrated that it was possible to be a woman and an artist; Colette's incarnation as a dancer echoed one of Sara's own early ambitions, a triumphant achievement of physical freedom. Immediately in 1910 Sara approached a Norwegian publisher about translating the book into Norwegian, and did in fact finally translate it, under the title *Omstreifersken*, although it did not appear until 1952. Isadora Duncan was also dancing in Paris in those years, and Sara was enthralled by her. The Swedish author Victoria Benedictsson, who had struggled to find her literary voice as the wife of a country postmaster and stepmother of many children, was another major influence, whose example could give her courage to carry on: 'If I feel really discouraged and hopeless about what I'm trying to do, I always reach for V.B. Her life and works are a "quand même" which never fail to have their effect on me.'[7] Creative women who defined their own parameters in defiance of social strictures were her ideals, although most of her time in Paris could be called an unsuccessful search for a room of her own.

In 1921 the Jönssons moved to Sweden, where Sara was to stay, with brief interruptions, for the rest of her life. In 1922 she had her first stories published under the name Cora Sandel: 'Rosina' in the left-wing newspaper *Arbeiderbladet* and 'Amors veie' ('Amor's Paths') in the even more left-wing *Mot Dag*. (Although she had no declared political allegiance, the socially critical content of her stories made it natural for her to seek an outlet in the left-wing press.) At the same time she was working on preliminary sketches for her first novel. Being published became not only artistically but financially necessary, as she got divorced in 1926 and had to provide for her son. Writing was always a slow process for her; her main series of novels, the 'Alberte' trilogy, was published over a period of thirteen years. Relations with her publisher Harald Grieg at Gyldendal were often strained; although he supported her, he made it clear that he would prefer novels to short stories, which did not sell well. She complained often that being a writer was 'a damned beggar's existence',[8] and it was a long time before it brought her a decent living. Like so many women authors, she also experienced in her most productive years an unremitting struggle between the demands of art and those of life:

> It is devilishly difficult to be an author, and it is no doubt devilishly difficult to be a male author. But it is 'a thousand demons' worse to be a female one. A male author usually has a wife, and she is – usually – an indispensable help to him. She copies manuscripts, answers letters, keeps a distance between him and all sorts of things. She functions as a secretary in other words, with or without payment, and is always there. In that role woman has often been praised and celebrated. But does anyone think about the female writer's position?[9]

Whether as muse or as secretary, the female helper is less accessible to a female writer.

Two of her early short stories which focus on women's fates are 'Nr. 31' ('No. 31'), which won a short story competition in 1923, and 'Lykken' ('Happiness'), first published in *Vor verden* (Our World) in 1924–5.[10] 'No. 31' is the story of a young Norwegian artist in Paris who falls in love. For her it is her life's adventure; for him, a passing affair. As he leaves for the south she realizes she is pregnant. He takes it for granted that she will have an abortion, but she is unable to. She is rescued from her passivity by fru Flehn, a busybody with the best of intentions, who arranges for her to have her baby secretly in hospital and leave it in an orphanage.

The story is told in part from the artist's viewpoint and in part from fru Flehn's, and there is no point of contact between them.

Fru Flehn represents sound common sense, spares no pains to persuade the artist to be sensible and think of her future, and collects her from the hospital expecting relief and gratitude; the artist is so numb with despair at the loss of her child that she can express nothing at all. The experience has reduced her to anonymity – she was 'No. 31' in a ward full of women in labour. The stark description of female suffering in the ward is one of Cora Sandel's crassest pictures of the negative aspects of female sexuality, its links with blood and death:

> From them there rose a chorus of lamentation, an unceasing, many-tongued complaint. If one stopped, another began. With every new arrival the electric lights were lit for a while, and when No. 31 on one occasion raised herself on an elbow in between two waves of pain and looked sideways, she closed her eyes in horror. Limbs which curled up in cramp and stretched out again . . . grinning masks, framed by hair which stuck in clumps during the struggle so that it looked like uncarded wool . . . foreheads pearling with sweat with hair plastered in strips across them . . . tongues which laboured in vain to moisten dry, thirsting lips . . . a sea swell of swollen shameless bellies, that was what she saw. (*SV* IV, pp. 91–2)

From the romantic illusions of spring in Paris we have moved to a Brueghel picture of the torments of hell.

The girl in the story 'Happiness' is also significantly nameless, one of those pale creatures who from the beginning has to accept that reality will never come up to her expectations: 'whenever she got five øre, she had been dreaming of at least a krone . . .' (*SV* IV, p. 97). She grows up with an unclear idea of what she wants, but becomes more and more certain of what she does *not* want: the 'good marriage' and well-regulated petit-bourgeois existence into which she is forced. Not until she has had two children does she discover from a chance meeting with a good partner at a ball what it is she wants: to dance. The partner himself is uninteresting; it is the chance to move her limbs freely which intoxicates her. She is refused further indulgence in such a suspicious activity, however, being reduced to searching for articles on Isadora Duncan in magazines, and one visit to the ballet in town. The repression builds up until it becomes too much to bear, and bursts out in the only form it can: in madness. Finally, in the asylum where no one tries to stop her dancing any more, she is happy.

Like many of Cora Sandel's stories, this one is told largely from the point of view of the 'compact majority', the well-adjusted members of society who cannot see what all the fuss is about; after all, the girl has a considerate husband, an attractive home, healthy children. Society's view is represented largely by 'the aunts', who behave as the conscience of the town: 'The aunts overlooked the square from their flat and took it in turns to sit in the window' (p. 107). They pity Karl Ludvig for his moody and unbalanced wife, and unfortunately they are proved only too right. No one attempts to understand the girl's viewpoint; the complete lack of communication between the individual and 'informed public opinion' lends a dramatic irony to the story which was to become one of Cora Sandel's most refined tools.

The 'Alberte' trilogy

The period between 1926 and the Second World War was Cora Sandel's most productive one, although compared with prolific authors like Sigrid Undset she did not publish many books. There were six titles in all: the 'Alberte' trilogy and three volumes of short stories. The stories were written in the intervals of work on the trilogy; they will be considered together in the next section.

The 'Alberte' trilogy is a study of the artist as outsider. It depicts the slow and painful maturing of a girl who from the start, like the protagonist of 'Happiness', knows only what she does not want to be: what her whole society tries to make her. The trilogy opens in 1903 when she is around sixteen or seventeen, and ends in 1920 when she is in her mid-thirties – there are few precise indications of age or date in the novels.[11] Yet it is not a normal *Entwicklungsroman* in the sense that it does not follow Alberte's development stage by stage; each volume covers not much more than a year, and many of the most dramatic events in her life happen in between two volumes. It is more a study of inner development; attention is focused on the periods in which her awareness of her own potential is maturing, or the pressures of existence become so intense that they cause a violent reaction.

In the first volume, *Alberte og Jakob* (*Alberta and Jacob*, 1926), Alberte is a teenager in a small northern Norwegian town, which has borrowed many physical and social characteristics from Tromsø. There can be few novel openings which convey such an intense impression of cold; like the description of hunger in Knut Hamsun's *Hunger*, it communicates itself to the reader like a physical sensation. Winter seems to last for ever, and Alberte is blue and pinched, living in a large house which the family cannot afford to heat properly. The cold is spiritual as well as physical; its main source is her mother, from whom Alberte constantly hears that she is not the attractive, domesticated girl fru Selmer wants. In her mother's eyes she is hopeless in every way; she is a scapegoat for everything that is wrong in the family's existence, stuck in a godforsaken small town without the money to make it bearable.

Alberte's brother Jakob is also under pressure to conform; although he is not interested in studying, he is kept on at school whilst Alberte, who is more intellectual, has to leave. But Jakob is more robust, and lacks Alberte's eternal sense of guilt. He can find a positive outlet for his rebellion; when he declares his intention of going to sea, his parents eventually give in. No such way out is possible for Alberte, surrounded by well-meaning 'aunts' and their exemplary daughters; she must conform, or face the dreadful fate of being an old maid – and the town can offer some terrifying examples of those. Although she does receive some appreciation – from a handsome working-class lad who first stirs her sexual feelings, from a visiting student who finds her difference interesting – it is little to set against the judgement best expressed in a letter from her uncle to her mother, which states categorically that as a 'less well endowed' girl there is no point sending her to Christiania to look for a husband.

Alberte tries to write, but is so dissatisfied with the results that she can see no future in it. When things look bleakest, her feeble attempts to obtain a post as a governess have failed and her mother is trying to persuade her into an engagement with her father's clerk, she decides the only escape is to drown herself. But on contact with the cold water, her defiance reasserts itself: 'They didn't drive her into the sea, and they won't. Something rose up in her down there in the icy cold which crept up around her body. It was uncontrollable terror, but it was also something bright and hard, a furious refusal. It was like touching bottom and being carried upwards again' (*SV* I, p. 288).

In this novel Alberte gets no further than rejecting all socially acceptable and unacceptable alternatives. By the beginning of the second novel, however, much has happened. *Alberte og friheten* (*Alberta and Freedom*, 1931) opens in Paris, where Alberte has already spent several years, in 1912. There is an almost total break with the first volume, and it is a long way into the novel before we discover what has happened in the intervening years. Alberte's parents have been killed in an accident, and after spending a short time in Christiania, Alberte has used her small inheritance to move to Paris. The money is long since gone, and she survives by writing articles home to the papers or posing as a naked model for an artist.

The latter fact shows how far she has moved in one sense from the puritanism of her upbringing – but in other ways little has changed. Despite a small circle of artist friends, she feels isolated, living in an attic which is frozen in winter and hot in summer. Her life still consists predominantly of negative attitudes: of guilt that time is passing and she is achieving nothing, and of longing for a fullness of life which seems beyond her reach. Finally she falls in love with a Danish schoolteacher, Veigård, and discovers her own sensuality. No sooner has their love been realized, however, than it is destroyed; Veigård leaves for Denmark promising to return, and she hears no more. This betrayal of her trust leaves her devastated. It is a long time before she learns by chance that he was killed in an accident on the way home – but by then she has abandoned her ideals and moved in with a Norwegian artist, Sivert, who has been pursuing her. The shock of Veigård's death makes her realize the extent of her compromise, and she moves out and begins to settle down in earnest to her writing – only to discover that it is too late, as she is pregnant.

The other women in Alberte's circle act as a foil to her. Potter, a cynical old maid, maintains that men are after only one thing; Alphonsine, a shrewd and perceptive friend, has had enough of unstable artists and marries a mechanic 'because you know where you are with them'; the Russian Marusjka lives comfortably by selling her favours discreetly to rich Americans. And there is Alberte's best friend Liesel, who follows a similar path: she lives with a Swedish sculptor Eliel, sacrifices her art for his and becomes pregnant. But she has a backstreet abortion, and is so damaged both mentally and physically that Alberte is frightened off attempting the same thing. All her women friends show her ways in which she cannot or will not go; the move back to Sivert at the end is not a positive choice but the result of the elimination of all other routes.

In *Bare Alberte* (*Alberta Alone*, 1939) the year is 1919; the narrative has skipped the First World War, as it has the birth of Alberte's son Brede, who is now nearly six. The war is peripheral to the Scandinavians in Paris; their lives have continued much as before, except for the food shortages. Alberte's time and energy have been devoted to caring for her sickly child; writing has been confined to scribbling in odd moments on scraps of paper, which have slowly grown into a bundle.

The novel opens in Brittany, where the family are spending a summer with Liesel and Eliel and another couple, Jeanne and Pierre. Pierre is a French writer, wounded in the war and struggling with writer's block as a result; he is the only one who encourages Alberte and makes sure that she has some free space in her life for writing. Their affinity grows into love; yet neither is free and nothing can come of it. Back in Paris, Alberte is sick with longing for Pierre; they meet again and the relationship develops, but when Jeanne appeals to her Alberte breaks it off. Sivert, meanwhile, has found comfort in a Swedish artist, and declares his intention of taking Brede and going to live with her; but she turns him down, so he returns home to Norway with the boy – and Alberte follows on sufferance. Back at the family farm, Brede finally finds an environment where he thrives, whereas Alberte feels more of an outsider than ever. Released from her worries over her son, she can at last turn wholeheartedly to her writing, and leaves with her manuscript in her bag to face life on her own:

She walks along, aware of only one thing. Now she has finished stumbling around in a fog looking for warmth and a safe harbour. It has lifted, the way ahead is clear and cold. No arms around her any more, not even a child's. Just life itself as far as she can see, struggle and an unclouded view. Now she will either perish or win such bitter strength that nothing will be able to reach her any more. She feels something of the strength of the one who stands absolutely alone. Then she thinks of Brede and knows that she has a long way to go to become invulnerable. (*SV* III, p. 335)

Her last thought in the novel is a memory of Pierre's exhortation to her as a writer: to tell a little of the truth. After half a lifetime of compromise, she has made her positive choice. Like many fictional women before her – Amalie Skram's fru Kant, Sigrid Undset's Jenny or Unni Hjelde – she has been faced with an ultimatum: it is not possible to reconcile creativity with the traditional female role, one must choose or go mad or die. The comparison of Cora Sandel with Sigrid Undset is an interesting one; the two women were in similar situations, combining single parenthood with writing in the 1920s and 1930s, yet their fictional conclusions point in different directions. In Sigrid Undset's novels, the choice falls out in favour of marriage or children, whereas Alberte, like Ibsen's Nora, leaves her husband and child to find herself. In this respect she can be compared also to Camilla Collett's Sofie in *The District Governor's Daughters*. Both are subjected to the tyranny of a mother's manipulations, reinforced by the social conventions of a provincial society; Sofie sacrifices her happiness to fit in with the social norm, whereas Alberte goes her own way. Despite her lack of articulateness, she is ultimately one of the strongest female figures in Scandinavian literature. The trilogy ends as it began, in coldness and isolation, but Alberte has made the life-threatening element her own.

The novels are narrated in the third person, but the point of view is to a large extent identified with the central character. In the first novel there is sometimes an ironic distancing which suggests a superior judgement to that of the unsophisticated teenager; but as the trilogy progresses, the narrative becomes more loyal to her observations. It is narrated in the present tense, which underlines

Alberte's sense of the static nature of life; she can see herself repeating the same meaningless actions year after year for eternity. In the first volume particularly, the physical setting plays a major part, and it is described in impressionistic glimpses, with a sharp eye for form, colour and light. Whereas Sigrid Undset's *Kristin Lavransdatter* starts in naturalistic fashion with a confident statement of time, place and characters – and with a family genealogy reminiscent of the opening of an Icelandic saga – the first paragraphs of *Alberta and Jacob* portray an anonymous townscape with noise and movement, but no people:

> The church clock gleams like a moon in the night. It strikes, and small, weak flares come to life in the darkness and burn dully, lost in its immensity, lonely and scattered. The clock strikes again, and the weak flares grow in number, group together, form lines and squares. There is movement between them, a horse-bell rings, perhaps one can hear an empty sledge slithering from side to side behind a horse on a hard-trampled road. Somewhere something drops into the sea with a splash, a chain rattles. Sounds of oars and creaking rowlocks come up from the darkness, a boat bumps dully against wood, heavy legs in sea-boots thump along a quay, someone shouts something. (*SV* I, p. 5)

This passage appeals to the senses of sight and hearing; the author's years as a painter have left clear traces in her descriptive prose.

Cora Sandel was precise about every detail in her manuscript. The history of the English translation of the trilogy provides an interesting footnote to her concern for accuracy: her English translator, Elizabeth Rokkan, had translated the novels into the past tense, maintaining that a novel in the present tense in English sounded unnatural, whereas in Norwegian the historical present is a not uncommon medium. Cora Sandel was upset about this, regarding it as 'misrepresentation and damage';[12] she insisted that the present tense conveyed a sense of the unceasing current of time. However, the books were printed in English in the past tense in the early 1960s and have been reprinted twice since.

In Norway the novels were a critical and popular success: the first volume sold 9,000 copies in the year of publication, and has sold over 100,000 copies since. They did sell much better than her short stories, which was a problem; the short story was a form which suited her, not least because she found it easier to fit into the interstices of everyday life. The slowness with which the novels appeared, despite their popularity, meant that for much of her life up to 1940 (when she was sixty) she was not at all well off.

Short stories

The short stories Cora Sandel wrote in the 1920s and 1930s, which were often first published in magazines, were collected in the anthologies *En blå sofa* (A Blue Sofa, 1927), *Carmen og Maja* (Carmen and Maja, 1932) and *Mange takk, doktor* (Thank You, Doctor, 1935). In addition, several which had not previously appeared in volume form were published in 1973 in the anthology *Barnet som elsket veier* (The Child Who Loved Roads).[13]

Few of Cora Sandel's short stories have such a positive conclusion as does Alberte's story. In her stories there are no female artists who succeed in their ambitions. Often they are women whose artistic gifts have never been allowed to develop, like the dancer in 'Happiness', or whose art is a caricature of talent, like the actress fru Lilja in 'Kunsten å tigge' ('The Art of Begging' from *Carmen and Maja*). Fru Lilja is a former trouper who is reduced to living in run-down boarding houses, giving recitals to hostile audiences, and borrowing money she can never repay. She is condemned by the respectable majority for her immoral behaviour and her unsuitable tastes – if she gets money she spends it on luxuries rather than necessities. The narrator, who is one of the guests at the boarding house, suggests an interpretation of events which differs from the general opprobrium: 'No doubt Helene Lilja thought that what she needed more than anything else, in order to recover after a long period of adversity, was a little enjoyment. But charity is not intended for that purpose, however much you pretend it is a loan' (*SV* IV, p. 290). This reservation, however, is communicated to the reader alone, and cannot assuage fru Lilja's sufferings. She can only travel on to the next place in the hope of prolonging her miserable little bit of independence a fraction longer.

Many of the central characters are outsiders. They are women of all ages and in all conditions of life, from the little girl in 'Evelyn' who is 'bad' because she has no one to love her to the sad old maids in 'Søstrene' ('The Sisters') who make what they can of an existence in which nothing happens. There are social outcasts like 'Lort-Katrine' ('Shit-Katrine'), the local prostitute whom everyone is entitled to scorn, and those whom no one needs to consider, like the servant in 'Klara' who is time and again persuaded by her hunger for affection to let a man into her bed – and loses her job because of it. There are those who have lost the respectability they once enjoyed by virtue of being the property of a man, such as the separated fru Arnold in 'En gåte' ('A Mystery'); she visits some family friends, who are so worried that she might think of abusing their hospitality that they practically drive her away – and register their own meanness only when it is too late. Even those who seem to be secure as respectable married women are often alienated from their surroundings. Fru Ludvigsen in 'A Blue Sofa' is out of her element in the dusty town in which her husband thrives, becomes moody and slovenly, and watches helplessly as he falls in love with another woman. The wife in 'Thank You, Doctor' is persuaded by her husband and his doctor friend to have an abortion; it is the only sensible thing to do for a poor artist couple like them, but she realizes after it is done that she will never get over it. For her husband it is a problem solved, but she feels victimized: 'Two men! Never before has she understood what two men means. A solidarity far beyond what any woman can grasp. She had thought they were together on her side. No, they were against her' (*SV* V, p. 22).

Often it is women themselves who are the most effective oppressors of other women. One of the best illustrations of this is 'Kusine Tea' ('Cousin Thea', from *Thank You, Doctor*), an account of the life of the daughter of a respectable family who simply will not conform. She scandalizes the family in every way, from getting involved with a married man to laughing and enjoying herself at the wrong time. She can do nothing against the power of the family, though, until her father dies and she inherits her share of the money – and then she refuses the respectable option of living as a spinster aunt with one of her married sisters, and uses her money to buy a small shop. Worse than that, she adopts a small boy and takes up her relationship with her married boyfriend. The scandal is complete. Ignoring all appeals, she lavishes money on the child, bringing him up with tastes which are quite unsuitable for a boy of his station in life. When he is a young man, she falls ill and dies, and it is discovered that she has been living on borrowed money for years; but she has achieved her aim of making sure that her adopted son does not settle for less than he is worth. What she herself could not achieve, she has made sure that he does, as the final sentence admits: 'But the boy is said to have become a clever man, strangely enough' (*SV* V, p. 140).

The last two words of the story indicate the tone of the whole. It is narrated at the outset by Tea's cousin, who fully endorses the family view that Tea is a cross and a burden: 'She was our family's sorrow from the start' (p. 130). The girl observes with suspense the struggle between Tea and the rest, and willingly allows herself to be used as a spy. As time passes, this identifiable narrator fades out and the narrative is taken over by a more generalized 'we', what one might call the collective 'aunts' voice' of the locality, which is totally in sympathy with the first voice. Tea's story is narrated in a consistent tone of disapproval; yet the subtext which emerges is one of sympathy and understanding. Tea's behaviour is not extreme, simply the expression of her desire to be free to choose her own path in life. That, of course, is the most dangerous thing of all to a social system which relies on the repression of its female members. There is irony in every line of the story, which must be read against the surface message.

Another example of a clash between the surface message and the deeper meaning of a text occurs in the story 'Kunsten å myrde' ('The Art of Murder', from *Thank You, Doctor*). The narrative of this story, set in France, is shared between two voices; it is told to the narrator, a young housewife, by her home help Francine, a war widow, and the narrator then passes it on to the reader with her comments. Francine tells the story of her sister, whose funeral she has just attended; and what seemed at first to be a simple, sad tale turns slowly into an account of persecution which is tantamount to murder. Francine's sister Germaine was an attractive girl who was seduced and abandoned by a foreign sailor. The family took care of her baby with the stern proviso that if it happened again, she would be thrown out with both children. Germaine toiled on a farm for a pittance, until eventually she gave in to an old man 'who was always after her' and became pregnant again. At this the family –

led by her mother – made it clear that she was no longer wanted, and practically forced her to hang herself in the clothes cupboard.

These events are coolly related by Francine, who has no doubt in her mind that her sister was entirely to blame: '"She should just have behaved herself. That's what the rest of us do. She could have done that too"' (*SV* V, p. 60). The narrator is horrified, and tries to suggest to Francine that Germaine was perhaps to be pitied rather than condemned; but Francine will have none of it, and her final judgement is uncontradicted by the half-persuaded narrator: '"It's no great loss, madame," Francine says again: "When a person is not in her right mind any more . . ."' (p. 63). The reader, on the other hand, is not at all persuaded. It is clear from Francine's description of events that Germaine was deliberately driven out of her right mind. Like 'Cousin Thea', the story exposes the mechanisms by which a society controls its members and the concealed violence of its reaction to deviance.

Repression is not always so direct; it can be much more subtle, as it is in 'Barnet som elsket veier' ('The Child Who Loved Roads').[14] The child of this story is a girl; although that is not apparent for some time, as the Norwegian for 'child' is a neutral noun, and Cora Sandel consistently uses the neutral pronoun 'det' ('it'), instead of 'hun' ('she') to refer to the character – a feature which is impossible to reproduce in English translation. It is some time before the reader is aware that the sex of the child matters; the story begins as an invocation to freedom expressed as a love of country roads which lead off into summer adventure. But the girl's sex catches up with her all too soon, when the surrounding adults start to talk about putting her hair up and letting her skirts down; she becomes aware that growing up means above all loss of free movement: 'But they got long skirts or trousers, and then they *walked*. Just *walked*. It made you wonder whether something happened to their legs at that thing they called confirmation. It must do, because then they hid them and walked. They *couldn't* run any longer' (*Barnet som elsket veier*, p. 144). Repression is expressed in her aunts' mild reproaches at her wildness, and allies itself with her own inner development, when she falls in love and suddenly realizes that she has been standing still and dreaming. In a panic she runs off again along her old beloved roads; but the reader is left with the feeling that it is only a matter of time. In this case there is no violent suppression, just gentle persuasion, but the ultimate result will be the same: deprivation of freedom of action.

Most of Cora Sandel's characters lose their battle with society, which becomes a kind of archetypal small-town milieu reminiscent of the fictional creation of her contemporary Aksel Sandemose, Jante.[15] The 'law of Jante' which encapsulates hostility to anything different, and which Sandemose felt had marked him for life, could be endorsed by Cora Sandel, with a codicil to the effect that it applies with double force to women, who cannot run away – like Alberte's Jakob, Sandemose's protagonist Espen Arnakke or Sandemose himself – to sea. The rules for good behaviour are absolute: some must learn the *art* of begging; some, if necessary, even the *art* of murder.

Later works

Cora Sandel's financial position improved towards the end of the thirties. She was given several Swedish grants, and in 1940 she was awarded a Norwegian author's stipend, largely due to the efforts of Nini Roll Anker. She lived in Norway again for a few years – 1936–9 – but returned to Sweden for good in 1939, making a permanent home in Uppsala in 1945. Thus she was in Sweden when the Germans occupied Norway. Although she took little direct part in the resistance, she reluctantly agreed in 1940 to give a lecture entitled 'Norway', which was a defence of her country for not being better prepared for conflict. The devastating effects of war on the individual had been apparent in her depiction of Pierre and Jeanne in *Alberta Alone* and in other earlier stories, such as 'Det er krig' ('There's a War On', from *Thank You, Doctor*), and the Second World War was to feature in yet others. Her unconditional opposition to Nazism was clear in the 1930s. But in her first published work after the war, *Kranes Konditori* (*Krane's Café*, 1945), she returned to her familiar timeless theme.

Katinka Stordal is a divorced mother of two who makes her living as a dressmaker. Despite being extremely talented, she is still, like the seamstresses of older days, overworked and underpaid; an important party is approaching, and she is under pressure from all the ladies of the town to finish their dresses. Exhausted, she comes into Krane's Café in the middle of the morning to relax over a drink. That is bad enough, but when she refuses to return to work and then later is joined by Stivhatten, a not very respectable Swedish individual, scandal is in the air.[16] Katinka refuses the efforts of well-meaning friends and family to persuade her to return to her sewing, and goes off with Stivhatten to spend the night at his place. He suggests that she should leave town with him, and she is tempted, seeing nothing around her but people who want to exploit her for their own ends. Yet she decides in the end to stay because of her teenage daughter; Katinka realizes that this is the one person who needs her absolutely, and that if she walks out on her the girl will end up on the streets.

Cora Sandel began writing this novel as a drama, and the finished form, which she called an 'interior with figures', has affinities with the dramatic genre. There is only one set, the café itself, in which all the action takes place. It is divided into two sections: the outer café in which the waitresses are stationed and the town worthies express their opinions about the progress of events, and the inner 'privaten' in which Katinka and Stivhatten meet. The action falls into two halves, corresponding to the two days of the story; the night at Stivhatten's happens 'offstage' in between the two parts. Much of the novel is dialogue. Its dramatic possibilities were immediately apparent to the critics when it was published, and it was soon dramatized by Helge Krog, who added a middle act showing the night at Stivhatten's. It was performed with great success in 1947 at *Det norske teatret* (The Norwegian Theatre – the major *nynorsk* company) in Oslo, and then in Sweden, Denmark and Finland. In 1951 it was made into a popular film.

Yet there is a vital aspect of the novel to which the stage and film versions cannot do justice: the narrative technique. The dramatized version spells out what is only hinted at in the fiction. This novel too is recounted consistently from a standpoint of disapproval, though not by an identified individual; as the critic Åse Hiorth Lervik puts it: 'What happens in the café's two rooms over this weekend is narrated and commented upon by a peculiar creature which one could be tempted to call the small town's soul.'[17] The narrative voice shows no sympathy for Katinka's desperation; she should do her duty like everyone else, and be grateful that the town's leading families have placed their orders with her. Again, it is from reading between the lines that one can deduce the author's attitude, which is diametrically opposed to the narrator's and, as usual, on the side of those who refuse to conform.

Cora Sandel's next publication worth noting was a collection of three long stories, *Figurer på mørk bunn* (Figures on a Dark Background, 1949). 'Nina' dates from before the war; it had won first prize in a competition in *Arbeidermagasinet* in 1939 for the best love story. It is the story of a meeting between the nervously distraught Nina and a failed painter-turned-farmer. He discovers her unconscious in the forest after taking an overdose; they become lovers, but she remains a mysterious figure until suddenly her husband arrives and explains that she is a spoilt neurotic who is always doing this kind of thing. Unusually, the story is narrated from the viewpoint of the man, trying to understand this secretive woman; he is a subjective but not an unreliable observer, who assesses the husband as a cynical manipulator. Yet the reader is left wondering at the end whether the farmer is not at least as vulnerable as Nina herself.

The other two stories in the collection are more directly related to the war. 'Den stillferdige gjesten' ('The Quiet Visitor') is about a Jewish women staying at a boarding house in the summer before the war, who is confronted by the prejudices – amounting in some cases to outspoken Nazi sympathies – of some of the guests. 'Til Lukas' ('To Lucas') was published in Sweden during the war, in an anthology of texts by Norwegian authors called *Utenfor norskegrensen* (Outside the Norwegian Frontiers, 1943). It takes the form of a letter written by a woman, a refugee from central Europe, to her husband, who has been taken by the Nazis and is probably dead. It tells of the difficulties of being a stranger in a strange land, and of being a woman whose part in the war is one of endurance rather than active involvement.

In 1950 Cora Sandel was awarded a yearly stipend by her publishers Gyldendal, and in 1950–51 her collected works appeared. She was to publish one more novel, *Kjøp ikke Dondi* (*The Leech*, 1958), when she was seventy-eight. She herself regarded it as her best work – but as is not uncommon with author's opinions of their own writing, it is an opinion shared by few. It is a competently told tale, but it lacks the passion of earlier works and fails to involve the reader to the same extent. It is the story of a family centred around the wife Dondi, an outsider who has never fitted in. But in this case the drift of the narrative is to inspire sympathy with the rest of the family rather than with the outsider herself; she is a greedy egoist, whose self-fulfilment involves the exploitation of everybody else. The woman who is nearly crushed by the pressure from other people to become what she is not has become the woman who nearly crushes other people to gain what she wants.

Cora Sandel lived until the age of ninety-four, dying in 1974; in her last years she led a withdrawn existence in Sweden, as private as she had been all her life. In 1972 there was an exhibition of her early paintings at Prins Eugens Waldemarsudde in Stockholm. Her works have remained popular. Her portraits of social repression have been used by modern feminists – not always, perhaps, as she intended; her harrowing studies of abortion, for example, have been used by both sides as ammunition in the conflict about the revision of the abortion laws. Throughout her fiction runs a sympathy with those who are marginalized by society, and an insistence on the absolute moral imperative of living authentically, which drives her female figures again and again to take a stance of opposition with a strength they did not know they had.

1. Camilla Collett.
   Statue by
   Gustav Vigeland,
   1911

2. Aasta Hansteen.
   Statue by
   Gustav Vigeland,
   1905

3. Amalie Skram ca. 1870

4. Ragnhild Jølsen ca. 1905

LES MEMBRES DU STORTHING ACCUEILLENT LEUR NOUVELLE COLLÈGUE

Le 17 mars 1911 sera une grande date dans l'Histoire de la Norvège : ce jour-là pour la première fois une femme vint siéger parmi les députés au Storthing. Cette femme, Mlle Rogstad, avait été élue députée quelques jours auparavant. Ses nouveaux collègues l'accueillirent avec les démonstrations les plus courtoises et les plus aimables ; en ouvrant la séance, le président du Storthing prononça, à son adresse, quelques paroles de bienvenue et il salua le triomphe du féminisme norvégien comme l'ouverture d'une nouvelle ère de prospérité nationale. Après quoi, un grand nombre de membres présents du Storthing vinrent serrer la main de la nouvelle députée : c'est cette jolie scène que notre dessin représente. — Peu de jours après, le 23 mars, Mlle Rogstad fit ses débuts avec un succès très vif à la tribune du Parlement norvégien dans la discussion du budget de la guerre.

5. Anna Rogstad,
   the first woman in
   the Norwegian
   Parliament
   (as deputy MP),
   1911

6. Sigrid Undset

7. Cora Sandel in Paris, 1911

8. Halldis Moren and
Tarjei Vesaas

9. Torborg Nedreaas

10. Bjørg Vik

11. Cecilie Løveid, 1991

12. A scene from Bjorg Vik's *Two Acts for Five Women*, National Theatre, Oslo, 1974

13. A scene from Cecilie Loveid's *Double Delight*, Central Theatre, Oslo, 1990

14. Herbjørg Wassmo, 1983

15. Gerd Brantenberg, 1985

16. Mari Osmundsen, 1989

8
Halldis Moren Vesaas (born 1907)

Becoming a poet

Although Halldis Moren was born and grew up in a rural community – the village of Trysil in Hedmark, not far from the Swedish border – her experience of that community was far removed from the oppressive 'Jante' attitudes suffered by an Aksel Sandemose or a Cora Sandel. Her supportive background stimulated a literary production of which the keynote is openness to experience, and the prevailing mood is life-affirming. Like Sigrid Undset she came from a home full of books, where reading and writing were valued activities; and like her, too, she conveys an earthy sensuality in her writings – though Halldis Moren's attitude to her own sensuality is less ambiguous, and expresses itself principally through poetry.

In many ways Halldis Moren stands out from the other authors whose writing receives detailed attention in this study. She is a poet; she writes in the second language of Norway, *nynorsk*; and she lived for most of her life in rural Norway rather than in an urban centre. Although she is not unique in being a woman poet in Norway, she is a representative of a genre which has traditionally been less attractive to women (see Chapter 5). When she began writing, there was a well-established poetic tradition in *nynorsk*, a language which is often characterized as being a more natural poetic medium than Norway's main language, *bokmål*;[1] but it was represented largely by male poets like Olav Aukrust (1883–1929), an important early influence. And she is different in another way too, a way which had consequences for her writing as well as her life, in being married to one of Norway's most lauded twentieth-century authors, Tarjei Vesaas (1897–1970).[2]

Halldis Moren was born in Trysil on 18 November 1907. Her father, Sven Moren (1871–1938), was a *nynorsk* writer, who published several novels, but is better remembered as a cultural personality than as an author. Her mother, Gudrid Breie

(1880–1963), was a qualified teacher and active in local politics, as well as having her hands full running the large farm; both parents encouraged their daughter's literary ambitions. Halldis was the eldest of five children, and the only girl; she was more conscious of the privilege of being the eldest than of any disadvantage because of her sex. She qualified as a teacher in 1928, but went to work as a secretary, largely to be able to travel. She worked first in Oslo and then in Hamar, and in 1929 she took a post in Geneva, where she remained until 1933. During those years her first two volumes of poetry were published. In 1931 she met Tarjei Vesaas; after several meetings in Norway and abroad (Geneva, Rome, Brittany) they married in April 1934 and settled on a farm at Midtbø, Telemark, not far from the Vesaas family home at Vinje. There they were to remain for the whole of their married lives, although with many and prolonged trips to other areas and other countries, often each on their own. Their son Olav was born in 1934, their daughter Guri in 1939. As they became more well-known, Midtbø became less of a rural backwater than a cultural centre as their wide circle of friends, including writers from all the Scandinavian countries, came to visit, and they participated in collaborative literary and educational projects.

The events of Halldis Moren Vesaas's life are not marked by dramatic upheavals; it flowed – or so it seems – smoothly and harmoniously. Over twenty-six years she published seven volumes of poetry, which trace stages on life's way; through the poems we follow her development from early youth, thirsty for experience, into maturity, marriage and motherhood, and then into a more reflective and troubled period of middle life. Outside events impinge more and more, as the rumblings of political upheaval in the 1930s are followed by war and occupation, and then by the atomic threat. Yet the poems never become propaganda; they remain anchored in the same warm sympathy for all life which prefers to understand rather than to judge.

There is no doubt that Halldis Moren's path to literature was easier than that of most women writers and, indeed, than that of many men. Yet it was not entirely free of hindrances. When she sent her first collection to the Aschehoug publishing house, it was returned with harsh criticism, and the romantic poet Vilhelm Krag (1871–1933) gave her the paternalistic advice: 'Why don't you get yourself a boyfriend, instead of producing all this nonsense?'[3] Instead she revised the poems, and made her debut the following year with *Harpe og dolk* (Harp and Dagger, 1929).

Poetry

When *Harpe og dolk* appeared in 1929, Halldis Moren was the first woman poet to make her appearance in Norwegian literature for almost a generation.[4] Not only that, but she was writing with a frankness which startled critics: 'Before her there was no female lyrical poet who had openly and joyfully expressed herself as a loving subject, fully aware of her feminine identity and of her absolute equality with a man.'[5] Looking back forty years later, she summarized her own feelings about her debut and about the new freedoms that women were experiencing:

> At that time there were so few women in this country who had written poetry that when you did so, you almost inevitably felt yourself to be a kind of 'echoing rock' that registered silent cries and gave them a voice. Women's feelings, women's viewpoints, women's lives had until then practically never found expression in poetry, so there was so much to draw on. I was extremely young too, and richly and joyfully aware of being a woman. There is probably no generation of young women who have been greeted by a brighter dawn than those of us who grew up between 1920 and 1930. We owned the keys of all kinds of freedom . . . [6]

Her poems express a Wordsworthian joy at being young in that dawn, when everything was possible for the confident poet; her 'song' makes her rich and generous. The poems give expression to female sexual desire – desire expressed not just as a vague longing or a spiritual communion but as an urgent physical need which is fulfilled by a real man in her bed. It is a mutual giving without reserve, in which the whole of nature becomes a participant. The man comes in from his work in the fields, of which their lovemaking is a natural extension:

You come and pull me close with your brown hands
and speak to me in words so wild and sweet.
Bewitched, I lie with you. Oh, I can sense
Through all my joy how rich you smell of earth!
The scent of earth and growth is on your skin.
– I lie in your arm and drink, so warm and wild,
like one who dies I sink into your soil
and sleep a spring night through upon your breast.

               'Jordange' ('Scent of Earth', *DS*, p. 29)[7]

Such poems created a minor scandal, written as they were by an
unmarried young woman in the 1920s. Yet the poet is not just
a passive recipient of a man's tenderness and potency; she has her
own strength, her own weapons if need be. The title poem 'Harp
and Dagger' expresses the other side of her nature: her harp plays
tender songs which express her heart's feelings, but she also wears a
dagger in her belt to take revenge if the man should tire of her love.
Equality means more than sexual permissiveness; it means being
able to meet strength with strength.

    Halldis Moren's first poems have been compared to those of
the Finland-Swedish poet Edith Södergran, who made her debut
only thirteen years earlier.[8] Södergran came to mean a great deal
to Halldis Moren, although there cannot have been any direct
influence here as she did not read Södergran's poems until after
writing *Harpe og dolk*.[9] Yet the same challenging female voice
speaks out of both collections; although a lover may come to the
maiden in Edith Södergran's 'The Day Cools' as a conqueror, he
soon finds that he is dealing with more than he bargained for:

You looked for a woman
and found a soul – [10]

The two poets differ, however, in the formal aspects of their
poetry; whilst Edith Södergran was one of the first Modernist poets
in Scandinavia, using free verse forms and relying on rhythm and
assonance rather than rhyme, Halldis Moren's poems are relatively
traditional in their use of regular stanza forms and rhyme schemes.
Occasionally she uses a freer form, but she did not herself see
that as an innovation, as free verse had been used by earlier Norwegian poets such as Wergeland, Vilhelm Krag and Obstfelder.[11]

Halldis Moren's second collection, *Morgonen* (The Morning, 1930), differs little from her first. The poems of this collection affirm her determination to drink full draughts of life; she also reveals an ability to take herself less seriously, as in the poem 'Forlat oss vår skuld' ('Forgive Us Our Sins'), in which she asks that all her sins may be wiped out – because the first sin tastes sweetest of all, and she wishes to enjoy that first taste again. There is no trace here of the pietism which still had a hold in many rural areas in Norway.

In 1933 came *Strender* (Shores), a collection in which love poems predominate, reflecting the poet's own experience at this time. Yet although the poems are intensely personal, they are not private, but express their jubilation through imagery which awakens resonances in the reader. As in 'Scent of Earth', nature is constantly present – not just as a framework or a sympathetic echo in the Romantic sense, but as an inextricable part of the relationship. Trees are a recurrent image in Halldis Moren's poetry, and often convey a sense of permanence, as in 'Tuntre', a poem about planting the special, almost sacred tree which stands in the middle of a farm and will send its roots down into the hearts of both man and woman. In 'Tre og mold' ('Tree and Earth') she herself becomes the tree and the man becomes the earth in which she is planted, drinking deep from the inexhaustible springs of his being. The poem 'Bølgje' ('Billow') begins with an awakening to the sound of the sea, which penetrates all their senses until the man himself becomes the sea, enveloping the woman like a force of nature and drowning every sense:

> Our house is filled like a conch shell
> With the swell of the sea. Ceaselessly the sea
> runs toward the land, today as yesterday
> – we heard its song through all our dreams.
> Still we taste of sea, we who were kissed,
> rocked and embraced by it all the long day,
> – you are like the sea as you take me in your arms,
> a wave breaking against mouth and breast.
> – Will you drown me? No, what you bring
> is the best that you know, wave from the wide sea!
>
> (*DS*, p. 77)

Lykkelege hender (Joyful Hands, 1936) is written by a woman in the first years of married life. Much of it is still turned towards the man, and to the expression of fulfilment through sexual union; he is rain falling on thirsty earth in a spring night, she is the earth which is drinking her fill ('Nei eg får aldri nok' – 'No I can't get enough'). But as the collection progresses, the woman becomes pregnant, and her senses turn towards her unborn child. These are the first Norwegian poems to express the physical feeling of carrying a child, feeling it growing as a part of you yet as a separate being, secret for a while but soon to push its way out to the world. The man is there too, a part of it even when he is not present, as in the strange poem 'Vår einsemd' ('Our Loneliness'), where the 'du' addressed by the poet slides from the child to the man and back.

Many of these poems are written in a freer verse form than the earlier ones. The poet has become more confident in trusting to the rhythms of the verse and sometimes abandons rhyme altogether, as in the title poem 'Lykkelege hender', which describes her busy hands and all that passes through them in the course of a work-filled day. Death is mentioned frequently in these poems full of fruitfulness and birth; but it does not disturb the harmony – it is a welcome peace to come, a fitting end to a life which has been lived to the full.

Although a sense of life's fulfilment is the central theme of these poems, it is punctuated by other moods and other themes. Halldis Moren Vesaas was not immune to the problems of combining a family with a career as a writer; the light-hearted poem 'Litteraturen og ungen' ('Literature and the Kid') describes mother trying to find a rhyme for 'gråt' ('cry') whilst baby is yelling in his cradle in the same room. (In Norwegian, 'gråt' turns out to rhyme with 'våt' – wet – whereas the English translator might be tempted to rhyme 'cry' with 'dry'.)

Not all the poems are located in the family; more prominent in this collection is an awareness of living in a community. In rural communities it is often the women who have the heaviest burdens to bear. In 'I bryllupet på Mo' ('The Wedding at Mo') a woman is regarded as lucky because she has borne 'only' thirteen children as well as supporting her drunken bull of a husband. 'I motbakken' ('Uphill') describes the thoughts of a woman toiling back to her mountain farm after a trip to the village; she has stayed too long gossiping with her sister and is making a panicky list in her head of all the jobs which will be waiting for her. Behind the slightly comic recitation of shopping lists and food for men and cows lies the grim reality of a life far from twentieth-century diversions, in which only unremitting drudgery can keep poverty at bay, and in which the woman bears the brunt of any oversights.[12] Echoes from the wider world are heard in this collection too, most clearly in the poem '1936', in which newspapers and radio intrude into the domestic idyll with their news of gathering storms, making the laughter of a child a poignant reminder of the fragility of life.

It was nine years before Halldis Moren Vesaas's next collection of poems, *Tung tids tale* ('Words from a Heavy Time', 1945), came out. These poems had to wait for publication until the end of the German occupation – although many of them were known in limited circles before that, as the poet had read them to friends and passed them around by hand. As the title suggests, most of the poems relate to the Second World War. They are ordered more or less chronologically from 1939 onwards, beginning with a poem about the Finno–Russian war, then the tense period of waiting, the experience of the occupation and finally the liberation in 1945. The subject matter has shifted from the experience of fulfilled womanhood of the earlier poems, though the change is not so radical as might be supposed.

These poems are not 'Resistance poetry' in the sense of patriotic appeals to fellow countrymen to resist the evil invader, and a bitter attack on Nazi aims and methods – the kind of poetry that Nordahl Grieg, Arnulf Øverland and Inger Hagerup were distributing during the occupation. There is no doubt in Halldis Moren Vesaas's poems that the invasion of Norway is to be vigorously resisted in word and deed; and yet the situation never becomes black and white – there is no glorification of Norway as a land of the free, or depiction of the Germans as a brutal mob. She emphasizes that war is a tragedy for both sides in the conflict, and that the human suffering takes no account of who is 'right' and who is 'wrong'. When she writes about the Finno–Russian war, for example – a battle in which Norwegians sided with the Finns – she recounts an episode in which Finnish soldiers desecrate a Russian corpse, which becomes a symptom of how war releases universal evil ('An

Incident from the War in Finland', *DS*, p. 110).

Her poems about the Germans in Norway reveal a similar capacity to stand back from her own sense of outrage and sympathize with the individuals who are caught in events over which they have no control, as in the poem 'Støvlane trampar' ('The Boots Are Marching'), which was written as early as the spring of the invasion in 1940. The poem begins with a description of the boots trampling down her native soil, killing all that grows, and with the poet's wish that the earth might send up briars that scratch; but suddenly she realizes that the boots are not empty, and that the weary men marching past have a heavier burden to bear than those who are watching – and she can no longer wish for thorns to hurt them. The second part of the poem enters the thoughts of those who are marching past, seeing the hatred on the faces they pass, and expressing a sense of powerlessness at being caught up in a machine which destroys their freedom too:

> We have no face. We were born too late.
> To be part of a war machine, that was our fate.
> We grew up, became men and soldiers the same day.
> *We are the ones who never had any say.* (*DS*, p. 118)

She sees the war with the eyes of a mother, and the awareness that in a few short years *her* son too might be involved is never far from her thoughts (e.g. 'Ein kveld av krigen' – 'An Evening in Wartime'). The predominant mood of her war poems is one of sadness, mixed with a growing sense of solidarity and of hope that the need to hate might soon pass and the world turn again towards spring. In keeping with the mood, the rhythms of these poems are slower and the verses longer compared with the quick, insistent rhythms and clipped stanzas of battle poems.

Nature is as close a part of human life in Halldis Moren Vesaas's war poems as in her love poems; rain falling becomes a flood to wash away the evil works of war, and the first spring of liberation will receive its confirmation from the appearance of the first anemone from under the snow. The hope at the end of the war is expressed in the simple act, so redolent with significance for this author, of a woman planting a tree. In her mind's eye she sees the branches spreading wide over future peace, but she is reminded of the fragility of her hope by a sudden tremor running through the earth – a reminder of the bomb falling on Hiroshima just as destruction seemed to be nearing its end.[13]

Trees are a central symbol of the next collection, called simply *Treet* (The Tree, 1947). The title poem evokes a tree in the snow which is different from those around it; they are all conifers, asleep in their foliage, but this is a leafless tree which bears only buds. It becomes a promise of future blossoming in the spring; becomes finally the poet herself, waiting:

> All on our earth which bears buds
> and knows its fulfilment is near
> has this shimmer around it
> of waiting and silence and dream.
>
> So strange to have seen that tree.
>
> So good to have been that tree
> – and to be it still, in a future dawn.

(DS, p. 144)

This identification is susceptible of several interpretations. For the poet it might be the hope of inspiration, of the gift of a poem – as Halldis Moren Vesaas has said that many of her poems 'came' to her rather than being worked on systematically. For the woman it can have a different significance; this reader, who first read the poem when she was pregnant, was in no doubt that it was about bearing a child. It can speak to everyone of their dreams for the future.

Several poems in this collection are addressed to individuals, friends who are celebrating or friends who have died. One of the most poignant is a poem on the death of the Swedish poet Karin Boye, who committed suicide in 1941. She must have seemed a kindred spirit, with her poems in which nature becomes one with her own feelings; her poem 'Ja visst gör det ont' ('Yes Indeed It Hurts') is, like 'The Tree', about buds waiting to open, but imbued with a fear of the pain of living which is absent from the Norwegian poem. To Halldis Moren Vesaas it seems that Karin Boye must have died of cold ('The frozen one has frozen to death'), and she contrasts this with the fire of her poetry which can warm others.

Halldis Moren Vesaas's final collection of poetry was published after another long pause in 1955, under the title *I ein
annan skog* (In Another Forest). With this collection we are
indeed in a different place – and at times a darker one. The
poem from which the title is derived, 'Den andre skogen'
('The Other Forest'), compares the forest of her earlier life,
with its strong, straight trees, to the one she has now sought out:

> Here it is narrow and dark
> with peculiar twisted trees,
> storm-tossed, bent and broken –
> never was I in such a forest.
> Can it be here that my heart
> must seek – and find its peace? (*DS*, p. 188)

The poem expresses a mixture of emotions: regret at leaving the
perfect trees, pity for the deformed ones, and at the same time
a feeling that in this new forest there is a struggle for life
which makes it more exhilarating than the forest where all is
achieved, arouse in the poet the wish 'that life, my life, might
be here'. Life is less secure than it had earlier seemed, yet the
poet welcomes the challenge out of which new growth can
come. The rain which had embraced her as a lover will now
fall 'black as cold coal' ('Regn skal falle', 'Rain Shall Fall'),
and the other who had seemed so known, so near, has again
become distant and unknown ('Ukjend', 'Unknown'.) In one
of her simplest and most moving poems, she acknowledges that
even the deepest love cannot overcome the ultimate loneliness
of each individual, but it can nevertheless provide a home on
this earth:

> You walk as far as my innermost gate
> and I walk as far as yours.
> Inside that we are each alone
> according to nature's laws.
>
> Never force yourself further in
> was the law that governed us two.
> Whether we met rarely or often
> I felt peace and trust in you.

If you aren't there one day when I come
turning back is easy to bear
when I have stood and looked at your house
knowing that you live there.

So long as I know you will come now and then
like now over crunching stone
and smile in pleasure to see me there
so long will my house be a home.

('Ord over grind', 'Words Over the Gate', *DS*, p. 180.)

It is the homely images from near experience, not abstract speculations, which best express her view of life in these poems. Sympathy
for the one who is alone, the one who is different, runs through
many of them, such as 'Voggesang for ein bytting' ('Lullaby for a
Changeling'), in which the perfect son has been taken by the trolls,
who have left their ugly brat instead – which the mother decides
to care for as her own; or 'Einsamflygar' ('The Lonely Flier'),
which uses the image of a bird lost beneath the stars, separated
from the migrating flock, as a picture of the outsider who must
go his own way without help. Behind these poems lie memories
of the outsiders the poet had known and who early went their
own way into self-chosen death – not only Karin Boye but also
more recently Tor Jonsson (1916–51) and the Swedish writer Stig
Dagerman (1923–54).

Death is a constant presence in these poems – no longer as a
distant peace at the end of a working day, but as a much nearer
reality. In the poem 'Den andre' ('The Other') her lover of this
earth, with the golden skin, must make way for a pale and cold
lover who 'kisses with wilder fervour' as he claims her; and in 'Det
sikre' ('Certainty') it is a comfort to a person tormented by life that
the coins which will close his eyes are perhaps already minted, the
cloth which will form his shroud is perhaps already woven. The
final poem, 'Skuggane' ('The Shades'), is set in the realm of the
dead, where memories of the earth slowly fade and those who
have been there longest have no words to recall what life meant;
yet paradoxically, the effect of this is to revive the love of the earth
in those who have recently left it, so that the poem ends with an
affirmation of the joy of life:

Then those who came here last began
again to speak, and their voices rose
and praised clouds, birds, green grass,
light and dark, warm blood, dreams
and all that the living possess.   (*DV*, p. 191)

Looking back over her poetry a decade later, Halldis Moren Vesaas summed up its dominant emotion as love for 'all that we living possess'.[14] Awareness of the transience of life makes its gifts that much more precious.

Other writing

Halldis Moren Vesaas's last book of poetry was published when she was forty-eight; after that she wrote only a few 'occasional' poems. The pressing need to write poetry, which arose directly from the changing phases of her life, had faded. This is how she describes it:

> The poems which 'came down' to me through the years were also a kind of by-product of the process of living. They have the closest connection with it, without therefore being an account of it. When life bubbled up in me most fully, in happiness or in pain, the poems took form, functioned literally as a safety valve, like the rapidly boiling water in the test-tube we learnt about in physics when we were children. At times when the water in life's test-tube was just simmering away happily there were no poems, or at any rate very few. They didn't announce themselves then, and as a rule there's no point trying to summon them up.[15]

Yet Halldis Moren Vesaas's career as a writer was by no means over in 1955. Although her poems qualitatively are the high point of her writing, quantitatively they make up only a small part of it; she also wrote in many other genres, including fiction, journalism, literary criticism, essays and autobiography. In 1940 she was first asked to translate a play to be performed at *Det norske teatret*, and has since translated and adapted so many plays – from French, English and German – that she has had a career as a translator which on its own would have satisfied many people.[16] Her translation of Racine's *Phèdre* into alexandrines was a major event at the theatre in 1960, and other authors she has translated include Shakespeare, Goethe, Molière, Pirandello, Kafka and Claudel. In 1982–3 she adapted Torborg Nedreaas's *Nothing Grows By Moonlight*, Sigrid Undset's *Dear Dea* and Cora Sandel's *The Leech* for *Det norske teatret*. It is a career which continues; her translations of Racine's *Bérénice* and Beaumarchais's *Le Mariage de Figaro* were performed in 1989, and in 1990 she was working on Sophocles' *Antigone* and planning to set about Molière's *Tartuffe*.

She also wrote several books for children, and one novel, *Hildegunn*, which was published during the occupation in 1942. This novel has been dismissed as 'teenage fiction', which it is not. It is the story of a young girl who wants to be an artist, and her struggles not only against her rural environment but particularly against her mother, who does not want to let her go. Finally she escapes to Oslo and a life of privation – until she meets the well-known artist Tormod Styrkson. She releases the dried-up creativity in him and finds her vocation in being his muse. When she develops tuberculosis he stays loyal to her, but although she recovers she decides not to return to him, for 'she would not have been able to give him anything more if they had spent their whole lives together'.[17] She returns home, where she discovers a new sense of belonging. She can see her mother with new eyes – for she also is a frustrated artist, who has never had the time to develop her talent for weaving but now, finally, after her husband's death, is able to create her life's work. Female creativity finds its way out in the end, although the channels along which it runs may be winding ones.

In 1951 Halldis Moren Vesaas published a biography of her father, *Sven Moren og heimen hans* (Sven Moren and His Home). In 1967 came a collection of her essays, *Sett og levd* (Seen and Lived). Some are accounts of her travels, mainly to Greece and Rome. She travelled with an open mind; but what interested her most was the people she met, either literally in the shape of a taxi-driving Greek philosopher or metaphorically through their writings. Thus a visit to Eleusis becomes a meditation on Plato and Socrates, and in Rome she follows in the footsteps of John Keats. Her essays on her contemporaries are equally full of empathy; she always writes about people she likes – or perhaps always comes to like the people she writes about. Writers she has known – Tor Jonsson, Einar Skjæraasen, Stig Dagerman, the Danish Martin A. Hansen – receive generous tribute. Of particular interest in the context of this study is her essay on Hulda Garborg who, like Halldis Moren herself, was married to a man who was acknowledged as a major author, and in the shade of whose talent her own may have felt oppressed:

> behind this sparkling story of an extroverted and incredibly active life one can glimpse a text of a quite different kind: the story of someone who wanted to be a writer and perhaps was, but who never quite achieved what she wanted.[18]

Finally the selection includes a couple of essays about Tarjei Vesaas, written in 1947 and 1964; the first one sounds much surer of what he is like than the second, echoing the movement in her poetry from confident intimacy with the lover with whom all nature comes to her, to a feeling that 'the other' will always be in some way irreducibly alien.

Tarjei Vesaas died in 1970; a few years later Halldis Moren published two books about their lives together, *I Midtbøs bakkar* (On Midtbø's Hills, 1974), which covers the period up to 1946, and *Båten om dagen* (The Boat in the Daytime, 1976), about the years 1946–70. The books are a mixture of biography and autobiography; they tell of her own life and tell it obviously from her point of view, but the centre of their focus is nearly always Tarjei. They were written in the consciousness of the fact that 'the author–apparatus Vesaas' had become something of a national institution, and that they were both seen as larger than life: 'That is one of the reasons I sat down to write the books of memoirs – which are really parts of one book: in order to kill off the worst untruths, to adjust the myths and to reveal that even idols have problems, just as much as anyone else.'[19]

This declared intention is only partly successful. Tarjei Vesaas emerges as a man not without faults, but one who persistently remains larger than life; he is portrayed with the eyes of love, and by a wife who admits to being constantly taken by surprise by the new sides of him revealed in his books, which made her wonder if she really knew him at all. There is an aura of mystery around him which never completely evaporates.

The picture the author gives of herself and her own writing in these two volumes is revealing. Like Hulda Garborg, she was aware of living – professionally, at least – in her husband's shadow, and despite her undoubtedly sincere acknowledgement of the superiority of his talent, here too one can catch glimpses of 'a text of a quite different kind'. Their marriage perpetuated the traditional gender divisions and implicitly relegated her work to a lower priority, as she good-humouredly but somewhat ruefully recounts:

> Tarjei . . . did not touch pen and paper that summer. I on the other hand had a lot to do. I had my translating work with me, and of course I kept house for the two men. It did happen that I felt a little sexually discriminated as I sat inside, hammering away at the typewriter and keeping one eye on the clock as it slowly and surely moved towards the next mealtime, whilst the menfolk went for a stroll or sat by the wall in the sun, philosophizing.[20]

In many ways she was fiercely independent, and determined to retain her own freedom of action; she was not going to become an appendage, and even intended to keep her own name – until practical difficulties persuaded her to add his. Yet with hindsight – and the benefit of the insights of the new feminist movement in the decade when she was writing her memoirs – she became more aware of the unspoken assumptions. The one 'writing room' in the house was automatically his, whilst she wrote in the bedroom – and eventually on the changing table, whilst the baby slept in a cradle beside it. It did not occur to either of them that she should have her own room; and ironically, it was not until 1955, the year that her final collection of poetry appeared, that she did get a workroom. What difference that fact might have made is impossible to know, but the different working conditions for the two halves of the 'author–apparatus' must be one factor in the different volume of work they produced.

The main impression left by these two autobiographical volumes, however, is that of a life lived fully and with few regrets. Her capacity for friendship emerges from her many sympathetic portraits of the visitors to Midtbø. Many were authors who formed part of the inter-Scandinavian cultural co-operation which was particularly strong in the years after the war; in places the account becomes almost a cultural history of modern Scandinavia. The acuteness of her observations of other authors – Paul la Cour, Martin A. Hansen, Tore Ørjasæter, Stig Dagerman, Solveig von Schoultz, Inger Hagerup – conveys to the reader an almost physical sense of their presence.

It was some time after 1976 before Halldis Moren Vesaas published any new work – although her collected poems appeared in 1977, and she continued to be busy with many other kinds of cultural activities; the number of educational and cultural committees she sat on during her life would be difficult to calculate. She not infrequently complained that she was selected because she could represent several 'minority' interests, being (a) a woman, (b) a *nynorsk* writer and (c) from a rural area.[21]

The next work she published, in 1987 – her eightieth year – was a collection of short stories, *Så nær deg* (So Close To You). All four stories in the collection are concerned with the relationships between parents and children, particularly mother and daughter, with that strongest of all bonds in which 'the two parts have once belonged together more closely than in any other human constellation'.[22] Yet it is a bond which should naturally loosen with time, otherwise it can become a chain. In the title story a mother travels with her daughter to Rome, and witnesses the daughter's falling in love so intensely that it is like her own experience: 'the mother . . . felt how what filled her daughter also filled her. The wall which separated them had been thin before, and now it was as if it had disappeared'.[23] In this symbiotic relationship she feels her daughter's bitter disappointment like a physical pain – which is a pain of separation too, as she realizes that she cannot protect her. She must allow the distance between them to grow, return to her own life so that her daughter may be freed into hers.

'Siste sandkorn' ('The Last Grains of Sand') is told from the viewpoint of a daughter who has come home to nurse her dying mother, and at the same time to sort out her unresolved jealousy from a childhood in which her younger sister was so much prettier and more popular than she. Although she is tempted not to tell her sister of the danger – so that she may at least have her mother to herself in her last moments – she overcomes her selfishness, and in so doing comes to accept the past and realize that her role has been equally important, if less visible. The daughter's viewpoint predominates also in 'Med pannelugg' ('With a Fringe'), about a girl who is trying to earn her mother's praise by emulating her skill with a needle. According to the author, these two stories were based on her relationship with her own mother, and the book was intended 'in general to act as a kind of positive counterweight to all the negative mother/daughter relationships in contemporary literature'.[24]

'Kore' [25] explores the feelings of a mother whose daughter has been killed, and whose grief is so intense that it has become a barrier between herself and her second husband. He helps to break down that barrier by confronting her with the past on a trip to Greece, which she had once visited with her daughter. When she realizes that he not only understands her grief but also needs her help, she is at last able to offer him mutual support.

All these stories work through a crisis in a relationship to a reconciliation. It is the kind of resolution which emerges from most of what Halldis Moren Vesaas has written, be it fact or fiction: 'Nothing which is natural is really bad'.[26] Conflict and misunderstanding can arise, but they are rarely purely destructive, and even war cannot wipe out man's essential humanity. The dimension of evil is almost entirely absent from her writings – and it is not surprising that it is those works of Tarjei Vesaas where it features most strongly which seemed to her most alien. Although she was by no means untouched by the problems of being a woman writer, she was never overwhelmed by them. Of the writers to whom earlier chapters have been devoted, Ragnhild Jølsen never married, Camilla Collett lost the love of her life, and Amalie Skram, Sigrid Undset and Cora Sandel all divorced. Halldis Moren Vesaas is the only one who achieved a stable and permanent relationship. The combination of a harmonious temperament and a congenial environment make her one of the few Norwegian women authors of whom it seems safe to say that life gave her what she wanted.

PART III
1960–1990

9
The Personal is Political

Norway in the modern world

The development of Norway since the end of the Second World War has been peaceful; the country has not been troubled by political upheavals or by armed conflict. It is often regarded along with the other Scandinavian countries as a model welfare state, with a just constitution and liberal laws. At the same time, it is perceived as peripheral to Europe, both because it does not belong to the EC and because the myth persists of a nation of fierce individualists living close to nature in silent, isolated valleys – a nation in which, as Ibsen maintained, 'every second man is a philosopher'.[1]

Like most myths, this contains an element of truth; both the history and the geography of Norway mark it off from its Scandinavian neighbours and from the rest of Europe. The brevity of Norway's history as an independent country in modern times is still apparent in its reluctance to compromise that independence, and the physical nature of the country, with its small population spread thinly over a rugged terrain, has created specific economic and social problems. The fierceness of the conflict between independence and interdependence was demonstrated by the EC referendum in 1972. Despite a desire to participate in both European and Scandinavian collaboration (e.g. through continued membership of NATO and of the Nordic Council of Ministers), Norwegians refused membership of the Common Market. Some of the reasons were economic, involving in particular fears for the future of the agricultural and fishing industries; some were more emotional, based on a perception of entry to the Market as a surrender of national sovereignty. As one modern historian – who believes that the decision was a misguided one – puts it: '[Norway] might perhaps be more fairly described in this period of stress as the involuntary prisoner of its history'.[2]

Politically there have been no dramatic swings in modern times, as the balance of power is fairly evenly divided between the parties of the left (mainly the Labour Party) and parties of the centre/moderate right. Paradoxically, this has resulted in several changes of government since 1965, when the long Labour rule was ended by a three-party coalition (Conservative, Centre and Christian People's Parties); in such an evenly balanced situation, a slight swing is enough to destabilize a coalition or minority government. In 1971 a minority Labour government was set up under Trygve Bratteli; it was forced to resign after the EC referendum, having made the issue a vote of confidence; Gro Harlem Brundtland (Labour) became Prime Minister for the first time in 1981, in a government which lasted only a few months; and in the elections of 1989, Brundtland's second Labour government was again forced to stand down in favour of a Conservative/Centre/Christian People's coalition led by Jan P. Syse – which had no absolute majority, but was forced to rely on the erratic support of the extreme right-wing Progress Party. That coalition lasted only a year, resigning in 1990 in favour of a new minority Labour government. If Norway nevertheless appears to outsiders to have had a fairly stable government throughout this period, this is due to the fact that there is less difference between the policies of the left and those of the right than there is, say, in England; both are committed to the preservation of the welfare state, and the Norwegian Conservative Party is closer to what we would define as Social Democrats.

Yet Norway has not escaped the problems of late-twentieth-century capitalism any more than the rest of the Western world. Industrialization and urbanization have continued to deplete the rural areas; many outlying farms and coastal settlements have become depopulated. This process is continuing despite vociferous protests in recent years, as the maintenance of communications to remote areas becomes increasingly unviable in economic terms. Concern for the environment is strong, as is evident from the frequent protests about the destruction of areas of outstanding natural beauty in order to provide hydro-electric power from waterfalls, or to build oil refineries for Norway's new oil industry. Norwegians are increasingly concerned about the international environment too, as is evinced by Gro

Harlem Brundtland's leading role in the production of 'The Brundtland Report', which underlines the urgency of seeking global solutions.[3]

Until the middle of the twentieth century, Norway was a country of emigration rather than immigration, particularly during the mass exodus to America between 1860 and 1910; but since the end of the 1960s immigration has increased rapidly, the largest body being workers or refugees from the Third World. (In 1988, for example, of the 10,000 long-term immigrants who entered Norway, nearly 6,000 came from Asia.)[4] In a population of just over four million, which is not increasing except as a result of the immigrant birth rate, the effect of the influx is noticeable, particularly in the capital. Racism has for the first time become a problem in Norway, with the unfortunate result that the Progress Party increased its share of seats in Parliament from 2 to 22 in the 1989 elections.

The modern media have become an important part of Norwegian culture. After a relatively late start – Norwegian television did not begin broadcasting until 1960 – mass communication spread rapidly, and with it the influence of other languages and cultures, especially English. Both in broadcasting and in publishing, the pressure of imports is unremitting; English-language series dominate television evening viewing time, and foreign literature floods in (in 1988, for example, of the total of 4,036 books published in Norway, only 2,266 were originally written in Norwegian.)[5] The Norwegians are divided between their desire for the acquisition of foreign languages, necessary for their communication with the rest of the world, and their concern for the preservation of their own language. A glance at the high percentage of recently imported English words in the national newspapers is enough to justify their apprehension.

Women's visibility in the public sphere, as demonstrated in Chapter 5, had not improved to any marked extent by the middle of the twentieth century. After 1913 there was a relative lull in activity, and improvements were slow. The system remained basically unaffected by the change:

Both gender equality and women's policies were devised within the confines of a tutelary, patriarchal political system dominated by men. The penchant for paternalism of Nordic welfare states, made palatable by a strong commitment to equality, is especially obvious in regard to women. . . . Universal suffrage had not provided women with political power.[6]

The lack of political power became a serious issue to women in the 1960s, in the period of prosperity after the post-war recovery. The increase of activity in this area is often associated with the more general protest movements of 1968, but it had begun earlier. During the 1960s researchers had become interested in the study of social conditioning and sex-role stereotypes, and a grass-roots movement emerged to secure more adequate political representation, at both local and national level.[7] This involved first ensuring that candidates were selected, and then that they were elected – both somewhat easier in a cumulative voting system than in a constituency one. The first push came with the local elections in 1967, at which the percentage of women elected increased from 6.3 to 9.5 per cent – the first time they had become a force to be reckoned with. From then onwards, percentages gradually increased over the next two decades, both in the general elections

Table 9.1   Percentages of women elected at general and local elections 1967–89

	Parliament	Local councils	County councils
1967		9.5	
1969	9		
1971		14.8	5.4
1973	16		
1975		15.4	24.9
1977	23.9		
1979		22.8	28.8
1981	25.8		
1983		24	32.8
1985	34.4		
1987		31.1	40.5
1989	35.7		

and in local council and county council elections (see Table 9.1).

Having got this far, it was important for women not just to remain on the back benches. The token Cabinet Minister appointed in 1945 was no substitute for a real say in decision-making. Norway's first woman Prime Minister, Gro Harlem Brundtland, was appointed briefly in 1981 and then ran the government from 1986 to 1989 and from 1990 onwards; equally important, she regarded it as a matter of prime importance to have women in her Cabinet – a significant difference from the situation in Great Britain at that time. Eight of the eighteen Cabinet Ministers she appointed were women. The principle became established independent of her influence; when Jan P. Syse named his Cabinet in 1989, eight of his eighteen Ministers were women. They were not concentrated in the 'soft' areas like health and family care either: the Ministries of Trade, Justice and Agriculture were headed by women.

Although the winning of political influence began as a grass-roots movement, it was not long before more organized women's groups appeared. In the early 1970s, two new feminist organizations were formed: *Nyfeministene* (The New Feminists) in 1970, and *Kvinnefronten* (The Women's Front) in 1972. They were different in their philosophies and in their approach. The New Feminists, following the American pattern, was a largely middle-class movement which concentrated on the freedom of the individual, and was organized into loosely knit cells aimed at collective consciousness-raising. The Women's Front was a more political organization with a central leadership, which linked the oppression of women to that of the working classes in a capitalist society, and concentrated on changing the system. Both organizations had internal conflicts; in 1975 a section from within the Women's Front formed a new group called *Brød og roser* (Bread and Roses), and in the same year a breakaway group from the New Feminists formed *Lesbisk bevegelse* (The Lesbian Movement). Despite their differences, however, they had many common goals, such as the right to abortion, better childcare facilities and equal pay and working conditions for women, and played a central part in the achievement of these aims.[8]

One of the first results of the new wave of feminism was the setting up of an Equal Opportunities Commission in 1972. The

Commission's report formed the basis for the Equal Status Act, which became law in 1979. The aim of the law is 'to promote equality between the sexes. Women and men shall be given equal opportunities for education, work and cultural and intellectual development. In present-day society the aim will chiefly be to improve the position of women.'[9] The law allows for positive discrimination, acknowledging that the removal of formal barriers is not enough to achieve real equality, but that more energetic measures need to be taken. The law was further amended in subsequent years, particularly with respect to representation on public bodies; from a cautious amendment in 1981 to the effect that women should be represented on all public bodies evolved a more far-reaching amendment in 1988 which stated that all public committees, boards, etc., with four or more members should consist of at least 40 per cent women and 40 per cent men. Despite gloomy predictions, it has not proved impossible to implement.

Laws in other areas have improved the status of women: in 1978, a law was finally passed allowing abortion on demand, and in 1979, a law giving the right of Norwegian citizenship to children born of a Norwegian mother. Women's Studies departments have been set up at several academic institutions; in 1978, for example, the Institute of Women's Law became a formal department of the University of Oslo, the first of its kind in the world. The Social Science Research Council has established a secretariat for women's studies.

Yet important as changes in the law have been, just as important are changes in practice. Apart from the representation of women on public bodies, the Equal Status Act did not introduce any radically new legislation; the principle of equality was already enshrined in Norwegian law, but it had demonstrably not led to an equal society. It was a question of moving from *de jure* to *de facto* equality.[10] As recent studies have demonstrated, Norwegian society is still a patriarchal system where the consequences of full equality have not been realized.[11] Childcare is expensive and far from adequate. Equal pay has not been achieved in any area of society; in 1988, the average pay of women industrial workers was 85 per cent that of men, that of office workers 93 per cent and that of shop workers 87 per cent.[12] Nevertheless, much has been achieved. Although Norwegian women were relatively late

– in comparison with the other Nordic countries – in taking up higher education in large numbers and in re-entering the labour force, by the mid-1970s they represented around 40 per cent of the non-agricultural labour force and 44 per cent of university students.[13] And they have achieved both formal recognition and social acceptance of equality in a way that women even in other Western industrialized countries can only envy.

From Modernism to commitment

In literary terms, the early 1960s were not a time of radical change; the most innovative works came from the pens of established authors like Johan Borgen and Tarjei Vesaas. Borgen's novels *Jeg* (*The Scapegoat*, 1959) and *Blåtind* (The Blue Peak, 1964) explored formally and thematically the problems of split personality and lost identity. Vesaas's *Brannen* (The Fire, 1961) and *Isslottet* (*The Ice Palace*, 1963) are studies in alienation and lack of communication which threaten the disintegration of society.

It was not until 1966 that a new literary generation appeared. The long-running literary magazine *Profil* (Profile) was taken over by an editorial board who declared themselves to be a new generation of Modernists. Authors like Tor Obrestad (born 1938), Espen Haavardsholm (born 1945), Jan Erik Vold (born 1939) and Einar Økland (born 1940) were to dominate the literary scene for the next decade. Chief amongst them was Dag Solstad (born 1941), who wrote a programmatic article in *Profil* I, 1966, entitled 'Norsk prosa – europeisk modernisme' ('Norwegian Prose – European Modernism'), urging Norwegian writers to escape the stranglehold of the traditional realistic novel and its illusion of probability, and to draw inspiration from Nordic myth and folk tale. Solstad's own early works illustrate his thesis: *Spiraler* (Spirals, 1965) contains Kafkaesque parables of man's struggles to find his bearings in a hostile environment; and *Svingstol* (Swivel Chair, 1967) is a collection of 'short fiction' texts which strip a story down to its essential – or, more correctly, inessential – elements.[14]

The 'Modernist wave' of the 1960s was as brief as it was intense; it was superseded – in the works of these authors, at least – by a new political commitment. The change is charted by *Profil*, which by the end of 1968 was urging authors to compose new models for the understanding of society. In the early 1970s Obrestad, Haavardsholm, Økland, Solstad and others joined the political organization AKP (m–l), the Marxist–Leninist Workers' Communist Party; and with post-Vietnam political awareness they resolved to commit their talents to the service of the new society. It was the first time since the 1920s that left-wing intellectuals in Norway had come to view a Communist Party as their natural home.

From the standpoint of the present study, the most striking aspect of these cultural-literary movements of the 1960s and early 1970s is the almost total absence of women. There was not one who played a central role in the *Profil* Modernist group or in the AKP (m–l) group. There were some women associated with *Profil*, in particular Liv Køltzow (born 1944), Eldrid Lunden (born 1940) and Cecilie Løveid (born 1951), who were all to become successful authors; but none of them made much impression on the male-dominated ethos of the group. Like their sisters in the French intellectual left of the late 1960s, they finished up, metaphorically speaking, yet again making the tea.[15] As Liv Køltzow later ruefully expressed it:

> It was a very active group, but I was only 'involved' to the extent that I was there, tagged along if you like. Girls didn't have very much to say there, and I wasn't used to saying very much anyway. It wasn't somehow the intention that girls should say anything. I became withdrawn from being with all those boys, even though in a literary sense I felt very close to some of them.[16]

The invigorating new atmosphere was liberating only for some. But it was not only a matter of traditional repression; as time went on, it became increasingly evident that the interests of many women writers were moving in a different direction. By the mid-1970s, they were visible in an entirely new way.

If they were not much in evidence in the *Profil* group, women were nevertheless active as writers in the 1960s, although more as individuals than as a collective movement. Many of the writers who had made their names earlier were still writing. Torborg Nedreaas was in the middle of the 'Herdis' series, and Ebba Haslund, Ingeborg Refling Hagen, Marie Takvam, Gunvor Hofmo, Halldis Moren Vesaas and others continued into the 1970s and beyond.

Solveig Christov (born 1918) also spans the whole period. After her allegorical novels of the 1950s, she returned to a more realistic narrative with *Korsvei i jungelen* (Crossroads in the Jungle, 1959). Most of the novel is narrated by Eva, a piano teacher and spinster from Oslo, who experiences a turbulent summer on her brother's farm in the country; it becomes a drama of jealousy in which two lovers are destroyed by society's victimization of those who do not conform. Eva is an ambivalent character: an independent woman who refuses to be patronized ('I'm not going to hang over the sea in order to be saved every time you need to save an Iselin. I am Eva. I can swim, I swim like a fish'[17]); she carries her wish for self-sufficiency to the extent of never allowing anyone to get close to her, and finishes as a sad and isolated figure.

Solveig Christov's next novel, *Elskerens hjemkomst* (The Lover's Return, 1961), is ironically titled; the unreliable narrator, Claus Lund, is returning to Norway after half a lifetime abroad to face a reckoning with the past from which he fled. He meets again the three women with whom he was involved, and is forced to acknowledge that he abandoned the one he should have loved out of cowardice, and cannot return the love of the one who has waited for him. The most sympathetic character is Claus's brother Holger, whom Claus despises since he discovered he was a homosexual, but who demonstrates an altruism which is beyond Claus's comprehension. This sensitive portrayal of homosexuality is remarkable in a novel written by a woman at the beginning of the 1960s. It includes an indictment in Holger's mouth of the indoctrination of men as well as women in a patriarchal society which foreshadows later attacks by French feminist theorists on 'phallogocentrism'[18]:

> You had a piece of tackle with which you would breed children in the fullness of time, and to that tackle you let them attach the whole system, man's honour, man's courage, man's will, man's duty, man's pride, man's . . . man's man's . . . I had the idea that I could do it over again, relive your and my growing up over again, I had the idea that I could turn them [his stepsons] into men without hanging all these leaden things on their breeding tackle. I wanted to turn them into human beings.[19]

Despite the fact that Holger is driven to suicide by his self-righteous brother, his words remain standing as a refutation of Claus's blinkered attitude.

Solveig Christov's later novel *Knivsliperens dagbok* (The Knife-Sharpener's Diary, 1976) won a prize in Aschehoug's novel competition. It is also narrated by a man, this time a surgeon who finds renewed joy of life in being able to lower his defences and open himself to a woman. Solveig Christov's novels often take men as their subject, questioning their socialization into a 'macho' self-image and suggesting that they have as much to gain as women from allowing more traditionally feminine values a greater place in their lives.

The major woman writer who made her debut during the 1960s is Bjørg Vik (born 1935). Her first volume of short stories, *Søndag ettermiddag* (Sunday Afternoon), was published in 1963, and the critics, with rare unanimity, singled her out at once as an original writer. These stories explore the dramas beneath the polished surface of life in modern society – dramas particularly in the lives of women, from the 'liberated' student who hides her uncertainties behind a façade of sexual liberation and cynicism to the semi-alcoholic middle-aged housewife who cannot articulate her own sense of futility, but turns her rebellion inwards in paralyzing guilt. Her stories were admired both for their erotic frankness and for their acute observation. By the mid-seventies she had come to be seen as a pioneer of new feminism, a role-model for later writers – a label against which she protested.[20] She has remained a central figure in Norwegian literary life up to the 1990s (see Chapter 10).

Liv Køltzow's first book was a slim volume of short stories, *Øyet i treet* (The Eye in the Tree, 1970), which did not arouse much interest at the time, though later it took on greater significance: 'Now that we are wise after the event, we might label this little book as a kind of beginning of the "feminist wave": the stories are about the moment before something happens.'[21] The title story is about a girl sitting in a tree, hiding during a game of hide-and-seek; throughout almost the whole story she sits still, observing the others and waiting for the right moment to move.

With Liv Køltzow's next novel, *Hvem bestemmer over Bjørg og Unni?* (Who Decides What Happens to Bjørg and Unni?, 1972), the 'feminist wave' had begun to roll. This is one of the first books to address itself to feminist politics, in the sense of investigating how political decisions affect the lives of ordinary women in ways of which the decision-makers are unaware, and how individuals can challenge those decisions. 'The personal is political'; as their male colleagues were analyzing the effects of the international political situation or internal industrial strife on a male-centred society,[22] women authors were becoming aware that their patterns were different and had been largely obscured by the emphases of men's committed writing.

Bjørg and Unni in Liv Køltzow's novel are two young women living on a new estate in Oslo. Bjørg is married to a warm-hearted man, who is an active trade unionist, busy with meetings and unaware of the extra burdens this imposes on his wife; they have two children, and her life revolves around them and their home. Her friend Unni is an unmarried mother, with a full-time job and a chronic shortage of time, money and adequate childcare. The catalyst for them both to take action comes when the local council decides to build a trunk road through their estate, bringing disruption and danger to the children. In their determination to oppose the threat, Bjørg and Unni make contact with the other women on the estate and realize that their problems are not isolated ones. They organize a sit-down in front of the bulldozers, and discover that they can stop the relentless march of the machines. It is only a beginning, not a solution; but it demonstrates how awareness of the way they have been manipulated is the first step towards collective action.

Liv Køltzow's later novels developed this theme. *Historien om Eli* (The Story of Eli, 1976) is about a girl who has been socialized into passivity, and slowly and painfully realizes that no one else can take responsibility for her life; she has to summon up the initiative to break out of her failed marriage before she can begin to work towards independence. *Løp, mann* (Run, Man, 1980) is a study of a group of friends and their loyalties and conflicts as teachers, partners and parents – the way in which patterns become set and difficult to break. In *Hvem har ditt ansikt?* (Who Has Your Face?, 1988), the central character, Helen, falls inconveniently in love and has to face the problems this poses for her well-ordered existence, at the same time as trying to find her way as an artist. She becomes conscious of her conditioning and begins to find the strength to oppose it, as her lover points out on the novel's final page: 'When you were born, all the masculine qualities had long since been shared out amongst the others. Then you arrived. And were given the role of the woman to play, the mild conciliator.'[23]

'Jentesosialiseringen', the conditioning of women into socially acceptable roles, is a central theme not only for Bjørg Vik and Liv Køltzow but for several other writers during this period. Margaret Johansen's (born 1923) *Det var engang en sommer* (Once Upon a Summer, 1974) portrays a girl who is released by her lover's efforts from her conventional straitjacket – and his subsequent problems in coping with the new liberated woman. Ebba Haslund's *Bare et lite sammenbrudd* (Just a Little Breakdown, 1975) centres on a middle-aged woman from the upper middle class who has been the perfect wife, and her discovery of the hollowness of that role.

More flamboyant figures are used by Bergljot Hobæk Haff (born 1925) in her studies of women's many roles. *Skjøgens bok* (The Prostitute's Book, 1965) is narrated by a prostitute who is used by her clients as an opportunity to act out their repressions, becoming confidante, mother-substitute, libertine or artist's model according to men's wishes. In *Heksen* (The Witch, 1974) the narrator is an outcast, fruit of a mismatch between farmer's daughter and gypsy, who in the religious fervour of the sixteenth century is forced into the role of a witch. In men's desire for her they see devilish temptation, and she becomes a scapegoat, victim of a whole society's irrational fears, as her mistress suggests: 'Just think if it is one day explained that our time was a time of darkness, and that we only needed the witch-burnings in order to light up our own fear of the dark?'[24]

The new 'sexually liberated' role can easily become as much of a straitjacket as the earlier conventional one, and it was most particularly a straitjacket for those who found the heterosexual role unacceptable. Literature with lesbianism as a major theme has been rare in all Western countries until recent times, and Scandinavia is no exception – although Sweden has been better provided than most. In Norway there was very little lesbian literature before 1970.[25] The situation changed, however, in 1973, when Gerd Brantenberg's *Opp alle jordens homofile* (*What Comes Naturally*) was published.

Gerd Brantenberg (born 1941) stood out publicly as a lesbian author from the start. Her major works are *Egalias døtre* (*The Daughters of Egalia*, 1977), a dystopian novel about a matri-archal society which was an international best-seller, and her semi-autobiographical trilogy about growing up as a lesbian in the 1950s and 1960s (1979–89). She has been and remains the most visible spokeswoman for alternative sexuality in Norway (see Chapter 12).

Tove Nilsen (born 1952) is an author from a slightly younger generation who placed a lesbian relationship at the centre of one of her early works, *Helle og Vera* (Helle and Vera, 1975). But it is only one of the themes of her wide-ranging authorship. Her first novel, *Aldri la dem kle deg forsvarsløst naken* (Never Let Them Strip You Defencelessly Naked, 1974), was a literary contribution to the abortion debate, whereas *Fritt løp* (A Free Rein, 1980) took up the question of sexuality as a means of contact and a means of oppression. The novel *Den svarte gryte* (The Black Cauldron, 1985) moved on to a different topic: the problems of political refugees from the Third World in Oslo in the 1980s, and the Norwegian authorities' callous treatment of people living under constant threat. Yet this novel is not so removed as might seem from the topics of her early books; the narrator is the journalist and author Tove Nilsen, who is forced to question her own prejudices when she encounters this society of outcasts; she casts an ironic glance back at her own past, wryly aware of the element of hypocrisy inherent in her behaviour as feminist *à la mode*:

> I was young, I was committed, I was ambitious. I was one of those who stormed ahead like a wild foal in order to overturn 'the macho society'. . . . A feminist with a sharp tongue and sexy boots, there was no better combination in the seventies. Angry attacks and sweet smiles, we were the ones for whom editors in their forties fell over backwards and opened all the doors. Girls who don't look like their opinions, great![26]

And she finds that having seen through all the clichés of the sexual game does not make her any less vulnerable to the urgency of desire. Tove Nilsen switches to a male narrator in *I stedet for dinosaurer* (Instead of Dinosaurs, 1987) to portray the vulnerability of a man unable to cope with the various roles that society would make him play.

Vera Henriksen (born 1927) stands apart from the younger, 'sexy-boots' feminists of the 1970s. She is principally a writer of historical novels, often compared to Sigrid Undset; meticulous studies of the literature of the period and of modern research lie behind her popular stories of Norway around the time of the Reformation in the novel series which begins with *Trollsteinen* (The Troll Stone, 1970) and ends with *Skjærsild* (Purgatory, 1977). It is the era of witch-burning, a dominant theme of the series and an instrument for the oppression of women. More recently, Vera Henriksen has returned to saga material for her themes. *Dronningsagaen* (The Queen's Saga, 1979) is a female pendant to Snorre Sturlason's *Kings' Sagas*, presenting the other side of the coin from Snorre's hagiographic portrait in *The Saga of King Olav*, and portraying the saint-king through the eyes of his widow Queen Astrid, whom he raped in the bridal bed. *Kongespeil* (The King's Mirror, 1980) takes as its central character Ellisiv, the wife of Harald the Hard, who plays such an incidental role in Snorre's *King Harald's Saga*. The novels give a different perspective on the sagas, with their celebration of male courage and honour, as do her non-fictional investigations into the role of women in medieval Scandinavian literature and folk belief, *Sagaens kvinner* (The Women of the Sagas, 1981) and *Skjebneveven* (The Weave of Fate, 1982). In the latter book she suggests that 'the female myth' has not materially changed since the days of the sagas. There is clear evidence of the same opposing pairs of images of women as modern psychology recognizes in the 'good woman/bad woman' syndrome, or nineteenth-century literature portrays as the dichotomy between the Madonna and the Whore.[27] Women in saga times were powerful in their possession of magic [seid] and of the gift of life; but they were conceived of as either 'good' like Unn the Deep-Minded, founder of a great dynasty, or 'bad' like Queen Gunnhild, wife of Erik Bloodaxe, who practised evil magic and was insatiable in her sexual lust.[28]

Among the most important of the older generation of poets still writing during this period are Gunvor Hofmo (born 1921) and Marie Takvam (born 1926). After publishing five collections of poetry between 1946 and 1955, Gunvor Hofmo was silent until 1971, when she again started publishing regularly – another eight anthologies by 1987. The *nynorsk* writer Marie Takvam has published a volume of poetry every five years or so since her debut in 1954. Her poetry is erotically charged and outspoken, and demonstrates increasing concern at man's wanton destruction of human and natural resources, and at the absurdity of living in a society overburdened by luxuries whilst half the world is deprived of the essentials of life. Her poems in the collection *Falle og reise seg att* (Fall and Rise Again, 1980) show a writer conscious of being a woman in late-twentieth-century Norwegian society, with all the attendant advantages and double-binds. There is an insoluble conflict between the desire for independence and the need for a love which still implies dependence. The poem 'Trø meg ikke på tærne' ('Don't Tread on My Toes') looks at the problem with a wry humour and a frankness of physical detail which are characteristic of the poet:

> It's fine that you drink the marrow out of my bones
> that you spurt your thoughts into my stomach.
> But don't tread on my toes!
> It's fine that you suck my willpower
> out through my lips
> and make it flood from my body's other openings.
> But don't tread on my toes!
>
> There's enough to help yourself to
> and there's room for your thoughts inside me too.
> But don't tread on my toes!
> I would so like to travel to the end of my own thoughts.
>
> So:
> do drink from me, do spurt into me,
> but never tread on a traveller's toes.[29]

New directions

In the two decades since 1970, there has been such a rich diversity of women's writing in Norway that any attempt to assess its long-term significance can only be provisional. The total number of Norwegian books being published rose steadily after 1965, the year when the government decided to implement *innkjøpsordningen*, an agreement whereby the state guarantees to buy 1,000 copies of each new work of creative literature for distribution to libraries. This eased the situation considerably for both authors and publishers, struggling against competition from imported works in a market which was not of a size to support many full-time writers purely on commercial terms.

The growing interest in women's studies also stimulated new authors. Women's literature became a topic for research, with the first centre emerging under the energetic leadership of Professor Åse Hiorth Lervik in Tromsø, and a new awareness of the importance of recovering 'forgotten women' on to syllabuses at all levels.[30] Theses were written about women's writing – initially mainly about older writers such as Amalie Skram, whose works experienced a renaissance in the 1970s, but also about living authors. Feminist literary criticism was recognized as a discipline. Norwegian feminist literary critics tend more towards the Anglo–American school of criticism, though there are a few who favour the more theoretical French approach.[31] The investigative techniques of structuralism have also been employed in the analysis of women's writing.[32]

Women began to move into areas where they had been little in evidence – e.g. as journalists and dramatists. Women writers had had little impact on the theatre since Hulda Garborg around the turn of the century. The list of plays premièred at Norwegian theatres during the years 1945–75 includes only 15 by women in a total of 221, including three by Aslaug Vaa, two by Solveig Christov, and one each by Inger Hagerup and Marie Takvam.[33] In the 1970s Bjørg Vik had the first of many theatrical successes with *To akter for fem kvinner* (Two Acts for Five Women, 1974). Since then she has become a reliable box-office success, and is also popular as a writer of radio and television plays.

Bjørg Vik's plays are not innovative in the technical sense; she embodies her conflicts in naturalistic dialogue. A dramatist who is more experimental in her approach to theatre is Cecilie Løveid (born 1951). Cecilie Løveid began as a writer of lyrical prose, with works like *Sug* (*Sea Swell*, 1979) which are difficult to assign to any genre. During the 1980s she moved almost entirely to writing in dramatic form, including both radio plays such as *Måkespisere* (*Seagull Eaters*, 1983), which won the Prix Italia, and stage plays such as *Balansedame* (Tightrope Lady, 1985) and *Dobbel nytelse* (Double Delight, 1988). Her stage plays demand a great deal of an ensemble, both physically and emotionally; and she has more often been performed successfully by small experimental groups rather than by large institutional theatres (see Chapter 11).

The last two decades have seen the debut of several women poets. Eldrid Lunden's (born 1940) compact, intense poems in collections like *hard, mjuk* (hard, soft, 1976) and *Mammy, blue* (1977) often employ unexpected combinations of words to suggest new perspectives:

> He who thrusts deep
> into her with a smile and
> finds her
> full to the understanding with
> tears.[34]

Her poetry, written in *nynorsk*, gives expression to the physical sensations of existing in a woman's body, experiencing the surrounding world and particularly other people – a lover, a mother, a child, a sister – through tactile impressions, sensations in the skin. The openness of women, and hence their vulnerability, is a recurring theme. In the poet's struggle to give form to this different way of experiencing, she is brought up against the problems of a language which does not accommodate the difference, and the poems become equally a search for a medium for the expression of female experience:

> Is it really true that women joyfully
> welcome the female touch
> with kisses hugs and right up close
> and that we are more open here than men?
> Why then has this joy never
> become visible in language?[35]

Eldrid Lunden teaches creative writing, and her *Essays* (1982) include critical articles on other authors such as Stein Mehren, Olaf Bull, Marie Takvam and the Icelandic novelist Svava Jacobsdottir. Particularly interesting is a commentary on the consequences of the split between the *bokmål* / capital city culture and the *nynorsk* / village culture of Norway for women's self-image.[36] In this essay she concludes that village culture has traditionally given women a more active role in social and economic life, and that the *nynorsk* language has been more resistant to the importation of foreign words which define women as objects to be judged solely on their outward appearance. Her own writing she defines not as 'women's literature' but as 'an attempt to speak a language which I believe can convey feminine values. And this language is one which does not belong to women alone' (p. 38). Reclaiming the feminine in language will liberate both men and women from the straitjacket of a discourse dominated by profit and power.

Cindy Haug (born 1956) created a sensation with her poetic odyssey, *Se deg ikke tilbake mot Europa og bli stein . . . O, Eurydike . . .* (Don't look back at Europe and get stoned . . . Oh, Eurydice . . ., 1982). The book recounts the tale of a love which proceeds from ecstasy to despair, through scenes of modern Oslo night life and with references to classical and folk mythology, in free verse forms which range from sentimental lyricism to contrapuntal jazz rhythms. She has continued to write an idiosyncratic poetry, ranging from concrete verse to dramatic dialogue, in collections which are sometimes private, sometimes funny, often explicitly erotic, with an undertone of irony which is constantly threatened by despair (e.g. *Mitt liv, fiksjoner* [My Life, Fictions, 1984]; *Blikket/Kniven* [The Look/The Knife, 1990]).

In the increased Norwegian book production since the mid-1960s, around two hundred new poets have been published. Other women poets of note include Sissel Bjugn (born 1947), Liv Lundberg (born 1944), Sidsel Mørck (born 1937), Åse Marie Nesse (born 1934), Annie Riis (born 1927) and Karin Sveen (born 1949). Many of them write in other genres too.

Despite the experimental nature of much modern writing by women as well as men, the dominant genre remains – in Norway as in other Western countries – the novel or short story. Broadly speaking, the focus of interest of the avant-garde in Norwegian literature had shifted by the end of the 1970s away from political commitment and towards a renewed interest in imaginative writing; the newly terminated 1980s had already by 1990 been labelled 'the decade of fantasy'.[37] Established 'political' writers like Dag Solstad and Edvard Hoem shifted from an analysis of class conflict to a more introverted form, although it could still be called committed in a broader sense. Typical of the new generation is a writer like Jan Kjærstad (born 1953); his novels, like *Homo Falsus* (1984) and *Det store eventyret* (The Great Adventure, 1987), are at one and the same time psychological thrillers and elaborate puzzles which the reader is invited to unravel.

A shift from directly 'kvinnepolitisk' (female-political) writing in the 1970s to a more imaginative form in the 1980s can – again, very broadly – be observed in women's writing as well. Mari Osmundsen (born 1951) is one of the younger generation of writers who most clearly exemplifies the change. Her first novels from the 1970s combine female politics with left-wing commitment, as in *Vi klarer det!* (We'll Make It!, 1978), about a strike in a factory which focuses on a girl who moves from trade unionism through the Women's Front to an AKP (m–l) study circle. It is one of the few attempts in post-war Norwegian literature to portray a working-class woman as a central character, others being Toril Brekke's (born 1949) novel *Jenny har fått sparken* (Jenny's Got the Sack, 1976) and Bjørg Vik's short story 'Liv' from 1972. Mari Osmundsen's later novels, like *Gode gjerninger* (Good Deeds, 1984), and *Familien* (The Family, 1985), although they do not abandon the earlier commitment entirely, move between the realistic and the fantastic worlds (see Chapter 12).

Fantasy plays a large part in the works of Sissel Lie (born 1942). *Tigersmil* (Tiger Smile, 1986) is a collection of short texts on the theme of sexuality, seen as a voracious force, in which the narrator cannot preserve her distance but experiences in her own body the rape she is describing ('Tiger'), or where a trip in a taxi becomes a voyage to a paradise of sensuality and the taxi-driver becomes the perfect lover ('Sjåføren', 'The Driver'). Her novel *Løvens hjerte* (The Lion's Heart, 1988) is a fantasy based on the medieval French poet Louise Labé, in which the twentieth-century narrator's sexual entanglements in her own time are interwoven with the provocative behaviour of the French poet. *Granateple* (Pomegranate, 1990) starts conventionally with a conversation between three women in a café, but soon departs into a world of fantasy where the characters take on a mystical dimension.

Karin Sveen (born 1949), a novelist as well as a poet, has published a collection of fantastic tales, *Døtre* (Daughters, 1980), as well as the novel *Utbryterdronninga* (Queen of Escapologists, 1982).

The latter tells of a girl who arrived from the sea, like Moses in a basket, to be adopted by a humble village couple; she grows up with the feeling that she is in the wrong element (she belongs in the water), and becomes an escapologist in order to act out her dream of escape. Biblical allusions hint that she is a modern Jesus (her parents are called Maria and Joseph); no more than Jesus does she belong in the society in which she has landed. Lisbet Hiide (born 1956) and Karin Moe (born 1945) are other authors in whose books the world of reality may suddenly give way to horror or chaos, but who retain a good portion of humour too. Karin Moe's short piece 'Kvinna som ville skrive litteratur' ('The Woman Who Wanted to Write Literature'), from *Kjønnskrift* (Sextext, 1980) takes the idea of 'female writing' to its absurd conclusion as the narrator drops into an Oslo bookshop to buy a pen that can be gripped by the vaginal muscles.

Such writing is often too esoteric to be popular with the general public. Far more successful in terms of sales figures are those authors who provide new variations on the well-tried formula of the realistic novel, such as Anne Karin Elstad (born 1938) and Herbjørg Wassmo (born 1942). Herbjørg Wassmo reached the public's notice with her best-selling trilogy about Tora (1981–6). It is the story of a 'German bastard' girl, an outcast in an isolated village in the north of Norway, who is sexually abused by her stepfather and slowly driven, despite her bitter resistance, into psychosis (see Chapter 12).

Anne Karin Elstad began by writing historical novels, a tetralogy about the life of a young village woman in the early nineteenth century (1976–80). Then she switched to writing about contemporary life – about the problems of growing up as a girl in modern society in *Senere, Lena* (Later, Lena, 1982) and about the experience of marriage breakdown and divorce in *Sitt eget liv* (Her Own Life, 1983) – novels which found an immediate response, and are constantly reprinted. After another historical novel in 1985, – *for dagene er onde* (– for these are evil days), she published *Maria, Maria* (1988), a novel based on her own experience of having a stroke after taking hormone replacement therapy, which occasioned a furious media debate.

Both Herbjørg Wassmo and Anne Karin Elstad, as well as possessing a talent for telling a good story in an absorbing

way, have taken up topics which have coincided with greater
public awareness on issues like incest and sexual abuse, marriage
breakdown and domestic violence, 'female ailments' and the
menopause. Their writings continue the tradition of female politics
of the previous decade, though in a more private way; they focus
on the problems of women's lives with which readers can identify.
Margaret Johansen's novel *Du kan da ikke bare gå* . . . (You can't
just walk out . . ., 1981), about the experiences of a battered wife,
also fits into this category; it was dramatized for the theatre and for
television.

One of the reasons why Norwegian literature is sometimes
accused of provinciality – by its own critics as well as by
outsiders – is that the vast majority of books are set in Norway and deal with Norwegian society. The Swedish concern
with the rest of Europe and the Third World – as expressed
in the 1960s in books by authors like Jan Myrdal (*Rapport
från kinesisk by*, *Report from a Chinese Village*, 1967) and Sara
Lidman (*Samtal i Hanoi*, Conversations in Hanoi, 1965) – has no
equivalent in Norway (Jens Bjørneboe being the major exception). But in the 1980s, partly because of increased immigration, awareness of other cultures was more in evidence. In
women's writing, there is now more interest in women of
other cultures, and more sensitivity about imposing European
values. Tove Nilsen's *The Black Cauldron* and Mari Osmundsen's
Gutten som slo tida ihjel (The Boy Who Killed Time, 1990)
present sympathetic portraits of women in the immigrant community, struggling to adapt to an alien environment. In 1985,
Toril Brekke published *Jakarandablomsten* (*The Jacaranda Flower*),
a factual account of a trip to Kenya in order to gather information about the conditions of women's lives. Although she
witnesses events which might horrify an emancipated Westerner
– women married off against their will to older men prepared
to pay the bride-price, and others rejected by their husbands
because they are ill or barren – she does not pass judgement,
but considers her own society's assumptions from a new angle.
Reading a glossy Kenyan magazine which is indistinguishable
from European women's magazines and irrelevant to the poly-
gamous society she is visiting, she realizes that oppression can take
many forms:

I look at Rachel and for some reason feel ashamed to have brought this magazine here, a Kenyan women's magazine that bears no relation to the Kenyan woman now facing me, a magazine from another world, my world more than hers, and it strikes me how far there is to go; for Rachel, for the élite women in Nairobi, for myself and my fellow sisters at home; a very long way to freedom and equality.[38]

Although the realistic novels of Elstad, Wassmo and others were runaway successes in comparison with other recent fiction, their success is only relative; the real best-sellers in Norway in recent years have been 'documentaries' about real people's lives, books about the royal family, political autobiographies.[39] And this study has not taken into account so-called 'trivial' literature, which has received more critical and academic attention in recent years; authors like Kjell Hallbing (born 1934), who produces the 'Morgan Kane' series under the pseudonym Louis Masterson, and whose books had sold six and a half *million* copies by 1977, or Margit Sandemo (born 1924), who has written more than a hundred novels, including the series on 'Isfolket' (The Ice People). Women's magazines also make up the reading material of far more women than read books. The most widely read weekly magazine in the early 1980s was *Hjemmet* (The Home), with sales of 375,000. The magazine changed its emphasis in the 1970s to reflect a greater awareness of the current feminist debate, so it should not be ignored in any survey of recent women's writing which takes account of its appeal to a broader public.

There has never been such a good time to be a woman writer in Norway. Publishers and readers are eager for new books by the many who have made a name for themselves, although one still cannot talk of complete equality in terms of either publishers' attitudes or critics' treatment.[40] As in politics and public life, however, Norwegian women authors have achieved a position in both élite and popular culture to which writers in most other countries must still aspire.

10
Bjørg Vik (born 1935)

'The pioneer of liberation'

If Halldis Moren Vesaas was an 'echoing rock' for women's experience in the 1920s, Bjørg Vik must have had a similar feeling forty years later. With her collections of stories in the 1960s, she was the first to give literary expression to the ideas of the 'new wave' feminism which did not gain momentum in Norway until the beginning of the following decade.

There was nothing in her early life which might have predisposed her for literary activity. Born into an unacademic family – her father was a waiter – she was brought up in a cramped Oslo flat during the German occupation and post-war austerity. Although she was encouraged by her parents and stayed on at school to take the leaving examination at eighteen, it did not occur to her to study for a degree. She took a college course in home economics, and after that a series of temporary jobs as a supply teacher, laboratory assistant or secretary. Yet from early on she had cherished a secret wish to become a writer, and decided to study journalism as a first step. She took a course at the College of Journalism in 1955, and in 1956 she began work for *Porsgrunns Dagblad*, the local paper in Porsgrunn, a small town 150 kilometres south-west of Oslo, just next door to Ibsen's birthplace, Skien. This temporary move became a permanent one, as she met her husband, the architect Hans Jørgen Vik, in Porsgrunn, and has lived there ever since.

During the end of the 1950s and the beginning of the 1960s she had three children and wrote the short stories which were to appear as her first collection, *Søndag ettermiddag* (Sunday Afternoon) in 1963. In several interviews since she has talked about the difficulties of those years: the struggle to find time to write and the struggle, familiar from the confessions of so many women writers – including Amalie Skram and Cora Sandel in this volume – against the guilt feelings induced by the conflict between doing her own work and being the 'perfect mother'.

From the start the short story was her preferred form, although she later became successful as a dramatist and has also written novels. The reason for this preference was partly that she discovered, like other women writers before her, that the short story was easier to reconcile with the demands of a young family, which permitted only short bursts of attention.[1] But there was another reason, too: she soon found that the form was the one best suited to her literary style:

> I myself chose this form both because the stories I want to tell require something other than the broad canvas of a novel, and because it suits my temperament. I like the concentration of the short story; it demands linguistic precision and intensity. The short story reveals just the top of the iceberg, but the subtext must always be there.[2]

Cora Sandel was a major influence; she was the one who opened the world of literature for the aspiring writer. Her reading of Cora Sandel's short stories may well have been a factor in her choice of form; she admitted that her first stories owed much to Cora Sandel's style.[3] The mood of *Sunday Afternoon* is reminiscent of the older writer, with its low-key studies of women trapped in frustrating situations. The family circle has become a prison which saps the energy even to wish for change, as in 'Ingenting er hendt' ('Nothing Has Happened'), in which the wife functions like a service machine, and slides slowly into apathy; or 'Barndom' ('Childhood'), where a destructive marriage is viewed through the eyes of a daughter who is made to feel guilty because she is not a boy. If she had been, her father would have taught her to be a car mechanic – but that is out of the question, and all she can do is to behave as much like a boy as possible to avoid upsetting him. Even when there is an attempt at breaking out of the trap, it usually fails, as in 'En lei historie' ('A Sorry Tale'), where Johanne's flight from her family and her dreadful fiancé ends in miscarriage and depression, or 'Sjung om studentens . . .' ('The Student Song'[4]), which tells of a lonely student whose attempt to find a little affection meets only contempt.

There is no overt message in Bjørg Vik's stories. In this way too they resemble Cora Sandel's; she makes visible the quiet desperation of people's lives, but without proposing a solution. The indignation is not articulated, but lies beneath the surface of the iceberg, communicating itself to the reader through the details with which the picture is built up. The objects, the sounds and the smells of everyday life are obtrusively present, underlining the drudgery or the preoccupation with things which replaces communication between people. The latter is particularly in evidence in the title story, 'Sunday Afternoon', in which a marriage is threatened by the emphasis on material acquisitions. The husband is away working all week, and the wife is lonely in her attractive house; she wishes they could spend more time together, but 'That was just not possible. Anyway, they wouldn't be able to afford the mortgage payments then.'[5] The idea that another way of life would be better is not articulated; but the wife's unhappiness and the husband's repressed aggression lead the reader to draw that conclusion.

Excessive materialism, resulting in alienation, is present in Bjørg Vik's next collection, as is suggested by the title, *Nødrop fra en myk sofa* (Cries for Help from a Soft Sofa, 1966) – a phrase which has been applied to her work as a whole. In the story 'Herre, ta i din sterke hånd . . .' ('Lord, stretch out thy hand . . .') the wife expresses her disillusion directly; she is living in a small flat on the sixth floor, becoming agoraphobic and dreaming of moving to a small place in the country, whilst her husband can think only of the fact that they have nearly reached the goal of their strivings: to buy a car. In the title story, in which a nervous employee and his wife are invited to the boss's house for dinner, he is impressed but she is appalled by the thought that their own aspirations might culminate in just such a glittering but barren showcase.

In addition to these studies of failed communication between couples, there are also many stories where the viewpoint is that of a young girl, observing the richness of life and the strangeness of adult behaviour with fresh eyes. 'Innerst i det mørke skapet' ('At the Back of the Dark Cupboard') describes the friendship and rivalry between two girls, already aware of class differences and the need to keep up appearances. Even simple things like a visit to the corner shop are described with a vividness of sense impressions which evokes the flavour of what is already a past age:

> Just the sound of the flour drawer being pulled out was such a lovely thing. A heavy, reassuring sound. And then the floury metal scoop which they filled the bag with, when it sank down into the flour drawer it was the quietest thing in the whole world. There was no sound, not even a sigh, as it sank deep down into all that soft whiteness. It was fine too when they held the bag by its corners and bumped it on the counter, several times, and the flour settled inside, and then the bag was closed.[6]

When this collection of stories appeared, however, it was other aspects of it than the author's meticulous eye for detail which attracted attention. It caught the tide of the sexual revolution of the 'swinging sixties', when contraception was finally becoming easily available to both married and unmarried women. Earlier heroines, like Sigrid Undset's Kristin Lavransdatter and Cora Sandel's Alberte, had enjoyed illicit sex only at the cost of unwanted pregnancy; Bjørg Vik's women could control their own fertility, and play a more active sexual role. A couple of the stories in this collection, 'Når en ung mann plukker mjødurt' ('When a Young Man Gathers Meadowsweet') and 'A Little Bit of Madness . . .' [*sic*] celebrate an older woman's freedom to take a young man as her lover. Both meetings are undertaken in the full awareness of their transience, and without guilt. The visual and tactile sensations of lovemaking are conveyed with an immediacy which gave Bjørg Vik a certain *succès de scandale*; it was not normal for a woman writer, even in the 1960s, to be quite so frank about physical sex.

The theme is continued in *Det grådige hjerte* (The Greedy Heart, 1968), in which the title story tells of two Norwegian couples who meet on holiday on the Mediterranean. Ena, wife of Einar, falls in love with Preben, and they become lovers. For him it is a shattering experience, but for her, deeply though she feels it, it is not a catastrophe but a natural event which is in tune with the view of life she explains to him:

'We're not made for just one person, that is my simple belief. Don't you see? Hardly any of us are, I believe. Perhaps we can change ourselves so that one is enough. For ever and ever. . . . But I can't, don't you see, don't want to either. I don't want a mean, impoverished kind of life.'[7]

She has managed to combine a stable marriage with an acceptance of each partner's freedom of action. A similarly uncomplicated approach to sexuality is described in 'Brev til en elsker' ('Letter to a Lover'), which takes the form of a letter written by Christl, in prison for drunken driving, to the lover who is accepted by her husband; both are essential to her happiness, she feels, and rejoices in the knowledge.

It is new for a woman writer to write positively about free love; but it is not done in the naive belief that it solves all problems. Ena knows that she has to pay, in pain and loss, for her brief ecstasy; and the story 'Lykkelandet' ('The Ideal Home') harshly exposes the other side of the brave new world. A middle-aged husband seduces the girl who has rented the house next door, and rediscovers a physical ecstasy he thought he would never find again. But when the affair threatens to upset his well-ordered life, he hastily retreats to his wife and family, and abandons Bella. She had earlier confided in him: 'no one has ever given a damn about me . . . Ever. Or at least not when it mattered' (p. 112) – only to be treated in exactly the same way by him. The step from liberation to exploitation is a short one, and it is still likely to be the woman who pays the heavier price.

Bjørg Vik was awarded an author's stipend in 1969. This gave her for the first time the possibility of planned free working time, after managing on a couple of mornings a week paid for by freelance journalism. She realized the necessity of having space of her own, and rented an office away from home, which became a real liberation, as she explained in an interview: 'If I were to give any advice to a woman who wants to write, it would probably be this: get yourself a room, preferably a good distance away from where you live.'[8] With this new sense of physical and mental space, she wrote her first novel, *Gråt elskede mann* (Cry, Beloved Man), which was published in 1970.

The feminist decade

Cry, Beloved Man is the story of what Norwegians would call 'a paperless marriage'. The newly divorced Nikolay, taking refuge from his sorrows in a friend's country cabin, meets a young hippie, Ilni, who is squatting there. Her first appearance is highly disturbing to the conventional Nikolay – she emerges from the sea wearing nothing but flippers – and she continues to unsettle him with her unpredictable behaviour. They begin to live together, and have a child; but he finds that he is unable to tolerate the insecurity of the situation. She refuses to become his property, lives in a mess, frequents some bizarre dropouts, and does not understand his ideas about fidelity; she admits freely that she goes to bed with other men 'if there is any point in it . . . if it can help someone. If we can't reach each other in any other way.'[9] Finally she leaves him, realizing that he will never be able to stop trying to make her into someone else, and he realizes that his attempts to confine her to one role have missed the point entirely: 'Child prostitute? Sea-rose? Tramp? With a sharp twinge of pain he saw that these pictures were no other than half-waking dreams and anxious lies, he had had a human being and he had lost it' (p. 218).

Critical reception of this novel was less positive; there was general agreement that the idea was not wholly successfully realized. The concentration which characterized the author's short stories could not be sustained through a novel. It also becomes problematic that the viewpoint is with Nikolay throughout; although the reader's sympathy at the end is intended to lie with Ilni, we never see the relationship from her point of view and thus she remains a rather shadowy figure, a myth rather than a real woman.[10] Bjørg Vik was less than happy with the novel, and disappointed with its reception, which laid so much stress on her depiction of unconventional sexuality that she felt it had distorted the work – and led her to a decision to write differently in future. Matters were not improved when a film was made of the novel in 1971; the author was so annoyed at the speculative soft porn to which it was reduced that she refused her fee, donating it to the Norwegian Authors' Association.

Bjørg Vik returned to the short story form with one of her

artistically most successful works, *Kvinneakvariet* (*An Aquarium of Women*, 1972). This cycle of short stories is arranged in three groups of three, each of which centres around a common experience, a time of crisis and conflict in the lives of the characters. The three stories in the first section deal with young girls on the threshold of adolescence, becoming aware of the fact that opportunities are not equal for all, and that they are being pressurized into a passive feminine mould which prohibits all kinds of freedoms – the freedom to be out after dark, to indulge in boisterous physical activity, to be open about stirring sexual feelings and their maturing bodies. Materialism is already at work in the central character of 'Portrommene' ('Back Yards'), Lillian, who deserts her lower-class friend Tora for the privileged Benedikte, who has a large house, beautiful clothes and an artistic mother. The setting of these stories is the lower-middle-class Oslo environment in which Bjørg Vik grew up. It is a world in which fathers are generally absent, out at work or socializing, returning home exhausted or drunk; the mothers, by contrast, are always at home, engaged in domestic activity and policing their daughters. They are the guardians of conventional values, often described standing at the windows looking out; both prisoner and jailer in one, they remain within their own restricted sphere whilst turning the wrath of the righteous on anyone who tries to step out of it.

The split between male and female worlds is sharply in evidence in another story from this section, 'På bussen er det fint' ('It's good to be on the bus'), about a town girl and her family visiting her uncle's farm. The male world is identified with nature: father and uncle go into the fields, discuss crops and animals, suggest a visit to the cowshed. The female adult world is the domestic sphere ('culture'); mother and aunt remain in the house, cook the food and provide comfort. The girl feels ambivalent, attracted to yet fearful of her father's world. She takes refuge in the female world, yet realizes its limitations, its inability to integrate the 'animal' side of mature sexuality.[11]

The second section moves to a later stage in women's lives. 'Climbing Roses' employs a series of shifting perspectives in order to portray simultaneously the lives of a group of families living in up-market Hartshill, and the rebellion of the teenage daughter of one family, Anja. All the families follow a similar pattern: the men pursue their careers to the point of exhaustion, whilst the women are 'kept' at home. Their parasitic nature is expressed in crass terms in Anja's diary: 'In the USA there are many who are like you. I can't think of anything more ugly than middle-aged American women with hard lips and blue hair. They look like just what they are: WHORES. They have sold their bodies and their lives for a nice house and a chequebook'(p. 36).[12] Anja links the exploitation of women with global exploitation; materialism induces selfish greed and blindness to the consequences for the individual and for the environment.

'Liv' and 'Emilie' are stories of married women with families who are nearing the point of breakdown. Liv is a low-paid factory worker, married to another low-paid factory worker; she polishes plates all day, and returns home to the housework – a double burden which so exhausts her that she has no energy even to think. She cannot analyze the source of her despair, but erupts at the end into inarticulate accusation of 'them', who have forced her to live like this. Emilie's story articulates the protest. She is comparatively well off, a librarian married to a teacher, but carrying the same double burden, and supposed to be grateful for the 'privilege' of combining a career with a family. The pressures on her culminate in a nervous breakdown; and in a letter to her husband she outlines how oppression is endemic in society. Like a latter-day Nora from *A Doll's House*, she is leaving her husband in order to work things out; nearly a hundred years after Ibsen's play, the choice between integrity and conventional marriage is still just as stark.

The third section of *An Aquarium of Women* moves into a sphere which is in various ways 'outside' – outside marriage and the family, outside the geographical locations of Norwegian town or village community. And the women in this section are freer and more independent. Yet the characters are still conditioned by the social structures which have formed them, and relationships with men are no easier because they are different. 'Greetings from the Land of the Weeping Willows' is set in an Eastern European socialist country where the protagonist is part of an official delegation. Her despair at the lack of freedom and her inability to make contact with the inhabitants become mingled with sadness at the impossibility of making contact with another of the delegates, Karsten, on any but a superficial sexual level.

'After All the Words' is narrated by a Norwegian in Paris who meets a fellow countryman and decides to start a relationship with him: an attempt – not for the first time – at an equal partnership. It fails because he cannot accept that she will not commit herself to declaring him 'the only one', and because she cannot accept the attitudes of the group to which he belongs, left-wing activists committed to achieving a just society but unable to see that they are all failing to liberate the person closest to them – the woman who cleans their house and takes care of their children. Yet the story ends on a note of optimism, a declaration of faith that women will one day awaken and take their destiny in their own hands:

> 'Listen, I can hear movement; thousands of feet on the asphalt and on the grass, listen to the laughter, they are coming, they are leaving the small rooms, the small houses and the large blocks of flats, they are coming from offices and factories, from hospitals and schools and department stores and studios, all our sisters; listen, I can hear movement . . .' (p. 107–8)

It is an ending that Bjørg Vik was uncertain about – 'my little vision', as she called it – 'which I was worried about, that it would seem artificially attached, that I hadn't motivated it properly. But on a purely emotional level, I felt it was motivated.'[13] Her anxiety is justified: the lyrical outburst does seem unmotivated by that particular story, and provides the one false note in a series of psychologically convincing portraits. Yet it is easy to see why the author wanted to end this particular work on a note of hope. *An Aquarium of Women* is her most outspokenly feminist collection to date, in which liberation has become more than an individualistic middle-class issue, and more than a matter of sex alone. Here she explores its implications for the working class – 'Liv' is one of the few portraits of a working-class woman in modern Norwegian women's writing – and its links with other political issues, including capitalism and socialism. She has deplored elsewhere the socialist tendency to see class as the central issue, and to obscure the fact that women are exploited regardless of class and need to unite to fight that exploitation;[14] it is a sentiment which is given fictional form in 'After All the Words.'

An Aquarium of Women was welcomed by the growing women's movement in the early 1970s; it illuminated many of the issues of topical debate. The first half of this decade was Bjørg Vik's most active period politically; she supported the women's movement in various ways – she was one of the founders of the journal *Sirene*, which from its beginnings in 1973 was one of its most influential mouthpieces. She wrote an article for the first issue entitled 'Er det sant at kvinner er undertrykte?' ('Is it true that women are oppressed?'), in which she pointed out how women had been conditioned into regarding their oppression as a privilege, how they were still defined by what their husbands did, and how school books and job advertisements perpetuated the divisions between 'women's work' and 'men's work'. And in 1974 she completed a play about women's lives which ran to full houses for months: *To akter for fem kvinner* (Two Acts for Five Women).

This was not Bjørg Vik's first attempt at drama; she had written a couple of radio plays in the 1960s. But *Two Acts for Five Women* was her first full-length stage play, and not an easy formula into which to breathe dramatic life. The five women of the title are the only characters, and the play covers just one evening – a reunion of old friends. All the women do is talk; there are no unexpected events or changes of scene. The tension is provided by the clashes between the personalities of the five friends, for three of whom the evening becomes a turning point in their lives.

The reunion takes place in the flat belonging to Hanna, who is the closest to being the mouthpiece for the author's views. Hanna is divorced, a freelance photographer who has achieved a sense of self-worth which is not just a reflection of a husband's. She has thought a great deal about the artificiality of women's roles, which she illustrates in a parodic mask-scene to her friends. She asks them uncomfortable questions, making them face conflicts they have tried to repress. At the same time, she admits to the conflict in her own life: she has made the decision to leave her son with his father, whilst her daughter lives with her, and has to face not only the shocked reactions of other women but her own painful feeling of estrangement from her son. Trying to live by one's own truth is not an easy option.

The other four women learn not only from Hanna, but from their interaction with each other. Lilleba has taken refuge in a 'little mother' role; she lives for her four children and husband, and feels 'stupid' compared to the others. She is pregnant again. During the course of the evening she admits that she uses the children to hold on to the illusion of her perfect marriage, and that she wants more from life than this; she decides to stop being Mother Earth and have an abortion. Anne Sofie also presents a façade of happiness, exulting in the ecstasy of passion with her new lover; her façade too is broken down, as she recognizes that her happiness is based on cheating her husband. And she is not really happy either; she suffers from back pains and headaches which are a physical reaction to her repressed tension. She also reaches a decision: she will be honest about what she is doing, whatever the outcome.

Ellinor seems at first to have succeeded on all fronts: she has a stable marriage and a flourishing career as an artist. Her self-image is also threatened, this time by Anne Sofie, who is provoked by Ellinor's condemnatory attitude to her own love affair into telling her that her husband has had an affair whilst she was away painting. Upset by the news, Ellinor goes home to confront her husband – and returns later to reveal that honesty has helped them to greater clarity about their relationship, to stop pretending that Anker was the stronger of the two when both really knew it was Ellinor. Gry is the quietest and the least attractive: a working girl and spinster, always short of money, who has had little contact with men. She tells of a childhood in which her father regularly beat her mother, imbuing her with a fear of men and sexuality which she has never been able to conquer. There seems little likelihood that her sad life will be radically changed as a result of the evening's events – but being able to talk about it may have had a therapeutic effect.

This sketch of the five women makes the play sound programmatic, like a collection of representative declarations from across the spectrum of modern female types. It is a rationalization which obscures the effect of seeing it performed – the conflicts are not presented separately but crisscross one another continually, and the lively dialogue keeps the action moving. A passage from the first act will illustrate this:

LILLEBA: No, I mean, I simply thought that if I ever was going to do anything like that [take a lover], I just don't see how I would be able to manage it. With the kids all round me and Hans popping in and out as the fancy takes him and –

ELLINOR: You have thought about it, Lilleba?

LILLEBA: Just for fun, don't get me wrong.

HANNA: All women think about it – or nearly all. Because there's so much we haven't experienced.

ELLINOR: Well, there must be something wrong with me then, because I don't think about it.

ANNE SOFIE: Saint Ellinor has spoken – from the heights of great purity. You'll soon be just as pious as your mother.

ELLINOR (*sharply*): Don't you say anything against my mother! You can say what you want and do what you want, but no snide remarks about Mummy, I won't hear of it.

ANNE SOFIE: Perhaps you had your sexual experiences whilst you were studying at the academy, but I didn't do that, that's the difference. Just don't try to spoil this for me!

ELLINOR: Fuck in peace, my girl.

ANNE SOFIE: Ugh, you have to use those words.

LILLEBA: I was falling in love with him, that's why I stopped going.

HANNA: There's something wrong somewhere, you've taken over the opportunities for cheating that male society provides. You're sailing under a flag of convenience.

LILLEBA: I did fall in love with him.

GRY: Who are you talking about?

LILLEBA: The course leader. Mister –

ANNE SOFIE: A flag of convenience?

HANNA: Loyal, wonderful housewife on one side, hot-blooded lover on the other. No reason for change. What you didn't get when you were younger you're cheating your way to now. But we've got to stop this cheating, can't you see? We have to show our true colours, Anne Fi![15]

This is a revealing exchange. Lilleba is beginning to admit her desire for something other than husband and family, Anne Sofie is tensely defending her right to experience passion and quarrelling with Ellinor, who reveals a vulnerable side, and Hanna wants to make them see their individual experiences in the light of the women's situation in modern society. All these things happen at the same time; the dialogue tends towards stichomythia, as the characters sometimes join in a general conversation and sometimes split into smaller groups, producing an effect of counterpoint as two or more conversations develop simultaneously. Bjørg Vik has mastered the art of making her characters talk past one another in a seemingly haphazard way; someone makes a remark which may be ignored but is then later taken up by another character and added to the weave. In this passage Lilleba stops listening to the others and goes off on her own track – and the two threads continue in parallel for a while, until they are taken up into a new pattern. The play is as close an approximation to spontaneous conversation as possible whilst still operating within the dramatic conventions of comprehensibility.

The fact that *Two Acts for Five Women* was a good play as well as a topical feminist statement helps to explain its long-running success, not only in Norway but abroad. It has been translated into several languages, and performed in many countries, including two 'off-Broadway' productions. Since 1974 Bjørg Vik has written several successful plays for radio, television and stage, though none has had quite the impact of this one. Immediately after this, however, she returned to short stories with *Fortellinger om frihet* (Tales of Freedom, 1975).

The title of this collection is ironic: most of the tales deal with the illusory nature of freedom. Two of the stories are studies of a group of girls growing up in post-war Oslo, in the typical Bjørg Vik setting of lower-middle-class small-flat family life. In 'Fisken i garnet' ('The Fish in the Net') the description of the mothers who imprint their lifestyle on their daughters has become stylized; they have lost their individuality and appear as a grey army, a regiment of the doomed:

The women never died.

The women were condemned to eternity in drying enclosures, stairs, kitchen windows, dustbins. They grew a little greyer in the face, a little fatter or thinner, their hair fell out slowly, but their eyes were unchanging, in a pact with eternity, enduring, brave and entirely without hope.[16]

Only the central character, Ingvil, manages to preserve her dream of a different kind of life, but it is a fragile one.

'Perleporten' ('The Pearly Gates') follows the fates of three girls further into adulthood, work and marriage – and shows how most of them fall victim to the familiar pattern. Only Torunn breaks out of an unsatisfactory relationship, and is possibly on her way into the women's movement at the end. (In an interesting comparison of this story with Sigrid Undset's story 'Småpiker' ['Little Girls'], Liv Riiser demonstrates how little the upbringing of girls changed in Norway between 1900 and 1950: in the middle classes, at least, they were still inculcated with a sense of their relative importance based on class, money and attractiveness, and there was still a rigid demarcation between boys' and girls' activities.)[17]

Three stories in this volume portray the effect on families of modern rationalization, which involves moving them from rural communities into little boxes in town – and their resulting alienation as family solidarity disintegrates. Particularly poignant is the story of a little boy whose father is away all week working, leaving him and his mother isolated on a bleak housing estate. His mother turns to drink, whilst his father keeps urging him to be a *real* boy – though never getting round to the fishing trip of which his son dreams – and takes out his pent-up aggression on his wife, culminating in a rape witnessed by his son. Driven to despair, the boy kills the only thing he loves – a pet rabbit ('Kaninene' – 'The Rabbits').

Freedom seems to have a better chance in 'Kvinnesak er menneskesak' ('Women's Liberation is People's Liberation'), in which the feminist Linda Solli visits a small town to lecture on the subject of rape as a symbol of the male-dominated society. Yet at the party after her lecture she is made depressingly aware of the distance between the new theories and the way men and women actually relate to one another, and is brought sharply up against the limits to her own freedom when one of the 'new men' attending the lecture tries to rape her. The anthology ends with a long story, 'Sensommer' ('Late Summer'), which is about an open marriage where both partners use their freedom to form new relationships – and shows how that freedom can become destructive. This story is unusual in that it experiments with the narrative viewpoint. Most of Bjørg Vik's stories are told by an omniscient narrator who often identifies with one of the characters; but here the narrative voice switches between a first person (the wife, Birgit), a second person (Birgit addressing herself) and a third person (a narrator who is loyal to Birgit's viewpoint). The effect is to vary the distance between Birgit and the reader; although her version of events is not contradicted, the reader can step back and take a more dispassionate look at the consequences of her actions.

Tales of Freedom is less straightforwardly positive about feminism than Bjørg Vik's works from earlier in the 1970s; although she is still sharp in her attacks on the indoctrination of young girls and the dehumanizing effects of materialism, she shows also that freedom for its own sake can be destructive rather than constructive. This collection represents a transitional phase in her works. In interviews from around this time she expressed her impatience with being regarded as a figurehead of the feminist movement, a 'liberated woman' who could write just as steamily about sex as men.[18] She also disagreed with the narrow politicization of the women's movement, with the arrogant attitude of the middle-class feminists in The Women's Front that it was their mission to liberate the women of the working class, and with their refusal to recognize any common ground with women at the top of the social scale. She was not interested in political solutions which were just as divisive as what they were trying to replace.

In return, even her most overtly feminist works were criticized by left-wing feminists for not being political enough; the journal *Kjerringråd* (Old Wives' Remedies), for example, printed an article on *Two Acts for Five Women* in 1977 which attacked its lack of recommendations for positive action:

> [Hanna] formulates a critique of male-dominated society, but she does not see that it is also a capitalist society. This is perhaps the reason why the play as a whole tells us more about repression, about myths and roles and visions for liberated women, than it tells about strategy, about how liberation might be realized.[19]

She was criticized for writing only about the private sphere, and concentrating on a limited section of middle-class society. She distanced herself increasingly from the more active campaigners as the decade progressed. Although her sympathies always lie primarily with women, the indignation of the early 1970s is softened in her later works. In moving from a 'political' phase at the beginning of the decade to a more individual stance by the end of it, she anticipated the move away from political commitment by many other Norwegian authors. Now as in the mid–1960s, she was not following a trend but preceding it.

'The poet of longing'

'Longing is the guiding light of our lives', Bjørg Vik declared in an interview in 1981;[20] and it is a major theme of her short story collection from 1979, *En håndfull lengsel* (*Out of Season*). Several of these stories are about women past their first youth, carrying on courageously with lives in which there is little sunshine, hoping against their better judgement that things might get better. Fru Fyrst Hansen in 'Bære sin skjebne' ('Enduring One's Fate') struggles through the death of one child and the crippling of another to maintain her independence; Soffi in the story of that name enters on her third marriage with a mixture of hope and a resigned feeling that it will not be that different from the first two; the Romanian Ileana in 'Utenfor sesongen' ('Out of Season') travels constantly around looking for romance, growing a little older and more desperate each year.   Friendship between women is a stronger theme than before; in some of the stories their practical solidarity provides a counterweight to an otherwise depressing picture. 'Enkene' ('The Widows'), a story of two old women with little left but to wait for death, becomes, paradoxically, the most positive story in the collection. This is not so much because of the friendship between the two women, Jenny and Maria, which survives mainly on the memories of their married lives, but because they are both drawn, reluctantly at first, into contact with the next generation of women. After Maria's death, Jenny passes on the stairs the young woman from the flat above, whom she had previously scorned as a loose-living flirt, and greets her for the first time, welcoming sunshine into a sunless life: '"Good day," said Jenny. Jenny Thorn held out her hand. The afternoon sunshine fell on the two women as it poured in a narrow stream through one of the windows on the stairs.'[21]

'Rosa og Ruth' ('Rosa and Ruth') describes a friendship between two women in their late thirties with very different lifestyles. Rosa is married with two children, helps her husband in his shoe shop and meets Ruth on occasional shopping trips into town; she is attractive, preoccupied with her appearance, and both fascinated and worried by Ruth's unconventionality. Ruth is divorced, surviving from hand to mouth as a freelance photographer and copywriter; she is a volcano of energy, knows everyone and wears a bewildering array of second-hand clothes. The story is told mostly from Rosa's viewpoint, with occasional glimpses of Ruth's; Rosa slowly realizes that Ruth's liberated life also contains loneliness and insecurity. The role of independent woman who has abandoned traditional family life in order to realize herself can become yet another failure behind a carefully preserved façade. This is the reverse side of the optimism of Hanna in *Two Acts for Five Women*.[22]

In between her short stories, Bjørg Vik carried on writing plays. The radio play *Døtre* (*Daughters*, 1979), which later transferred to the stage, is a study of relationships between three generations of women: 'grandma', who has devoted her life to the traditional duties of wife and mother, and expects a return in kind, and her daughter Miriam, a publisher's consultant struggling under the double burden of career and housework; between Miriam and *her* daughter Siv, who resents her mother's compulsion to excel and envisages a life less burdened by responsibility and guilt; and between grandmother and granddaughter. It is a precisely observed study in failure of communication, the way in which people talk past each other and fail to express what they really mean, as Miriam realizes: 'We don't really talk *to* each other, just at –. Underneath all that nervous stream of words she's actually calling out something quite different: look at me, turn towards me, say something to me, do I matter to you.'[23]

The play *Fribillet til Soria Moria* (Free Ticket to Soria Moria) was published in 1984, though it was written earlier.[24] A mutually supportive relationship between two women is at the core of this work: between Elise, the domestic and dependable spinster, and the divorced Mabel, an extrovert who wears smart clothes and takes lovers. Elise depends on Mabel to fight her battles and bring excitement into her life; but it does not emerge until Elise finds a man and thinks of marrying that Mabel depends equally upon Elise's care. In the end their friendship is more important to both than precarious love affairs.

An autumn mood prevails in Bjørg Vik's two collections of short stories from the 1980s, *Snart er det høst* (Soon It Will Be Autumn, 1982) and *En gjenglemt petunia* (A Forgotten Petunia, 1985). In many of them the characters have moved on to a later time of life – in tune with their author. The title story of *Soon It Will Be Autumn* describes a mother's adjustment to the fact that her children have left home, and 'Ung gutt i motlys' ('Youth Lit from Behind') is about the turmoil of a boy who has left home a little too soon, and his mother's anxiety. Two stories from *A Forgotten Petunia*, 'Den lange reisen til et annet menneske' ('The Long Journey to Another Person') and 'Ubekreftede meldinger om lykke' ('Unconfirmed Reports of Happiness') describe enduring marriages, which do not gloss over the problems but where the couples conclude that theirs has, despite everything, been the better course.

These collections, however, are more than nostalgic continuations of familiar themes. There are new departures here too, and experiments with narrative. 'Amandabakken' is a collective study of a whole street, the changing houses and gardens, and the changes in the lives of those who live there. There is humour in the recounting of the oddities of people's lives and attempts to 'keep up with the Joneses' (here the Carlsens); and the narrator preserves an ironic distance, slipping in comments about what 'people' think and gently puncturing the posturing of her characters. 'Gamle piker må holde sammen' ('Old Girls Must Stick Together') is another story of two female friends of opposing types; but there is a refreshing air of absurdity about the machinations of the impecunious Matilde, and her sheet-anchor Terese is no doormat, but a sprightly spinster who refuses to adopt the general view and regard herself as exploited: 'Without Matilde, my life would have been poorer.'[25]

A Forgotten Petunia contains two stories which are imaginative excursions into a less familiar world. 'Kystlandskap' ('Coastal Landscape') is about a family where the sexual tensions are extreme. The parents live in barely concealed enmity, and the father's affection is concentrated on his daughter Sara. She is approaching puberty, and reacts by trying not to grow up – she becomes anorexic. In her loneliness she spends her time taming a black-headed gull – only to return from a trip one day to find that it has disappeared for good. Only by looking back over the sequence of events can the reader work out that it was killed by her father. A quasi detective-story framework is used too in 'Kall meg Jutta' ('Call Me Jutta'), one of Bjørg Vik's rare stories with a male central character, an educationally subnormal, grossly overweight young man, Rune. His overeating is a reaction to grief over his mother's death, which he and his father cannot discuss. The major event of his life is meeting Jutta, a middle-aged woman who becomes his lover – until she meets someone more attractive. Her precocious little daughter, whom Rune dislikes, suddenly accuses him of interfering with her. The police come round – but we never know whether it happened or not, just that it seems unlikely. It is a bleak study of stunted sexuality.

Bjørg Vik's final work from the 1980s, *Små nøkler store rom* (Small Keys Large Rooms, 1988), is a return to the novel form which she had tried and abandoned in 1970. It is also a return to familiar territory, being a semi-autobiographical account of the author's childhood. Through the medium of the little girl Elsi she tells of early memories of bombardment and occupation, of growing up in an Oslo flat, and of summer holidays with an aunt in the country. Again it is the details of rooms and stairways, clothes and implements which give a sense of immediacy to the narrative, from the intricate sleeping arrangements which fitted five people into a small flat to the moth-eaten pre-war swimming costumes used by the older women. The keys of the title represent the knowledge Elsi slowly acquires as she gets older - keys to unlock the rooms of experience, some of which she wants to know, others which she is frightened to see into. Rooms are also to do with a sense of self, like that of her father, with whom she has a particularly close bond: 'When she and her father are together, they have found a key, they can open doors, know about each other's room, without going into it. But the door is open.'[26] As she starts to mature, however, she finds that her father's door becomes closed to her, and begins to discover a new relationship with her mother. In trying to make her rebellious daughter aware of the need to be careful, her mother tells her about her aunt Agnes, who had suddenly produced an illegitimate child whilst still a child herself. Elsi is horrified – 'Mother had opened the door to a room she didn't want to look into' (p. 254). She feels that she has been initiated into a female knowledge that has been handed down; she has been passed 'a burden which she must carry onwards' (p. 254). She is growing up into a female tradition in which transgression of acceptable codes of behaviour can still bring swift retribution.[27]

The critical spotlight shifted away from Bjørg Vik in the 1980s – partly as a result of her own decisions about her priorities, as she felt she had been overexposed to its glare in the 1970s. She no longer felt the need to be a public figure, although a new book from her pen always sells well, and she has been entered several times for the Nordic Council prize.

Her range as an author is precisely defined; the majority of her works centre on the private lives of women and girls in a fairly narrow social band. She has little to say about women and work, despite the growing importance of work in Norwegian women's lives since 1970; with a few important exceptions, most of her female characters either do not work or are not seen working – we meet them in their leisure time or in the domestic sphere, and it is not work they talk about. The only women characters who have a real commitment to their work are the artists and writers. Yet within her self-imposed limits, Bjørg Vik has mapped out the experience of women in post-war Norway from the 1950s to the 1980s with a painstaking accuracy which makes it a unique record.

11
Cecilie Løveid (born 1951)

'An angel walks through all the books . . .'

To move from Bjørg Vik's short stories to Cecilie Løveid's texts is to adjust one's vision from a meticulously observed realistic painting of everyday life to a multipatterned fresco or collage, where it is not easy at first sight to distinguish the various shapes and their relationship to one another. This is an author who takes a delight in being elusive, evading categories and definitions. It is often impossible to assign her texts to any recognized genre, as she mixes prose and poetry, dramatic and epic techniques, and is frequently involved in a collaborative performance where her text is intimately linked with musical and visual art to form a whole which cannot be conveyed on the printed page. The texts themselves often differ from the work in performance, so that the text that is printed represents an almost arbitrary choice from a number of possible texts, and thus suggests the contours of a work caught at a certain stage in its evolution rather than a definitive version. It is part of an ongoing dialogue.

The texts are open in another way too, in that they are open to other texts, sometimes almost forming a dialogue with other authors. Cecilie Løveid's writing is full of literary echoes, both from Scandinavia (e.g. folk songs, Ibsen, Garborg, Skram) and from abroad (Shakespeare, Blake, Woolf, Gertrude Stein, Kipling, Hesse, Provençal troubadour songs). She also draws freely on other kinds of texts, using everything from modern pop songs and magazine articles to public notices as a sounding board for her writing. Often the allusions, like those in Eliot's 'The Waste Land', are identifiable to those who are prepared to do a little literary detective work; sometimes they are not – either because they are so deeply buried in the subtext that hardly a word of the original remains, or because they are a transmutation of experience so private that it would be inaccessible to anyone but the author without her explanation.

This combination of formal experimentation and broad intertextuality has given Cecilie Løveid the reputation of being a 'difficult' author; paradoxically, although she has won many prizes, she is rarely a commercial success at the theatre, and critics appeal to her to express herself more clearly. The label 'post-modernist' has been applied to her; she confounds traditional expectations of rationality and logic. She has often expressed her unwillingness to provide explanations of her work, and discouraged critics from doing so; when she was asked in a television interview what we should think about her latest play, she replied: 'You shouldn't think – you should take away some impressions, you should play.'[1] Her pictures should not be dissected by intellectual analysis, but should communicate directly with the feelings: 'When I have done a dive down for them, and want to give my pictures to those who are to receive them, then they have a kind of mathematical formula. It is important that the pictures are shown, not analyzed. The reader or the audience can't read them as I see them in any case.'[2]

Born half a generation later than Bjørg Vik, Cecilie Løveid started publishing at the height of the new women's movement in Norway, in the early 1970s. She resists the label 'feminist' as she does all other categorizations; she has never written to a specific political programme. In common with others of her generation, she has suffered from the backhanded discrimination involved in being included on a literary panel or commissioned to write a play because 'we must have something from a woman'. Yet she realizes that what she writes is inevitably influenced by 'the fate of women in the twentieth century'.[3] In her works, woman is the subject – both in the literal sense that her central characters are women and in the more general sense that they are written around women's desire, women's rhythm and women's bodies. Here if anywhere one can find in Norwegian literature an equivalent of the writing of the female body, the *jouissance* that Hélène Cixous and other French writers advocate and practise.[4] Cecilie Løveid plays with and subverts lineal structure, fixed character and logical meaning; her works are open-ended, offering a variety of possible interpretations, and her dialogue is multivalent, full of *double entendre*, puns and even sometimes words used for their sound rather than for their meaning. She is aware that writing must be a political act, and also that it is futile to try to change the structure of society without changing the way we perceive ourselves and the world as it is expressed in language. She wants to concentrate attention on the medium: 'I believe that my books are first and foremost language.'[5]

Cecilie Løveid was born in 1951 in Mysen, a town in eastern Norway, but she was only a few days old when the family moved to Bergen, where she was to spend the next thirty-five years. Both her father and her mother worked at sea, and Cecilie rarely saw them; she was brought up by her grandparents. Her grandmother was a housewife, her grandfather a streetcar worker with literary ambitions who had once been a member of Norway's Communist Party. She read and wrote avidly from an early age. Asked later why she had become a writer, she emphasized the importance of her grandfather's influence, as well as the fact that her mother had once been a professional actress – and that she had suffered from asthmatic bronchitis as a child, which meant that she stayed at home and read a great deal.[6] This also helps to explain the breadth of her literary references.

To begin with, however, she was drawn to art rather than literature. When she left school, she began studying textile design at the Bergen College of Art and Design, although her main interest was painting. At the same time she came into contact with the Communist sympathizers in the *Profil* group. Although, like Liv Køltzow and Eldrid Lunden, she was a passive member of the group, it was one of the influences which drew her back towards literature again. Then, at the age of seventeen, she had a baby – a daughter, Live. As she explains it, the birth of her child was the main reason why she decided to concentrate on writing; like Cora Sandel before her, she found the mess associated with painting and printing difficult to combine with the daily care of an infant. Whatever the ultimate reason, the stress she places on visual imagery in her writing suggests that this dimension is always vividly present in her mind's eye.

Some of her early short pieces were published in newspapers, and then in anthologies: in *Gruppe 68* (Group 68, Cappelen 1968) and *Åtte fra Bergen* (Eight from Bergen, Pax 1969). In 1972 her first book, *Most*, was published.

'the distinctive ring of shattered language'

Most is the name of an invented place where this multiple story unfolds; it is narrated by a succession of women's voices, those of Veslemøy, Marit and Inger. Veslemøy's voice is the dominant one; her name is an echo of the heroine of Arne Garborg's *Haugtussa*, who was deceived in love and assailed by seductive demons, and resisted them by virtue of the innate common sense of a country girl. Cecilie Løveid's Veslemøy is abandoned by her lover, John Wesley, a sailor with a girl in every port, who is also the lover of Marit and Inger – the archetypal wandering seducer, irresistible and faithless. (His name, as well as being similar to that of the lover Jon in Haugtussa, also contains an allusion to a modern text: Bob Dylan's ballad of John Wesley Harding.[7])

The stories of the three women are fragmentary and overlapping, woven together in such a way that it is not always clear who is speaking; chronology breaks down, as all speak in the present about episodes which cannot be simultaneous. There is no conclusive ending, but in the last section Marit and Inger find a home together, and Inger expresses a hope for the future which must be seized *now*, 'whilst everything in our bodies is alive', not postponed to some future socialist utopia; the concrete things around us offer us an immediate joy, if only we are open to it: 'Truth shines through the curtains each morning. The postman leaves truth in all the mailboxes. We must open them and read the letters.'[8]

Most announces themes which recur in many later works: that of abandonment by or absence of a man, who may variously be husband/lover/father, and that of the sea – the central male figure is often a sailor, and there is a cluster of images around the sea theme. It is not difficult to find clues to the insistent presence of these themes in the author's private life; but more interesting from the point of view of this study is the way in which they contribute to modern feminist discussion of the ambiguity and universality of sexuality, and of post-Freudian sexual imagery.[9] Although all the girls are left by their universal lover – and all three undergo an abortion afterwards – the dominant tone of the work is one not of bitterness, but of pleasure, even joy. Nearly everything Cecilie Løveid writes is a celebration of sensuality; her language is centred in bodily experience – concrete and direct at one moment, widening to express a more generalized sense of physical well-being the next. The water imagery is interwoven with sexual experience as nature becomes the lover's body and the woman is pierced with pleasure in every pore:

> The trout. Who sees the trout. The cat sees the bird.
> The bird whirls up. The cat flees. The girl
> wades out naked. Between her legs she gets the
> fat trout. Squeezes the fat trout.
> Joyfully the mosquito pricks. (p. 10)

The sensual harmony is disrupted by Jernkjeve (the Iron Jaw), which tears through the forest and 'rips my heart from me' – an image both of the destructive force of mechanization and of the potential for destruction of male sexuality when it becomes depersonalized aggression, and not a tide which meets the woman's.

The critical reaction to this novel throws an interesting sidelight on the development of feminist criticism in Norway. When it appeared in the early 1970s, it was assessed as a political statement; along with works by Bjørg Vik, Liv Køltzow and the Swedish author Marit Paulsen, it was seen as a contribution to the debate about the necessary development of modern society in a more female-orientated direction – although it was admitted that its political commentary was addressed to individual experience rather than to institutions.[10] Later, when feminist criticism had become less directly political in its orientation, it was interpreted as a criticism of aesthetic form, and a necessary corrective to a purely intellectual feminism:

Parts of the women's movement take a different view of sexuality from that in *Most*. Løveid's insight into the social function of sexuality is in clear opposition to moralistic and self-denying ordinances in parts of the women's movement. Many seem to have fallen back in their argumentation on an intellectual sexuality where the ideal becomes a kind of rational meeting between the sexes. But physical and aesthetic attraction is an essential form of communication which political movements which are working towards liberation must take up seriously.[11]

Cecilie Løveid's next book, *Tenk om isen skulle komme* (What if the Ice Should Come, 1974), is set in modern Bergen, and is partly a novel about the town itself. Developers are moving in, and parts of the old town are disappearing under soulless new offices and flats. The central character Julia, who at the beginning was powerless and exploited – she was used as a model for pornographic photographs – discovers a sense of purpose in becoming a photographer herself in order to record the old town before it disappears. Commercial and personal exploitation become linked as she simultaneously frees herself from her chauvinistic lover Keff to form a more open relationship with Jak, who has broken out of stereotyped sex roles and consults her needs as well as his.

Alltid skyer over Askøy (Always Clouds Over Askøy, 1976) also has a Bergen setting. Bergen is Kjersti's town, and more than a backdrop to her drama, it is a part of her experience; the book begins and ends with her standing on a bridge and taking in the panorama of the city and seascape. With its long maritime history, Bergen is a town which seems closer to the sea than any other in Norway, and the sea theme runs strongly through the narrative. Kjersti's father was a sailor, and her childhood was marked by his absence. In the course of the narrative, she is abandoned again – by her lover Harald, who leaves her and their daughter. She has to learn self-value after being rejected, and to discover that female sexuality is a positive force after being made to feel inferior by Harald; in a scene halfway between sadness and laughter she relates how he enjoyed having her kneel and suck him, whilst refusing to return the favour, because 'I am much more dangerous between the legs than he is'[12].

As in *Most*, Kjersti's narrative is one of several female voices. The work is episodic, moving between different times and characters; thus one section is mainly concerned with Kjersti's mother and aunts, whilst another centres on her grandfather's account of *his* mother. It can be read as a history of women through several generations, and their progress from a struggle to gather together the bare necessities to a more existential concern for the quality of life.[13] No more than any other of Cecilie Løveid's female characters does Kjersti sit around feeling sorry for herself; she is determined to find a way of living in which she can be fulfilled both as a woman and as an artist. Art, like sexuality, cannot be confined in an enclosed space and practised in isolation; it is another way of making contact with other people.

This novel was followed by a collection of texts called *Fanget villrose* (Captured Wildrose, 1977), of which it is even more difficult to give a coherent summary. There is no identifiable fictional character at the centre to hold it together; it is a collection of pieces, often halfway between poetry and prose, which can be grouped around a cluster of themes. Some refer to current political events, some to art and literature, some to childhood memories and some to dreams. The filtering consciousness is usually female and often openly feminist, as in the subsection called 'Captured Wildrose', where the theme of entrapment emerges. Women are trapped in a variety of roles, in the 'female socialization' of the growing-up process or in male expectations as sexual objects; they are also trapped into art, as in 'Kyss' ('Kiss'), in which a woman is modelling for a sculpture in 'a pose of fear'; or 'Film', in which she is commanded to smile for a photograph.

The theme is taken to extremes in a couple of texts, where women's heads are actually divided from their bodies. 'Hodet har fritt utsyn' ('The head has a free view') describes how the woman's lover has taken her body and left her head behind – a parodic image of the desire to possess woman as a sexual object without being bothered to take account of her as a thinking being, but which in this case suits the woman quite well too: 'He has got rid of my pestering. In a way he's got rid of me, but has me, and I've got rid of him, and have myself and am with him. I know that many women envy my situation. I have a free view, I don't have to go out and labour.'[14]

Having your head separated from your body is part of a long female tradition; in 'Brev' ('Letter') the narrator relates how her grandmother used to walk around with her head underneath her arm. In those days, women were less likely to complain about the split or try to tape their heads back on 'discreetly', as the narrator does. 'Female Writers of the Past' explores the history of women's writing, which also transgressed male ideas of femininity and consequently had to be done in secret at night, anonymously or concealed behind a male pseudonym. It is one of Cecilie Løveid's most explicitly feminist texts:

> Female writers of the past were not like those of the
> future: liberated and self-aware. Anonymity was
> necessary to conceal the unladylike activity of
> publishing books and articles. Names like

> John Oliver Hobbes, John Strange Winter,
> Martin Ross, George Eliot, Kåre P

> were all created to lie beneath a man
> had to have a good lay
> waistlength hair
> by night

> Education had only prepared them to get and keep a
> husband. Milkwhite sheets with monogram. Manuscripts
> had to wait until the author's coast was clear,
> encapsulated in fear or hung out of the window to air
> in the form of a colourful exquisite patchwork quilt.

> At night the quill pen leapt into her hand
> before she had sat down with her light. (p. 46)

Cecilie Løveid's artistic activities during the 1970s were more wide-ranging than the texts which she actually published. She was involved in projects with other media: theatre, TV and film. Many of these were by their nature ephemeral, and not all came to fruition, but out of them developed the more substantial drama of later years. They also gave her contact with other artists at a time when she might otherwise have been isolated, and provided an outlet for her continuing fascination with the plastic arts: 'the need to visualize rises up in me from time to time, I have never quite

managed to repress the artist in me, even though I don't believe
I would have been all that good . . .'[15]

It was with the 'novel' *Sug* (Sea Swell, 1979) that she had her first
major success. The book begins with two quotations from English
authors: William Blake's poem 'What is it men in women most
desire?' and a passage from Virginia Woolf's *To The Lighthouse*, in
which Mrs Ramsay, gathering up the children's debris from the day
and finally alone with her thoughts, rests in the feeling that she is
not being called upon to respond to any demands, that she can for
a while exist just for herself, 'a wedge-shaped core of darkness'.[16]
The two quotations prefigure the themes of the book: desire –
active female desire – and the need for autonomy, for space out
of which creativity might arise.

The title *Sug* can be understood on many levels, and can hardly
be translated adequately; a more literal translation would be 'Suck'.
It can have reference to the movement of the sea, and to the
emptiness of gnawing hunger or of urgent sexual desire; it can
also refer to the suckling of a child or the sucking which forms
part of adult sexual play. All these meanings are woven into the
fabric of the book, which is formed into poetic prose episodes
around the life of Kjersti, the central character from *Always Clouds
Over Askøy*.

The absent sailor father of the earlier book returns as a figure she
is not finished with, precisely because of his absence. Her feelings
towards him are sexual; half-fearing, half-desiring, she fantasizes a
scene of childhood rape, which not only violates her physically but
also literally silences her, deprives her of a language in which to
express female experience:

THE BELOVED FATHER WENT INTO TOWN TO BUY A REEL OF
WHITE COTTON JUST FOR HER WHILST SHE CUT UP ALL HER
CLOTHES AND THREW THEM TO THE DOGS HE WANDERED
QUIETLY DOWN FOR A REEL OF WHITE COTTON

Not so that her mouth should be sewn up. But so that her life
should hang together, he wandered. Nevertheless she awoke
next morning with her mouth sewn up. Next morning she
awoke and was used, slit open between the legs and sewn up
across her mouth. (If you say anything to anyone you won't stay
here any longer.)

EVERYTHING COULD SUDDENLY BE TURNED UPSIDE DOWN[17]

In true Kristevan fashion, the Order of the Father has deprived her of speech.[18]

Sea Swell represents in part Kjersti's attempt to come to terms with this figure of authority and maleness. In another fantasy scene she visits him in a home and finds him old, blind and powerless; she is now able to take charge and act out her feelings of love and hatred in a scene with elements of both incest and parricide. She must be free of him in order to enter a mature relationship with a man.

The book further relates Kjersti's attempts to embark on a new relationship with Mats, who seems to be able to fulfil her desires, both physical and emotional. They spend a happy summer by the sea; but gradually their happiness is poisoned by the fact that Mats is unable to break free from his wife Eli, who threatens suicide. Kjersti reacts with anger and jealousy, and Mats finally leaves to return to his wife. The rest of the novel explores Kjersti's coming to terms with her loss, which involves the miscarriage of the child she was carrying. She retreats into depression and silence; she is sought in friendship by another woman, Monika; she tries art – joining Monika in making ceramic angels; she undertakes fantasy journeys into her own past and to unknown destinations. She has to work through the passivity induced by feeling objectified and rejected towards becoming an active subject again. The novel ends with a new meeting with a man, and a meditation about language and the problems it causes; if only one had a completely new language to begin a new kind of communication, she thinks:

> Both with a wish to reach out of ourselves, over to the other. So many languages. Is it easier to have a language without words? Without colour? One with a fine 'touch me' structure? One with warm 'come into me' calls. Or a language which rises up like a racing cycle in a rainy street in town. (p. 119)

The novel is as much about language as about sexuality – two means of communication which are inextricably bound up with each other. Despite its concentration on the destructive potential of relationships with the father or the lover, it does not present a negative attitude towards men. The most vivid parts are those which celebrate sexual meetings, which tell of the triumph of female desire which rises to meet the male. One of the texts, which might be called a poem, is called 'Rug' ('Rye'), and was earlier published separately with a dedication 'For Sigbjørn Obstfelder'. It is a reply to his poem from 1899, 'Rugen skjælver' ('The Rye Trembles'), in which the field of rye hides the daughter of men, who has been discovered by the father to have been sinning; she is disgraced, and the rye is trembling in shame. In Cecilie Løveid's poem, the daughter has become the field of rye, and the trembling is one of desire, not shame:

> If I were a ryefield not a daughter and you were a man
> on a walk.
> Were I sown so early and grown so fast that the east wind caught
> hold so I became waves.
> Would you come into my waves then?
>
> Yes suddenly you stood there as I dreamt in blue
> clothes dark whiskers and high boots at my edge.
> Then you flew
> with your belly close over ryeflick so warm that it smelt of
> newbaked bread.
>
> I opened myself new places in long swaying passages, higher
> waves. Then you had to look at your watch as you flew. Had
> to know how long you had been hovering.
>
> You left a hollow in broken ears your body's fluttering
> impression in the moment of fall.
>
> But I have many acres of earth and a fantasy which has
> survived an unending number of adventures. (p. 59)

Here the woman takes the active part, issuing an invitation to the man to 'come into my waves', and the man comes, flying close over her. But he is unable to sustain the flight, distracted by his desire to measure his own achievement, or by the intrusion of the world outside, or by his own orgasm which curtails his love-making as it does not the woman's. He becomes a faintly ridiculous figure in comparison to the woman, who stretches out ripe and abundant, undisturbed by a few broken stems, able to satisfy many lovers and refus-

ing to be devastated by the fall of this one. The form of
the verse echoes the new spreading freedom the woman has
won. Obstfelder's poem was written in a tightly controlled
verse form: three verses of four lines each with the insistent refrain 'The rye trembles' repeated on every other line
throughout the poem. Løveid's text is written in a free form
somewhere between verse and prose, and can be printed in
different ways; the original version from 1978 was printed in
shorter lines so that it looked more regular than the version
later printed in *Sea Swell*, and which I have quoted here.[19]

'I find a new way of being for each project'

The publication of *Sea Swell* marks the end of a phase of
Cecilie Løveid's writing. She later called it 'the last book I
have written'.[20] This is true in the sense that most of her
texts since then have been written not primarily to be printed,
as a communication from one writer to the reader, but as part
of a collaborative project involving other media, particularly
the theatre. She is the kind of dramatist who is very much
involved in the production of her plays, and many of her texts
contain several layers of rewriting. Her relationship with theatres
in Norway has often been marked by frustration at projects not
reaching performance or what she felt was a lack of understanding
of what she was trying to do, an unwillingness to experiment
with new forms. She is not the only contemporary dramatist
who has suffered from the tendency of the larger Norwegian
theatres to opt for 'safe' plays which will bring in the public –
which usually means either Ibsen or imported works from Britain
or America.[21]

Some of her first plays to be printed were written for the
radio. *Måkespisere* (*Seagull Eaters*) was first broadcast in 1982
and printed in 1983.[22] It tells the story of Kristine Larsen,
a poor Bergen girl who dreams of becoming a great actress.
Like Shakespeare's sister in Virginia Woolf's fantasy, being born
who and what she is, she does not stand a chance.[23] She
cannot afford to go to drama school, or even to buy books;
her father encourages her dreams, but gives her no help towards

realizing them. Successful actresses and theatre directors treat her with condescension, and eventually she is employed in vaudeville because she has 'pretty legs'. Nearly starving in the German occupation (it is the 1940s), she is seduced by her landlord, who offers her delicious food. When she bears his child, she is persuaded to hand it over to the 'Give the Führer a child' campaign. In the end she is stripped of everything; her dreams of a theatrical career, of love, of motherhood are all destroyed.

Kristine's story is woven around with many other voices, and with music too, setting the mood of the different scenes as the text cuts swiftly from one to another. It is intercut with quotations from the cookery book of Henriette Schønberg Erken, the Mrs Beeton of Norway. Her book provides detailed instructions not only about the preparation of food, but about the economic running of a household; it is a kind of middle class housewives' bible. As the tale unfolds, her cultured voice becomes an ironic commentary on Kristine's plight. The suggestion that the starving Kristine might be reduced to eating seagulls is accompanied by a recipe for preparing them, and her fattening up to produce a child for the Führer introduces a description of the best way of carving a goose. The play's last words, about the wringing out of wet cloths, become a comment on her final state:

> ERKEN: Wash rags must be rinsed and hung up to dry. A wet rag left bunched in a corner or on a wash tub, is a sure sign of slovenliness.[24]

Critics in Norway were enthusiastic about the play, noting how much twentieth-century social history could be read between the brief lines of dialogue. The 'collage' technique worked well for those who heard it on the radio: 'The form makes it new. There is something dreaming, sensitive and delicate about Cecilie Løveid's way of forming a text. In addition she has a sense of humour, so black that it gleams.'[25] International success was also beginning to come the author's way; this play was translated into several languages and won the Prix Italia for the best radio play of 1983.

Vinteren revner (The Ice Breaks Up, 1983), Cecilie Løveid's first play to be staged, returns to the theme of rejection and the absent father/lover figure of earlier works. Inger, mother of Hilde, has been abandoned by her husband, a 'man of salt'; he never appears in the play. She in her turn becomes an absent parent; she is a 'sailor', always departing for foreign ports and leaving her daughter. The only other character in the play is Jak, identified in the dramatis personae simply as 'a doctor and a man'. He becomes a kind of universal male, an Adam to Inger's Eve and a psychiatrist and father figure to Hilde. As Hilde grows up, she and her mother become rivals; an Electra conflict develops, in which Hilde acts out both incest with the 'father' and then matricide. In a quasi-rape scene, Jak provides her with what she lacks – a penis – which frees her from the winter into which she is frozen and gives her the strength to 'kill' the mother figure and grow up into mature womanhood. But the solution is only a partial one, for the *real* father is as absent at the end as he has been throughout. There has been no resolution of conflict with him, so all that Hilde can do at the end is to take over her mother's role as a wandering sailor, unable to take permanent root. It seems that the whole cycle will begin again.[26]

This is a play full of violent emotion and physical violence, which alternates with dreamlike sequences in which foetuses are projected on the backdrop or characters act out slow-motion parodies of themselves with masks. It is written in short lines of free verse, in repetitive, declamatory style, becoming almost a ritual chant at times. It makes great demands on the actors and on an audience used to naturalistic theatre; nevertheless it has been one of Cecilie Løveid's most successful plays on stage. It was staged at *Den Nationale Scene* in Bergen in January 1983, and again later that year – in *nynorsk* translation – on one of the stages of *Det norske teatret* in Oslo. The main theatre critic of the Oslo newspaper *Dagbladet*, Erik Pierstorff, welcomed it as 'the most original piece of new Norwegian drama I have seen since the première of Finn Carling's *Gitrene* (The Bars) in 1966. . . . The tension in this play lies between the great, universal mythical-psychological conflict on the one hand and the concretely ironic and often teasing depiction of the three people who are to embody it on the other.'[27]

Following this success, Cecilie Løveid was commissioned to write another play for the Bergen theatre. The result was *Balansedame* (Tightrope Lady, 1984), a play based on a short story, which in its turn grew out of an idea from an unlikely source: an article from the Swedish magazine *Damernas Värld* (Women's World) about a woman who refused to live in the present: 'I would prefer to have lived in the eighteenth century. The time we're living in now is no good for me.'[28] It also draws on the author's own private experience, in this case the recent difficult birth of a mongoloid son. Out of all this – and other strands too – grows the idea of a woman balancing between the uncertainties of the modern age and the relative certainties of the Rococo period, between the demands of man (first father, then husband) and child, and of her own self-fulfilment. It is a play which takes place in the mind as much as in real time, as the playwright comments on the title page: '*Tightrope Lady* takes place in our time. It can be reality, it can be the journey a woman undertakes within herself whilst she is lying in childbed, waiting for her new life.'[29]

The play begins with Susanne's early pregnancy and ends with a dead child, another in the long line of aborted, miscarried or stillborn children which must form part of Cecilie Løveid's nightmare world. Sexuality is often connected with conception in her writing – unusually for a contemporary author in an age where there is no longer a necessary connection. Carrying a child is an essential part of a woman's physical fulfilment. At the same time, the act of childbirth is more than just a biological event; it can stand for the act of creativity in general, or be symbolic of successful communication. When a relationship breaks down, a vital spark is extinguished which can transform its fruits into death rather than life.

There are many threads to be taken up in this story; there is no clear linear development to the plot. It was a play the theatre had problems with; although they had asked Cecilie to write it, they found they were not prepared to stage it. It had not been performed when it was published in 1984 with an Afterword from the producer Tom Remlov explaining why:

As a novelist and poet Cecilie's voice is unique, and the same is true to an even greater extent of the dramatist. It is difficult to know how much she has actually been influenced by modern international forms of theatre, such as the visual tableaux of 'performance art', or neo-Expressionism in the German theatre à la Botho Strauss. But the point is that she has a lot in common with such directions, and that makes her unique in a Norwegian context. We should of course be prepared to encourage this in our theatre. We need such stimulus, such challenge. Drama should function creatively in this way. But precisely because she is like this – so special – she cannot automatically find a place in the repertoire of our national commercial theatre. (p. 144)

This is a pretty damning indictment of modern Norwegian theatre from one of its producers: Cecilie Løveid is too creative, too much in tune with exciting international developments, to be risked on a Norwegian stage. The play had its première in Sweden; like Jens Bjørneboe before her, Cecilie Løveid found Swedish theatre better equipped to cope with experimental productions. However, the Norwegian theatre did then pull itself together, and Bergen's *Den Nationale Scene* staged the play in 1986. The critical reception was also symptomatic of the different theatrical milieu in the two countries; the Swedish press gave it a positive reception, whereas the Norwegian was mixed and at times downright confused.[30]

By this time Cecilie Løveid was becoming used to the idea of her plays having more success abroad. Her depression at the way dramatists are treated in Norway shows in an interview from 1986: 'If I sometimes toy with the idea of giving up writing plays, it is because the theatre is so slow-moving, it's so difficult to be spontaneous.'[31] But she did not give up writing plays; in fact her next play was directly inspired by the frustrations involved in staging *Tightrope Lady*: 'One day I just felt completely shattered. Then I wrote *Fornuftige dyr* just like that. Straight on to the page. I began to think about the situation, the hotel room – the child. Eilert Løvborg's manuscript, and my manuscript, became the child. The hotel room milieu became my situation. As banal as that.'[32]

Fornuftige dyr (Rational Animals) is another full-length stage play. Without Cecilie Løveid's comments above, there is no obvious connection with Ibsen's *Hedda Gabler*, just as there is no allusion to it in the play; it is a buried reference which resonates beneath the surface. Yet it is a useful reminder to the critic that babies in Cecilie Løveid's works may have more than a purely literal meaning, and that an aborted or abandoned child may signal a failure of communication in an area other than the sexual. More obvious points of reference in the play are to Pre-Raphaelite art and to William Blake, whose texts are woven into the dialogue.

The motto for the play is Blake's poem 'O Rose thou art sick', and the play is about a love that fails because communication fails. It begins with a meeting in a hotel room between Jan and Elisabeth; he has already left her for another woman, a 'Pre-Raphaelite beauty', and since he left she has had their baby – a child he would rather have had aborted. She loves him still, and uses the baby and her own seductive powers to call him back – and he responds, but will not stay. In Act II Jan returns three years later, interested in taking up the relationship, to find that he had made her pregnant again, and she aborted the baby this time – an act to which he objects as strongly as to the birth of the first. The final act takes place when their daughter is grown up; Elisabeth is now running her own hotel, and Jan comes in to seduce his daughter, leaving Elisabeth and his Pre-Raphaelite lover as lifeless marionettes in the foyer. Once again the mother has been superseded by the daughter in the relationship with the father – but this time the daughter has not been empowered by it; she appears at the end carried over Jan's shoulders 'as they used to carry calves in antiquity when they were to be sacrificed'.[33]

The play was staged in Bergen in 1986, and transmitted in a television version the same year. It was a moderate success, and in the meantime Cecilie Løveid had decided to move away from Bergen, where theatrical possibilities were limited. She moved to Oslo, where her next play, *Dobbel nytelse* (Double Delight) was staged at the small *Centralteatret* in 1990.

This play takes place on an archaeological dig; Guy and his wife Siri are excavating the medieval nunnery of St Catherine, together with Tutti and Frutti, two unemployed dancers who are their assistants. Siri is nursing a baby. A visitor arrives, a girl called Catherine, who has been brought up by Siri's mother as her own child, though she is in fact Siri's daughter, a child she had when she was still a child herself. The use of the same name is not coincidental; Catherine is a parallel to the historical St Catherine, and Siri's excavations become a digging back into her own past and women's past in general – she gradually adopts a medieval costume during the course of the play. But Catherine is also a young feline creature (her name abbreviates to Cat) who wants a man, and more particularly wants Siri's man – she is jealous of her sister/mother. Guy is a passive character between these two, loving Siri but unable to follow her back into the past, desiring Cat but unable to consummate his passion. Finally he is killed by Cat and the two women are left alone; Siri steps into the boat they have excavated, dressed as a medieval bride for her voyage into the past, and Cat picks up the baby and is left standing alone centre stage 'like a Madonna' (stage directions).

It is a significant development in this play that it is the father/lover who is destroyed by the daughter, not the mother; the final tableau suggests a female tradition of birth and rebirth, handed down through the ages, to which man is incidental. Power and mature womanhood have been bestowed not by the man – who has failed in this play in the act of symbolic incest – but by the sister/mother who has handed on the baby, the sign of fertility.

Around these central characters are grouped others who comment on the action.[34] The two dancers Tutti and Frutti are a kind of chorus, acting out a balletic commentary on the action and speeches of the other characters, making visually explicit what is veiled in the dialogue. Another important character in performance is a singing pig, who wanders on to the stage in the interstices of the action to sing medieval love songs, which are translations of authentic texts by Provençal troubadours. The pig also acts as a visual commentary on the problems of gender and the potential bestiality of sexuality, being grotesquely androgynous with sagging breasts and a plastic penis. The combination of its absurd appearance and the plaintive way it sings its melancholy love songs is a masterpiece of stagecraft.

Comedy in this play is not confined to the visually parodic; it contains much verbal humour as well. Although it depicts a life-and-death struggle, it is also a more playful play than earlier ones; perhaps it represents a release for its author, as the subject matter resolves some earlier tensions. There are dialogues which consist of a competition to produce the most absurd rhyming words, and others where sexual innuendo and double entendre produce pun after pun, which makes the reading the text itself a 'double delight' – and the translator's despair.[35]

The performance of the play in 1990 was a sparkling one; but the author was probably not much surprised that the critics' welcome was as usual rather grudging. It was poorly attended, and did not have a long run.

1990 also saw the enacting of a different kind of theatrical event in which Cecilie Løveid was involved, *Badehuset* (The Baths).[36] This was a 'visual performance' project, written for a group called *Verdensteatret* (World Theatre) and staged in an open-air theatre consisting simply of a round space in Grünerløkka, the industrial district of Oslo, left by the demolition of a factory, with three fountains constructed in it. The cast were a group of women, with three women (young, middle-aged and old) as the three 'Graces', speakers of the text. The text was based on conversations between women overheard in a swimming pool, in which little was said directly, but which impressed on the author a feeling of women's 'incredible secrecy'.[37] There is no linear plot, but a collage of overlapping voices with music and dance. It was a deliberately ephemeral event, which lasted one week only.

Cecilie Løveid is in the middle of her creative career, and still developing. She recently moved into children's books, with the publication in 1990 of *Lille Pille og Lille Fille i den dype skogs teater* (Little Pille and Little Fille in the Deep Wood's Theatre), a story of two lonely girls finding contact through the medium of the theatre in the wood. It is a work which owes much to the well-known children's writer Torbjørn Egner,[38] and in which there are echoes of many fairy tales. A new play, *Tiden mellom tidene* (Time in between Times, 1991) was performed by a women's theatre group, *Lilith teatergruppe*, in Oslo in 1990, and in 1991 she was appointed Festival Poet to the Bergen Festival.[39]

Cecilie Løveid's way to the public as a playwright has been as difficult as that of many women writers from earlier generations; though the reasons – on the surface, at least – are different. It is not directly because she is a woman that her plays have been held back or badly received, as theatres and critics have made some effort to welcome women's writing in recent years. Yet in another way it may still be the fact of being a woman writer that lies behind the difficulties; she is trying to write in a different way, and in a way which is intimately connected with giving expression to women's experiences. Her project is language, and a new language has to struggle to create an audience for its message.

12
From Documentary to Fantasy

It is difficult to choose representative authors from the contemporary scene, where the profusion of works obscures clear lines of development; it is invidious to focus on one author when there are so many exciting women writers. This last section will therefore present three writers: Herbjørg Wassmo, Gerd Brantenberg and Mari Osmundsen. All are principally writers of fiction, still by far the most popular genre; and all are consciously feminist writers. Yet they differ in their approach to the genre, in their political aims and in their public profiles. My choice has also been influenced by the availability of their work in translation, as much recent work has still to be translated; Herbjørg Wassmo's *The House with the Blind Glass Windows* and Gerd Brantenberg's *The Daughters of Egalia* have recently appeared in English.

Herbjørg Wassmo (born 1942)

Herbjørg Wassmo is a 'regional' writer as much as a feminist writer; these are the two axes along which her work can be plotted. She comes from the north; she was born on the remote island of Skogsøya in Vesterålen, near the Lofoten Islands, and has remained in her home district. She has used the landscape and the life of north Norwegian farming and fishing communities as the setting for all her books. Geographical coincidence is one fact which has led to frequent comparison with Cora Sandel, who was an important model for her: 'She showed that it was possible to be an ordinary person from the North and yet to dare to write novels.'[1]

Like Cora Sandel, Herbjørg Wassmo made a late debut; she was thirty-four when her first book was published. She began with two volumes of poetry, *Vingeslag* (Wing Beats, 1976) and *Flotid* (Rising Tide, 1977), which attracted favourable but limited comment. It was not until she turned to novels in the 1980s that she caught the attention of critics and public, and although she has carried on experimenting with drama and documentary writing, it is as a novelist that she has found her form. Her novels during the 1980s were a runaway success, giving her the means to stop teaching and devote herself full-time to writing.

Herbjørg Wassmo's major work during this decade was her trilogy about Tora, *Huset med den blinde glassveranda* (*The House with the Blind Glass Windows*, 1981), *Det stumme rommet* (The Silent Room, 1983), and *Hudløs himmel* (Flayed Heavens, 1986). It fits into the tradition of multivolume studies by women writers of the development and socialization of girls who feel at odds with their milieu – Sigrid Undset's Kristin Lavransdatter, Torborg Nedreaas's novels about Herdis, and especially Cora Sandel's 'Alberte' trilogy.

Like Alberte, Tora feels mentally and physically frozen; the coldness of the climate becomes a metaphor for the lack of warmth from other human beings, beginning with her mother. Yet Tora is more of an outcast than Alberte; the illegitimate daughter of a Norwegian girl and a German soldier during the war, she is her mother's shame and a constant reminder of a time society would prefer to forget. As if that were not enough, she is a victim of sexual abuse by her stepfather Henrik, who is himself damaged both physically and mentally, and vents his bitterness on anyone weaker than himself. He terrorizes Tora and her mother Ingrid, and Tora's awareness of her mother's wretched life prevents her from asking for help. She can go to no one with her secret, not even her Aunt Rakel, Ingrid's sister and her opposite, warm and outspoken where Ingrid is silent and withdrawn. Bekkejordet, where Rakel and her husband Simon share a loving partnership, is a thriving estate, in contrast to the house of the title where Tora and Ingrid live, a decaying mansion which houses the most inadequate members of society. Bekkejordet is the bright point in Tora's life, but also attracts the bitter envy of Henrik, who twice burns down Simon's warehouses. The second time he is surprised by Tora; he falls into the sea and would have drowned if she had not saved him. Much as she hates him, she cannot watch him die. But he is convicted of arson and sent to prison.

The second volume opens more hopefully, with Tora alone with her mother, trying to establish a closer relationship. Yet she soon realizes that Ingrid cannot change – she has chosen Henrik once and for all. Tora moves closer to her aunt and uncle, but this relationship too becomes problematic: she cannot unlearn what she has learnt by force, and feels both sexual fear and sexual attraction for her Uncle Simon, of which she realizes he is totally unaware. The shame has taken root: 'The shame of knowing the dangerousness. Whilst he – a grown man – knew nothing of it' (*SR*, p. 97).[2] Rakel and Simon, who cannot have children, offer to help pay for her further education on the mainland; but before she can get away, Henrik returns from prison and rapes her one last time. This time she hits back, and leaves feeling she can fight victimization. On the mainland, she begins to become an ordinary girl like the others, doing well at school and even finding a boyfriend – until she realizes she is pregnant. Desperately she hides her pregnancy from everyone, and gives birth alone in her room. The baby dies almost at once, and she struggles out to the shore to bury it.

At the beginning of the last volume, she is just going through the motions of living. Rakel realizes that something is wrong, and arrives unexpectedly – to find a girl half-crazed with grief, able to talk about what happened only as a story about a dead bird. When Rakel grasps the truth, she determines to save Tora, to get her to see that it is Henrik's shame, not hers, and to make sure Henrik leaves her alone. Tora fights her way back to reality, and returns home, living at Bekkejordet in a brief interlude of happiness; she even confronts Henrik and warns him that Rakel knows. But her grasp on reality is tenuous, and it finally snaps when Rakel, who has stomach cancer, dies – she is washed overboard whilst in a small boat with Henrik, and despite his attempts to save her, she decides to drown, having first made him promise never to touch Tora again. Henrik is devastated, and ceases to be any threat to Tora; but it is too late. Tora's identification with her beloved aunt, whom she strongly resembles, becomes absolute, as she abandons the unbearable incarnation of Tora and takes on her aunt's personality instead. She is drawn deeper and deeper into a fantasy world, dressing and talking like Rakel, and even trying to take her place with Simon. Rejected by the gentle but grief-stricken man, who has no way of understanding her desperation, she slips into paranoia, tormented by voices in her head and by objects which take on a life of their own. With 'Rakel' for company, she returns to her baby's grave and lies down in the snow, waiting for the boat to come and take her to her father's family in Berlin.

The narrative is related in the third person, with the viewpoint often with Tora, but also moving around the other characters, particularly Rakel, and including direct comment on the action.[3] For much of the time it is a traditional realistic narrative, setting Tora's story against a detailed background of life in a north Norwegian fishing community in the 1950s, with the repressive views of any small and self-sufficient community, where the worst sin is to be different. There is a sharp divide between the 'men's world' of fishing, labouring and drinking in the local pub, and the 'women's world' of domestic routine and childcare, and when necessary (as in Ingrid's case) low-paid work at the fish factory. It is almost unthinkable to cross this divide, even when a mother of many children is incapacitated: 'Children were always a woman's thing . . . There might be heaps of unemployed fathers around. But it made no difference' (*HBG*, pp. 126–7). The story is related in a low-key, matter-of-fact way; despite the horrific nature of some of the incidents, the author does not brandish her indignation, but lets it emerge from the account itself.

Yet to describe the trilogy as realistic fiction is only part of the truth, as it incorporates an increasing amount of fantasy. It is symptomatic that it is discussed in the recent history of Norwegian women's writing both in the chapter on 'Psychological Realism after 1965' and in that on 'Breaking the Bounds of Realism in the Novel'.[4] Fantasy is a necessary escape for Tora from her degradation, as in her dreams of being rescued by her father – and, when she finds he is dead, of travelling to Berlin to find her German grandmother. But it is also the only way she can deal with her experiences, as there are no words in her language for what happens to her. She is haunted by the image of a dead cat which had been tortured by the local boys, which encapsulates her feeling that being a victim is her fault: 'No doubt it was the cat's own fault. Because no one owned it and no one looked after it. It had that effect on people, that they flayed it' (*HBG*, p. 54). She can cope with the dead child only by imagining it as a dead bird, and transfers her grief to pity for the starving birds during the winter. Bird imagery becomes dominant during the later part of the story.

In the final phase of her crisis, fantasy becomes more real to Tora than reality, the voices in her head sound louder than the voices outside. She has lost control not only of her actions but of her identity, which is invaded in a nightmarish scene in Rakel's kitchen by Christmas gingerbread men:

> They climbed up the stool legs, up her legs and thighs. Inside her clothes. . . . They would soon reach her neck. Millions of them. . . . Then she realized they were inside her mouth. Her ears. Inside her head. They were eating their way into her brain! And Simon wasn't there! It was nearly Christmas, and they hadn't fetched the tree! And the birds were sitting hidden in the rowan tree, waiting for daylight. Each alone with its head beneath its wing. Waiting for its chick. (*HH*, p. 235)

Authorial comments and the other characters fade away as the narrative parallels Tora's schizophrenic consciousness by losing all reference points except the dreamlike logic which leads her back to the grave from which the last volume began.

The trilogy was a best-seller; by 1987, 400,000 copies of the series had been sold. The first volume won the Norwegian Critics' Prize, and the third volume won the Scandinavian equivalent of the Booker Prize: the Nordic Council Prize. Herbjørg Wassmo was only the second woman to win the prize in its twenty-five-year history (the Swedish writer Sara Lidman won in 1980 for her novel *Vredens barn*, The Children of Wrath); the other Norwegians who had won it were Tarjei Vesaas (1964), Johan Borgen(1967) and Kjartan Fløgstad (1978).[5] Yet Herbjørg Wassmo has not become a media personality, preferring to communicate through her books – although she has been an active member of the Authors' Association.

In between the volumes of the trilogy, she produced other works. The effect of the Second World War on northern Norway, which was particularly devastating, inspired *Veien å gå* (The Way To Go, 1984), a factually based account of the flight of a Resistance fighter and his family in midwinter over the mountains to Sweden. It is the family she is interested in, the women and children who are a part of the suffering of war but seldom share in the glory.

She also wrote a couple of radio plays, *Juni–vinter* (June–Winter, 1983), a study of the meeting of two generations, and *Mellomlanding* (Stop-over, 1985) which describes a chance meeting between a woman and the man who fathered her child seventeen years before; he wants to take up the relationship, but she realizes that there is no going back, they must stand by the choices they have made.

Herbjørg Wassmo's other major work so far is her historical novel, *Dinas bok* (Dina's Book, 1989), set in the mid-nineteenth century, but in the familiar northern Norwegian fishing and farming community. It is a woman's story – but a very different woman from the hapless Tora. Dina is a strong-minded character who acts rather than being acted upon, and the novel opens with an act breathtaking in its decisiveness: on her way over the mountain to the doctor with her enfeebled husband, who has gangrene in one foot, she pushes the sledge to which he is strapped over a precipice. When his body is found, she refuses to attend the funeral, using the opportunity when everyone else is away to seduce the stable-boy in the master bedroom.

Dina is a law unto herself, flouting convention at a time when it was a cause of scandal for a woman even to ride astride or smoke a cigar. She runs the estate, treats people according to her judgement of them rather than their social standing, and takes what she wants – be it wine, music or men. Where Tora is associated with defenceless creatures, flayed cats and fledgling birds, Dina's image is a horse; her nearest companion, Svarten, is a black horse no one else can ride, and in her sexual encounters it is clear who is in the saddle: 'Their bodies were horses on the wide plains. They rode and rode. The woman was already an experienced rider. But he rode furiously after. The floorboards sang, the rafters cried . . .'[6]

Yet this passionate woman who seems in total control of her own life is also a betrayed child. When she was five years old, she accidentally killed her mother by tipping a cauldron of boiling lye over her, and her grief-stricken father sent her away to live with a cotter's family. She grew up with a burden of guilt, unable even to grieve properly, because 'you couldn't grieve for someone you yourself had sent on her way' (p. 40). By the age of fifteen she is a wild creature, whose only friend is her teacher Lorck, who has discovered her gift for music. But she is also beautiful and sensual, and when her father's friend Jacob Grønelv sees her, he knows he must have her. They marry, and things go well for a while, but in the long run this 'young mare' is too much for a man older than her father. She kills him, without emotion; having gone over the boundary once, it is easy to do it again. Yet both her mother and Jacob become her constant companions, as real in her fantasy life as her actual household. Finally she meets a man who is her equal, Leo Zjukovskij, a mysterious and unpredictable Russian visitor. Although he reciprocates her feelings, he refuses to be bound, announcing his departure again when she thinks he has returned for good. The pattern of betrayal of her early life reasserts itself, and she responds as she has always responded – with violence.

The novel is also about language. Dina has an uneasy relationship to language, which she feels is full of deceit; she prefers numbers, or music. She literally loses her own language twice; she becomes dumb after her mother's death, and begins to talk again only when she hears Lorck playing the cello. Similarly, she stops speaking after Jacob's death; this time the shock of her son's birth restores her speech.

The narrative incorporates different registers of language. Each chapter begins with a quotation from the Old Testament, the book which dominated Dina's early childhood and whose patriarchal prohibitions are a constant reminder of the law she has transgressed. The story is told in the third person, focusing on dialogue and action rather than introspection; yet it is punctuated by short diary-like excerpts with Dina speaking in the first person, where her motives become clear. Herbjørg Wassmo explains their inclusion thus: 'I felt as if I was not doing full justice to her, didn't fully understand her. She is seen through other people's eyes the whole time.'[7] With this experimental counterpointing of different kinds of texts, the author provides different perspectives on the story of a woman struggling to find her own language rather than to be defined by the traditional, 'phallic' discourse of law and religion.

Gerd Brantenberg (born 1941)

Gerd Brantenberg is not a regional writer in the same sense as Herbjørg Wassmo; although she grew up in Fredrikstad, a town at the entrance of the Oslo fjord, she was born in Oslo and returned to live there as an adult. In two of her novels, Fredrikstad plays a central part; her other works are set elsewhere. Central to everything she writes, however, is an active engagement in sexual politics. Indignation at society's treatment of women and of those whose sexual preferences are considered deviant recur constantly in her writing; she is the most visible of the writers who has openly declared herself lesbian. She has made an important contribution towards the establishment of a greater openness in Norwegian society towards alternative sexuality.

Although she had been writing since childhood, it was not until she was thirty-two that Gerd Brantenberg published her first novel, *Opp alle jordens homofile* (*What Comes Naturally*, 1973).[8] Part of the reason for her relatively late debut was the difficulty of writing about lesbianism even in the so-called liberated sixties; the liberation applied to heterosexuals alone. The novel is about the experience of being a lesbian in Oslo in the sixties, and the convoluted strategies necessary to disguise otherness. More unusual than its subject matter is the tone of the novel, which consistently conveys the funny side of the problem. It is addressed in mock-pedagogic style to a curious reader, whom the narrator second-guesses the whole time, and who varies between titillation and disapproval – as does the narrator herself, imbued as she is with the moral values of her society:

> we were so bourgeois we didn't even have the nerve to embrace each other without having turned out the light. Then we didn't have to see how peculiar it was with two girls. Because it is. Don't deny it. I can see you're trying to put up a front, saying you don't think it's peculiar in the least. But that's a lie. You aren't so tolerant. You can't be more tolerant than I was. And I was pretty intolerant of what I felt and did. But I did it. (p. 14)

Even the view expressed above that it is unusual to write a funny book about lesbianism is second-guessed by the narrator; lesbians are not supposed to have a sense of humour, any more than people in wheelchairs. It is difficult to make any comment on the novel which has not already been rendered absurd by the narrator. Thus by means of the humour Gerd Brantenberg achieves her serious purpose: to confront the reader with the extent of her own prejudices.

Unusually for a Norwegian novel, Gerd Brantenberg's next book was translated into many languages and became an international best-seller before its importance was recognized in Norway.[9] *Egalias døtre* (*The Daughters of Egalia*, 1977) takes place in an imaginary world, Egalia, a matriarchy in which women literally wear the trousers; they sit in government, run businesses and roam the world freely. Yet this is no utopia; it is a parody, which turns our familiar society on its head to expose its absurdity. In a world in which God is female, society was founded by Moulding Mothers and the glorious battles of the past were won by female leaders, it is the men who are oppressed, forced to wear tight skirts and uncomfortable shoes, to curl their beards and remove their chest hair, to stay at home and look after the children. Selective breeding has favoured men who are short, fat and gentle, and women who are tall and strong, and any protest about inequality is countered by a reference to nature's laws. The novel describes a revolt against this inequality which leads to the founding of the masculist movement, and the burning of pehoes (penis holders, restrictive garments in which men from adolescence onwards must encase their penises).

It is not only visible signs of oppression with which Gerd Brantenberg takes issue in this novel, however. Language, as modern feminist theorists have observed, is one of the subtlest forms of oppression, which structures the way in which people conceive of themselves; you cannot change the way people think without changing the language in which they think.[10] Gerd Brantenberg came independently to this conclusion whilst writing her novel; having started writing in 'normal' (i.e. phallocentric) language, she soon realized that a society based on matriarchal premises would develop a different language, and invented a new one accordingly. Thus the dominant form becomes the female rather than the male; instead of deriving 'woman' from 'man' and 'female' from 'male', she derives 'manwom' from 'wom' and 'mafele' from 'fele'.[11] Petronius's tentative suggestion in the opening chapter that he might become a mafele seawom is ridiculed by his aggressive sister Ba, whilst Director Bram demands peace to read the paper and her housebound Christopher tries to placate everybody. Petronius's thoughts are soon directed in a more seemly fashion towards his debut at the maidmen's ball, in which the young lordies hope to be swept up by the wom of their dreams, to escape the dire fate of ending up an elderly spinnerman and find a safe haven in fatherhood protection.

Petronius is not a conventionally attractive ladsel, being tall and slim and with hair on his chest; he is drawn towards the incipient revolt of the masculists. He wants to be a writer, and publishes a novel called *The Sons of Democracy* – which begins with a repetition of the first chapter of *The Daughters of Egalia*, with the language and sex roles revised to our 'normal' ones. Yet by now, the world of the novel has come to seem normal, and the society that Petronius describes seems bizarre. The critics' reception of it is a parody of the reception the author foresaw: 'The reviewer added that the word "woman" was, incidentally, quite funny, but wasn't it rather unlikely, or at least awkward. And how did the author imagine it should be pronounced?' (p. 264). *The Daughters of Egalia* is the best example in Norwegian literature of the effectiveness of humour as a weapon in the fight for sexual equality.

Gerd Brantenberg returned to realism with the first novel of her trilogy about Inger, *Sangen om St. Croix* (The Song of St Croix, 1979). Much of it is a collective novel about Fredrikstad and particularly the school at which Inger starts on the first page. The class of little girls are followed through the seven years of first school by an omniscient narrator. It is a small town in which class differences are marked, and the children's potential is limited by their home conditions; but it is limited equally by their sex. The education system begins from an early age to discriminate; 'unlucky' girls have teenage abortions or finish up on the streets, and the strongest force of all, social pressure, stifles independence:

> What happened to the rebellion in these girls?
> It was daubed over by lipstick.
> It disappeared in curls and hairdryers.
> It wasn't school that curbed the rebellion. It was make-up.[12]

Their mothers too share a common fate, in that their lives are dictated by their husbands' behaviour. This is obvious in the case of Ågot Tangen, Fanny's mother, whose husband is an unemployed drunkard and whose existence is a grey round of toil to feed and clothe her many children. It is less obvious in the case of Inger's mother Evelyn, who gave up her acting career to marry Ørnulf and have two children too young, and now lives a half-life, subject to her husband's tyrannical demands for constant admiration: 'How could it be that she, Evelyn Gjarm, who had once stood on the stage of Carl Johan Theatre and sung cabaret songs, was now going around shaking with fear at the very fact of existing?' (p. 190).

The second volume, *Ved fergestedet* (At the Ferry Crossing, 1985), continues the story of Inger and her friends through the next six years of secondary education, where class and sexual differences become more marked. Many children from less prosperous backgrounds leave school; girls study humanities subjects and boys science. The maths teacher states openly that 'It was not possible to teach maths to girls',[13] and the one girl who takes science has to fight to be allowed – and then fails, which just proves what everyone always knew. Amongst the pupils it is an accepted axiom that girls cannot think; they are secretaries of the school newspaper, but not editors. To her disappointment, Inger discovers the same attitude to women in the great thinkers of the past like Schopenhauer and Rousseau, and is forced to the conclusion:

> That meant that the women's movement – the irritating, dreadfully boring and unbecoming women's movement – was necessary. It was unworthy. There shouldn't have to be a women's movement. Did one have to devote one's time and energies to something so simple? Something that should be self-evident. That a woman was a person. (p. 180)

Inger becomes the focus, as we follow her gradual discovery that she is different; although she is seemingly well-adjusted, she suffers an inner exile. She falls in love with girls and, in an atmosphere where homosexuality is just not mentioned, feels that she must be the only one to suffer from this perversion. She keeps hoping it will go away, but it does not. By the beginning of the third volume, *For alle vinder* (To the Winds, 1989), she is carrying the knowledge around with her as 'her catastrophe'.

This volume, subtitled 'A novel about a girl (1960–65)' follows Inger on her apprenticeship to life after leaving school. She spends a year as an *au pair* in Edinburgh – a devastating experience of exploitation, but redeemed by the author's sense of humour in her description of her battles with the Hoover and the sweeper. She then begins her studies at the University of Oslo, faced continually with the same problem: she keeps falling in love with girls, but can never do anything about it. What is worse, she cannot even talk about it; there are no words for what she feels. Her situation deprives her of her language, until she begins to write what she cannot say. Finally, at the age of twenty-two, she starts to tell one or two people, and finds she is not alone in the world – but all, like her, have thought they were alone. Women who love women are those who are reached last of all by the tide of liberation:

> What was the deeper meaning in being hounded out into the world with scorn and curses like the ugly duckling? When would the ice finally break up so that they could see themselves, mirror themselves in the water and see that they were fine? When would a flock of youngsters stand on the shore and call to them: 'There's a new one!'[14]

Inger's mother's story ends in this novel. Evelyn's experience of being slowly crushed by her husband culminates in flight, which brings with it an exhilarating sense of freedom: 'She could take down a book from the bookshelf there, sit down, smoke a cigarette, go to the loo, have a wash and clean her teeth and then make the bed. And no one would come and tell her that she ought to have done it all in a different order' (p. 117). But she returns to Ørnulf, for there is really nothing else she can do. She loses her will to live, and dies - officially of liver failure, but Inger is in no doubt of the real cause: 'Papa got the woman he loved. Mamma. And then he destroyed her' (p. 219). It would be simplistic amateur psychology to say that Inger's lesbianism is caused by her parents' conflicts, but her experience of men in the home strengthens her determination never to be subject to one – either like her father or like the mild-mannered Mr Mayfield in Edinburgh, who never raises his voice but is treated like a potentate by the family, and is the only one allowed both butter and jam on his bread.

Gerd Brantenberg has drawn much of the material for this trilogy from her own background, although she maintains that the novels are not strictly autobiographical. There are obvious similarities between her and Inger, not least in their discovery of the power of words: 'Adolescence was for me precisely that: a conquest of words!'[15] And as well as forming Inger's *Entwicklungsroman*, the three novels present a detailed portrayal of life in one of Norway's provincial towns in a recently past but already vanished age.

In the last volume, Inger ponders why it is that homosexuals can understand heterosexual love, but heterosexuals cannot understand homosexual love. She concludes that it is because there are no great homosexual love stories, with which readers can identify even if they cannot focus on the same object; there is no homosexual version of *Kristin Lavransdatter* (p. 229). With the novel *Favntak* (Embraces, 1983), Gerd Brantenberg has done something towards rectifying that lack. It is a story of love between two women, which attempts to convey without the flippancy of earlier novels the force of homoerotic attraction; and it succeeds so well, according to one reviewer, that the reader forgets it is about homosexual love.[16]

The two women start from widely different premisses. Aud is a single woman who lives openly as a lesbian, and has had several relationships with other women; Irene is married with three children, and always thought of herself as heterosexual, until the meeting with Aud. They fall in love at a women's seminar in Denmark; this overwhelming feeling is then confronted by the circumstances of their different lives – Aud in Oslo and Irene in Trondheim, where she cannot bring herself to tell her husband Torgeir. They keep the relationship secret for a while, until Aud finally persuades Irene to tell Torgeir. He reacts with jealousy and disgust; it is true that he has a mistress on the side, but that is a different matter entirely. Thus he becomes the linchpin in the lives of three women, until his mistress tells Irene the truth. She decides to leave and move to Oslo and Aud.

Irene leaves her marriage not just because of her husband's hypocrisy, however, but because she becomes aware of his strategies to control her. He dictates her letter breaking off with Aud, and assumes responsibility not only for what Irene does but also for what she thinks; in the end she is reduced almost to silence, deprived of the power to speak. In a symbolic act, trying to burn her letters from Aud, he sets fire to the room she has furnished for herself in the cellar, the room which is the only place in his house where she can be herself:

He could have a thousand lovers. It was not all that important for her. She might perhaps get worked up enough to be jealous of their youth and beauty, that was all. But the letters he had burnt, the room he had destroyed, they were her slow journey towards understanding herself.[17]

Thus Irene's choice is ultimately not between Torgeir and Aud, but between him and herself; to renounce Aud would be to renounce her own chance of development. At first she decides to choose him; but the fact that he is not willing to face up to what has happened means that the whole basis of their relationship has become false, and in the end there is no choice. In this way the novel becomes a conflict not so much between heterosexual and homosexual love as between an exploitative and an honest relationship, between a destructive passion and one which allows room for growth.

Mari Osmundsen (born 1951)

Mari Osmundsen is younger than the other two authors in this section, and more difficult to place. This is partly because she consistently uses a pseudonym; her identity has not been disclosed and neither, therefore, have facts about her background. It is only recently that even a photograph has appeared on her books. But she is also difficult to place in that she is a writer who has gone through a considerable evolution in the twelve years she has been writing, and has developed an idiosyncratic style.

Her first novel, *Vi klarer det!* (We'll Make It!, 1978), could be called a typical left-wing seventies novel – except that it is untypical for it to have been written by a woman and to have women as the central characters. It is reminiscent of Tor Obrestad's *Sauda! Streik!* (Sauda! Strike!, 1972), or Dag Solstad's *25.september-plassen* (The 25th September Square, 1974) in being about working-class life in a modern factory environment, and about the necessity of political organization. It could be classed as social realism, and draws a clear AKP (m–l) (Marxist–Leninist) political moral. In the course of a wild-cat strike at a metal factory, the workers discover that organized solidarity is the key to fairer working conditions.

At the same time, the novel is more than a political tract; it offers a sympathetic view of the workers, especially the women. Magnhild Svendsen has been cutting out the same metal part for more years than she can remember; like Bjørg Vik's worker Liv in the short story of that name, she wonders what the full total might look like, and feels that her hands are the only part of her that is needed: 'Magnhild's hands meant working capacity, more than any other part of her. . . . Woman's hands. Mother's hands. Working hands.'[18] Her daughter Ann leaves school to become a factory worker, and grows up during the novel, going through teenage pregnancy, abortion and loneliness to become drawn into the political fight; she realizes that abortion, as well as poverty, is a political as much as a personal issue.

The novel mirrors the different aspirations of different parts of the women's movement in the 1970s, juxtaposing the official Labour Party line, which concentrated on improving opportunities for middle-class women, with the more radical Women's Front [*Kvinnefronten*], which stressed solidarity with the working class in the achievement of a more just society for all. Anne Birte, the representative of the latter viewpoint, discovers the ramifications of political involvement in her personal life; her marriage, which had been going through a crisis, is strengthened when both find a common political goal instead of concentrating their energies on creating their own little idyll.

The optimism of the ending of *Vi klarer det!* is modified in *På vei mot himmelen* (On the Way to Heaven, 1979), a study of disaffected modern youth in Oslo and of teenage pregnancy, prostitution and drugs. The story centres around two sisters, Signe and Helga, who leave an unloving home as early as they can; Helga ends up a drug addict on the streets of Copenhagen, but Signe survives as an unmarried mother, determined to cope for her daughter's sake and entering on a new relationship, but with a strong dash of cynicism in her hopes for the future.

Oslo is the setting for most of the stories in the anthology *Wow* (1982), which was Mari Osmundsen's critical breakthrough. The stories are about 'kvinnestyrke', women's resourcefulness in various areas of life. Some depict women in a typical 'victim' situation who manage to turn the tables; Ellen in 'Om å si nei' ('How to Say No') is nearly raped, but knifes the rapist and leaves him in cold blood; Berit in 'Byttingen' ('The Changeling') is a battered wife who reports her husband for hitting the baby, when actually she did it, in order to be able to get rid of him and give her children a better life. 'En av gutta' ('One of the Lads') is about a woman coping with a man's job – loading crates of drinks – and 'Wow' is about a marriage crisis in which a woman rejects her husband for a while in order to create space for herself. None of the figures is idealized, but they all take their fate in their own hands.

Two stories are particularly arresting. 'Sju minutter på seks' ('Seven Minutes to Six') is about two adolescent girls and sex. Kajsa, who is twelve, is out shopping for Christmas and thinking of nothing but what she will buy; Anne, seventeen, is desperate for money for drugs. Both are accosted by a pervert looking for a 'Lolita' to take to a hotel, who sees no difference between them; Anne, who fails to get any money out of her mother, takes up the offer, whilst Kajsa is terrified by her first glimpse of perversion, which changes her childhood world for ever: 'She shut out the memory, and inside her it was just as if a clock had stopped; it said seven minutes to six, and time would never be the same again.'[19]

'Marilyn' deals with a very different female experience. The awkward Marilyn, burdened with a ridiculous name, is on holiday as a maiden aunt looking after her sister's children when she meets Jørgen, the only man who has ever treated her as a woman. She meets him alone in the forest, and a warm friendship springs up. Finally he asks for her help – and reveals that he is actually dead. He is the driver of a truck that crashed carrying a lot of money, and his body has never been found; he cannot rest easy until it is known that he did not steal it. She leads the police to his body, and then he disappears for good – and she has a breakdown. The story is narrated in a matter-of-fact way by Marilyn, so that the reader is left in no doubt that the events she describes are real; the borderline between the realistic and the fantastic is crossed before one notices.

This story heralds a change in Mari Osmundsen's writing. By her next novel, *Gode gjerninger* (Good Deeds, 1984), she has moved from social realism to an idiosyncratic mixture of realism and fantasy, all related in the same straightforward tone. The novel depicts two friends, Karianne and Rut, who both combine life in Oslo with contacts with another dimension. Karianne lives in her grandmother's flat and works as a technical drawer; but from an early age she has had meetings with 'nissen', a demon she can summon up by calling down curses, and to whom she has sold her soul in return for the life of the baby she had at the age of fifteen. Rut works in a playgroup, and her contacts with the other world are involuntary; she starts to 'travel' to an unknown dimension – she literally disappears, and returns a few minutes later with the physical traces of the other place on her body. She is confined in a mental hospital until she learns to control her trips so that they happen only at night, and is allowed home as cured. Karianne meets Daniel, a Romany with whom she feels immediate psychic rapport; but in a sickeningly violent scene he is clubbed to death by a group of Oslo boys out 'Paki-bashing'. She calls up her devil to help her take revenge, and having found the group she shoots them all. With the police on her heels she takes refuge with Rut, who rescues her by taking her over into the other world – and having returned, finds she cannot get back, so that Karianne is left on her own in the other dimension.

Rut reacts to her experiences with predictable panic; such things just cannot happen. Karianne, on the other hand, regards her demon as a tiresome acquaintance; he pops up whenever she says a spell, and they argue like a couple of grumpy old partners. This is his first appearance in the novel:

> 'So the young lady is not afraid of walking home alone at night,' came a voice from the pavement beside her. She started; when she saw who it was she frowned, pursed her lips and carried on walking.
>
> 'Such a hurry, such a hurry,' it sighed. 'It's not easy to get rid of me, you know.'
>
> 'But not impossible,' said Karianne. 'It's several years since I saw your ugly snout last.'
>
> 'You've restrained yourself for quite a while now,' nodded the figure on the pavement. 'But everything has its price. You know that well.'
>
> 'That little verse!' said Karianne. 'Is that anything to make a fuss about?'
>
> 'You know more about trade than that,' he said. 'You'd better find time for a chat, at least.'[20]

The experiences are not given any coherent explanation. Rut's other world remains an undefined limbo, with no hints as to whether it might be the future or some kind of parallel dimension. Although Karianne is the only one who sees her demon, Rut is seen to disappear by others besides Karianne; her travelling cannot be simply hallucination. Both women are in touch with other forces over which they gain some control, but the price for supping with the devil is high.

Alongside the demonic, social and political issues have a direct impact on the girls' lives. Racism is responsible for the death of Daniel, and Karianne spends some time infiltrating a neo-Nazi group. Adoption is a recurrent theme, as Karianne was forced to give up her baby for adoption, and then finds that Daniel was adopted; he was taken from his Romany parents and raised by a Norwegian couple, and feels that he has lost his roots. The theme widens into a discussion of the moral justification of Western 'aid' to the Third World, as Daniel's sister intends to adopt a baby from Colombia, and Daniel attacks egoism masquerading as charity. The motto of the novel, from which the title is derived, is a quotation from Bjørnstjerne Bjørnson: 'It is good deeds which save the world'; the sentiment seems more ironic as the novel progresses, and good deeds are less in evidence than selfish or evil ones. Brutality is answered by brutality, and there is no cheating the Devil of his souls. Yet Karianne remains positive in her refusal to be beaten, as does Rut in her determination to save her friend, so the novel does not end in darkness. It ends, in fact, with sunrise.

The demonic and the everyday coexist in the novel *Familien* (The Family, 1985). It begins normally enough with life in a large house in the (invented) village of Bjørnebekk; it is a women's house, owned by a widow and made into flats for single or divorced women and their children, a place full of creativity and growth. But the harmony does not last, as various threats encroach, particularly to the children; loss of children and battles over child custody are almost obsessive themes. Men have no place in this house, and their intrusion is disruptive; the central character, Marit, becomes pregnant, but tries to convince her boyfriend that the baby is not his, as she fears he will claim rights over what is a part of her.

Alongside this female community is the male community, the 'coffee plantation' at Bjørnebekk. Only men work there – no women or children are allowed inside – and from the start the narrator drops hints that it is not what it seems. The area is enclosed in a vast greenhouse which, as well as coffee bushes, contains a wild area of jungle, with birds and crocodiles. The work is hard and dangerous, and the workers are treated like slaves – literally whipped; their skin turns dark blue, and sometimes they just disappear. They do not know themselves what it is they produce, and the reader never discovers, though the obvious inference is chemical weapons or nuclear arms. It is a world apart, in which the harsh forces of violence and sudden death are opposed to the softer values of nurture and art of the women's house.

Witches are abroad in this novel too. It is set in Easter week, when there is a tradition that all the stoves must be cleaned out the night before Maundy Thursday, in order to destroy the witches' nests. But many forget, so the witches grow strong. Their strength empowers the women in the community, who begin to make decisions about their own lives. Those who had lost their children come at dead of night to carry them off. Gunhild collects her four-year old Marthe and takes refuge with her inside the greenhouse; after rescuing a witch with her nose stuck in a tree in true fairy-tale fashion, they find their way to the wild zone.[21] This has become a community of refugees from the world, including pin-up girls from the wall of the men's rest-room, who have escaped to try to find souls of their own:

> The forest grew dark, night birds cried, high and far off. Slowly the fires burnt down. Gunhild remained sitting with the wrapped-up child in her lap long after the others had gone into the caves to sleep.
>
> 'Just stay here if you want,' said the old woman as she got up and went to lie down too. 'There's no danger here.'
>
> There was no moon. The sky was black. The river was black. The ashes of the fire glowed on the sand.
> Marthe slept.[22]

The book does not end with an escape into idyll, however; the others must go on living in the real world. Vibeke and Finn must solve their tug of love over their children, and Marit has to have her child and cope with its need of a father. The novel ends with her shooting her pregnant cat, whose kittens have died in its womb. It is only in fairy tales that there is a happy ending; in real life there is grief and cruelty too, in the natural as well as the human world. The women need all their strength in order to preserve their own space, to find room for their souls to grow.

Mari Osmundsen's latest works have been less well received. She has written several children's books, and in 1986 came the short story anthology *Drageegget* (The Dragon's Egg), in which she moved completely into the world of fantasy, creating a mixture of *The Arabian Nights* and modern science fiction. *Arv* (Inheritance, 1988) is a novel about four grown-up children at their mother's funeral who suddenly realize that there must be a great deal of money hidden in the house, and set about searching for it. It is related in a more or less realistic vein (although the narrator intrudes now and then), with fine insights into the characters of the four heirs – until the last section, when the 'plot' is wound up, and the characters suddenly turn on the narrator to complain:

> 'But it can't end like that,' says Frøydis behind my back. . . . 'You haven't solved a single problem . . .'
>
> 'Can't you come back tomorrow instead?' I ask, 'It really isn't very convenient right now. I have to correct the whole manuscript tonight, and get it in the post tomorrow morning,' I explain, but it doesn't look as if they are in the mood to listen.
>
> 'The money,' says Sveinung harshly. 'That was a *rotten* thing to do. We need that money, all of us . . .'[23]

The narrator gets out of her tight corner in typical fashion: she endows them all with the gift of flight and sends them out through the window to swoop about as she sits down at her desk once more. Yet again Mari Osmundsen is playing with narrative viewpoint and with the expectations of the reader of fiction.

Thus the form in which Mari Osmundsen writes has spanned the whole gamut from social realism with a straightforward political message to free flights – literally – of fantasy. She has followed a general trend in moving from the political seventies to the fantastic eighties,[24] but she has also discovered a greater freedom in her writing as she has liberated herself from the constraints of party politics. Her works still demonstrate a political consciousness, but in a more general sense of a critical awareness of the conditions of life in late twentieth-century Norway and of the need to inject other values into a Western civilization which is crumbling from inside. Her most recently published novel, *Gutten som slo tida ihjel* (The Boy Who Killed Time, 1990), reinforces the need for other values by bringing into sharp contrast the lives of two women – one a terrified refugee from the Third World, the other an independent middle-class Norwegian who cannot imagine a world so different from her own safe normality.

Conclusion

From a British perspective, women in the Scandinavian countries enjoy considerably greater equality today in nearly all areas. They are better represented in public life, particularly at the top; they have stronger family and equal opportunity legislation. Literature is the one field in which the difference is less marked, as British women writers are as successful as the Scandinavian ones. In the twentieth century, Norway, Denmark and Sweden have developed the welfare state into an egalitarian society in which class differences have been minimized and the economically weaker members of society have been protected; this has had the effect of combating the disadvantages under which women laboured as an economically and politically oppressed group.

In Norway, it has been a long battle from a position of extreme weakness. Before 1880, women's voices were so quiet that they had difficulty being heard, and such public debate as occurred was largely conducted on their behalf by male champions. It is symptomatic of public attitudes that the Norwegian appeal for women's liberation which was heard all round Europe was Henrik Ibsen's *A Doll's House* (1879); the challenge of the slamming door still reverberates daily in theatres worldwide. By comparison, Camilla Collett's *The District Governor's Daughters* has had little impact abroad; but in Norway its importance has recently been recognized, and it has been placed alongside Ibsen's play not only as a historical document, but also as a psychological study and an aesthetic achievement.

After 1880, women became more visible both as writers and as campaigners, and began to find their own language; they moved from the fight for the right to be heard to aiming for specific political goals, and their writing mirrored the new freedoms opening to them. With greater autonomy came the dilemmas of choice, in an effort to reconcile the domestic with the public sphere; as the double moral standard lost its force, double work and double binds replaced it, and many literary heroines are presented with a stark choice between fulfilment in a career and fulfilment 'as a woman'. It is a dilemma which even modern reforms have not entirely solved.

Since the 1960s, society has become more open in many ways which have been good for women. Greater openness about physical sex has had a liberating effect on their writing, as has a relaxation of taboos in areas which were previously kept private and hidden, such as incest, sexual abuse and homosexuality. Women have created their own space. Both before and after Virginia Woolf defined it, the motif of 'a room of one's own' surfaces in the writings of nearly every Norwegian woman writer, as a primal need; but as well as a refuge, it can also be a restriction. As in Bjørg Vik's aquarium, women can become trapped in their rooms like fishes looking out of a tank and knocking against the glass; framed in their windows, they watch as life goes on outside. More and more, they are coming out of their rooms to wider, wilder spaces. As the Danish writer Suzanne Brøgger puts it:

> But since [Virginia Woolf] wrote those words, more and more women are finding out that a room is simply not enough!
> At any rate I don't want a room.
> Not in that house.
> Not with those house rules.
> I won't live in the square patriarchal room.
> I won't live in patriarchal linear time.
> I want the whole earth under my feet.
> Be on it
> Before I have to go under it.
> (in *No Man's Land*, ed. Annegret Heitmann, p. 111)

The patriarchal room opens up into a female landscape, as the patriarchal tongue yields to a multiplicity of female voices. Language is the last, the innermost bastion, the stronger because the assumptions it incarnates are often deeply below the level of consciousness; they have to be hauled to the surface before they can be tackled. That is why what Cecilie Løveid calls 'the distinctive ring of shattered language' is such a potent force in modern women's creative and critical writing, and Norwegian writers are joining in the shattering with glee.

Notes

All translations from Norwegian in this volume are my own, unless otherwise stated.

INTRODUCTION

1. T.K. Derry's *A History of Modern Norway 1814–1972* (1973) provides eloquent illustration of the invisibility of women in nineteenth-century Norwegian history. In line with my remarks about the historical role of literary figures, he accords central importance to writers like Wergeland, Ibsen and Bjørnson; but he mentions women only as wives, sisters and mothers – with the occasional actress. The single exception in the nineteenth century is Camilla Collett; *The District Governor's Daughters* merits a short paragraph.

2. See Richard J. Evans: *The Feminists* for a survey of the early feminist movements in different parts of the world.

3. 'One must recognize the central significance of the franchise in that it aroused the greatest opposition and mobilized the greatest consciousness and effort. Yet in many ways it was the red herring of the revolution – a wasteful drain on the energy of seventy years. Because the opposition was so monolithic and unrelenting, the struggle so long and bitter, the vote took on a disproportionate importance. And when the ballot was won, the feminist movement collapsed in what can only be described as exhaustion.' Kate Millett: *Sexual Politics*, pp. 83–4.

4. See Elisabeth Aasen (ed.): *Vår bestemmelse er å giftes* (Our Fate Is To Be Married); *Fra gamle dage* (From Olden Days); *Kvinners spor i skrift* (Women's Tracks in Writing); Irene Engelstad *et al.*(eds): *Norsk kvinnelitteraturhistorie* (A History of Norwegian Women's Writing), vols I–III.

5. See, for example, Irene Engelstad: *Sammenbrudd og gjennombrudd* (Breakdown and Breakthrough) (on Amalie Skram); Liv Bliksrud: *Natur og normer hos Sigrid Undset* (Nature and Norms in Sigrid Undset).

6. See Toril Moi: *Sexual/Textual Politics* for a fuller account of these two trends. Toril Moi is one of the Norwegian critics who most strongly espouses French theory, and has indeed written largely about French writers.

7. The only survey article in English of which I am aware is Janet Rasmussen's 'Dreams and Discontent: The Female Voice in Norwegian Literature', in Sverre Lyngstad (ed.): *Review of National Literatures 12: Norway*, pp. 123–40.

8. See my Bibliography, Section 3, for fuller details of recent editions.

PART I 1850–1913

CHAPTER 1 Finding a Voice

1. The town of Oslo was called Christiania/Kristiania until 1925.
2. For example in T.K. Derry: *A History of Modern Norway 1814–1972*, pp. 73–4.
3. Aagot Benterud: *Camilla Collett. En skjebne og et livsverk* (Camilla Collett. A Fate and a Life's Work), p.17 (quoting from C.W. Schnitler: *Slegten fra 1814*).
4. Much early women's writing has only recently been chronicled by Elisabeth Aasen in *Kvinners spor i skrift* and Irene Engelstad *et al.* in *Norsk kvinnelitteraturhistorie*, vol. I (1600–1900).
5. The biography of Aasta Hansteen, *Furier er også kvinner* (Furies Are Also Women), is a collaboration between five researchers in different fields, to cover her wide interests.
6. Anne Caspari Agerholt: *Den norske kvinnebevegelses historie* (The History of the Norwegian Women's Movement) charts the development of women's organizations in Norway.
7. See Harald and Edvard Beyer: *Norsk litteraturhistorie* (A History of Norwegian Literature), p. 217.
8. Quoted in Agerholt: *Den norske kvinnebevegelses historie*, p. 133.
9. In the most widely used single-volume literary history, Harald and Edvard Beyer's *Norsk litteraturhistorie* (last revised in 1978), Camilla Collett and Amalie Skram are the only two women before 1890 accorded separate entries. Camilla Collett merits just under two pages, Amalie Skram just over two – as against Henrik Wergeland's fourteen and Jonas Lie's five and a half. Magdalene Thoresen and Aasta Hansteen have two sentences each, and Laura Kieler is not mentioned.
10. For a collection of critical writings by women from this period, see Åse Hiorth Lervik's *Gjennom kvinneøyne* (Through Women's Eyes), vol. I, 1880–1930.
11. Frederick and Lise-Lone Marker's *History of the Scandinavian Theatre* does not mention any of the female dramatists discussed in this chapter.
12. There is some disagreement about the reception of *Aino*. Kari Gaader Losnedahl, in *Norsk kvinnelitteraturhistorie I*, maintains that the play was not a success, and quotes the negative comment of a male theatre historian; Elisabeth Aasen in *Kvinners spor i skrift*, says that it was enthusiastically received, and quotes a review from *Nylænde*. Perhaps quality was in the

eye of the beholder.

13. Quoted from the introduction to the 1953 edition of *Som kvinder er*, published by Aschehoug, pp. 11–12.

14. See Virginia Woolf: *A Room of One's Own*, pp. 46–8.

CHAPTER 2 Camilla Collett

1. All quotations from Camilla Collett's works are taken from *Samlede Verker* (= *SV*), her collected works in three volumes. Mindeudgave, Gyldendalske Boghandel (Nordisk Forlag), Kristiania and Copenhagen, 1912–13.

2. From *Mod Strømmen* I (Against the Current, 1879). *SV* III, p. 79.

3. Camilla Collett's early letters and diaries have been published in four volumes: Camilla Collett and P.J. Collett: *Dagbøker og Breve* (= *DB*), ed. Leif Amundsen (Gyldendal norsk forlag, Oslo 1926–33). The correspondence with Collett from 1838 to 1841 is in volume III: *Frigjørelsens Aar* (The Year of Liberation, 1932) and volume IV: *Før Bryllupet* (Before the Wedding, 1933).

4. 'En sen, men fornøden redegjørelse' ('A Late but Necessary Explanation'), published in *Nylænde*, 16 February 1895. *SV* III, pp. 499–500.

5. Kristian Elster the Younger: *Illustreret Norsk Litteraturhistorie* (Illustrated History of Norwegian Literature) II, p. 311. Francis Bull: *Norges Litteratur. Fra februarrevolusjonen til første verdenskrig* (Norwegian Literature: From the February Revolution to the First World War), p. 83.

6. Compare Gordon Haight's remark about Virginia Woolf: 'It is not too much to say that to him [Leonard Woolf] we owe the whole of her contribution to English literature.' (Review of Quentin Bell: *Virginia Woolf*, *Yale Review*, Spring 1973, p. 429.)

7. Camilla Collett's diaries from the 1830s were published as volume I of *Dagbøker og Breve: Optegnelser fra Ungdomsaarene* (Memoirs from the Early Years, 1926). Her letters from 1827 to 1838 were published as volume II: *Breve fra Ungdomsaarene* (Letters from the Early Years, 1930).

8. Otto Hageberg, in his essay on the novel in Sigurd Aa. Aarnes (ed.): *Søkelys på Amtmandens Døtre* (Spotlight on AD), points out how the action is always precipitated by minor characters; Kold and Sofie, who are meant to represent the potential for a true marriage, are paralysed by a passivity which makes them incapable of realizing the ideal in their own lives.

9. The third revised edition from 1879 is now accepted as the standard text, and is the one which is included in *Samlede Verker*. Apart from the addition of the preface, there are no major differences from the first edition.

10. For a full account of the critical reception of the novel and its place in contemporary literary history, see Ellisiv Steen: *Diktning og virkelighet* (Literature and Reality), pp. 265–85.

11. In 1848 the meeting of American women at Seneca Falls demanded the right to work, to equal pay and to universal suffrage.

12. According to Gyldendal publishers, the third edition of 1879 has been reprinted eleven times.

13. I am indebted for the next section of this chapter to the following articles: (a) Sigurd Aa. Aarnes: 'Grotte-symbolet i Camilla Colletts *Amtmandens Døtre*' ('The Grotto Symbol in AD', printed in *Søkelys på Amtmandens Døtre*); (b) Asbjørn Aarseth: 'Erotisk idealism i Camilla Colletts *Amtmandens Døtre*' ('Erotic Idealism in AD'); (c) Jorunn Hareide: 'Grottesymbolet nok en gang: En polemisk analyse av *Amtmandens Døtre*' ('The Grotto Symbol Again: A Polemical Analysis of AD').

14. See Aarseth, 'Erotisk idealism'.

15. See Hareide, 'Grottesymbolet nok en gang'.

16. The term 'female landscape' derives from Ellen Moers's *Literary Women*, in which the final chapter ('Metaphors: A Postlude') explores the concept as applied to various women writers.

17. See Jorunn Hareide: 'Forsøk på å lytte til "Grundtonen". Camilla Colletts selvbiografi *I de lange Nætter*' ('An Attempt to Listen to the "Undertone". CC's Autobiography *In the Long Nights*); Erik Østerud: 'Kjerringa mot strømmen. Camilla Colletts liv og forfatterskap' ('The Old Woman against the Current. CC's Life and Writings').

18. Maurice Gravier: 'Camilla Collett et la France', p. 51.

19. 'Like Henrik, Camilla had the ability to comprehend large things through the medium of the small.' Ellisiv Steen: *Den lange strid* (The Long Struggle), p. 18.

20. See, for example, Sandra M. Gilbert and Susan Gubar: *The Madwoman in the Attic*, chapter 1: 'The Queen's Looking Glass'.

21. For a fuller account of Camilla Collett's relationship with other Norwegian authors, see Janet Garton: 'Women of Letters: Nineteenth-century Norwegian Authors in their Correspondence'.

22. 'Mrs Collett is not a nice character, believe me', Bjørnson wrote to his publisher Hegel in 1857. See Steen: *Den lange strid*, p. 101.

23. Letter to Camilla Collett, 3 May 1889. In *The Oxford Ibsen*, vol. VII, p. 469, transl. J.W. McFarlane.

CHAPTER 3 Amalie Skram

1. A full account of Amalie Skram's early life and her family is given in Antonie Tiberg: *Amalie Skram som kunstner og menneske* (AS in Life and Work), and more recently in Liv Køltzow: *Den unge Amalie Skram* (The Young AS).

2. Quoted in Irene Engelstad: *Amalie Skram om seg selv* (AS About Herself),

pp. 21–4.

3. A selection of Amalie Skram's correspondence has been published as *Mellom slagene* (Between Battles), ed. Eugenia Kielland (Aschehoug, Oslo 1976).

4. Letter to Erik Skram, 31 January 1883; quoted in *Amalie Skram om seg selv*, p. 80.

5. A selection of Amalie Skram's literary criticism has been published under the title *Optimistisk Læsemaade* (Optimistic Readings), ed. Irene Engelstad (Gyldendal norsk forlag, Oslo 1987). This quotation is taken from that edition (p. 15).

6. Letter to Arne Garborg, 6 January 1885 (*Mellom slagene*, p. 70); letter to Peter Nansen, 22 December 1892 (*Mellom slagene*, p. 92).

7. Letter to Arne Garborg, 11 August 1885 (*Mellom slagene*, p. 74).

8. For a full account of the sexual morality debate and Amalie Skram's contribution to it, see Elias Bredsdorff: *Den store nordiske krig om seksualmoralen* (The Great Northern War of Sexual Morality).

9. *Optimistisk Læsemaade*, p. 91.

10. All quotations from Amalie Skram's fictional works are taken from *Samlede Verker* (= *SV*), her collected works in six volumes (fifth edition, Gyldendal, Oslo 1976).

11. See her letter to Professor Ernst Sars, 29 May 1881 (*Mellom slagene*, pp. 46–7).

12. 'What a ridiculous suggestion it was, to want to employ a woman in a position like that.' Letter to Bjørnson, 7 July 1892. Quoted in the edition of Amalie Skram and Bjørnson's correspondence, *Brevvekslingen mellom Bjørnstjerne Bjørnson og Amalie Skram*, ed. Øyvind Anker and Edvard Beyer (Gyldendal norsk forlag, Oslo 1982) (p. 64).

13. See Note 12. For a fuller investigation of Amalie Skram as a letter-writer, see Janet Garton: 'Women of Letters: Nineteenth-century Norwegian Authors in their Correspondence.'

14. Anne-Lisa Amadou: 'Madame Bovary i Constance Ring'.

15. 'Om *Albertine*' (About *Albertine*), in *Optimistisk Læsemaade*, pp. 101–11 (p. 110).

16. *Mellom slagene*, p. 83.

17. Letter to Bjørnson, 19 January 1899; *Brevveksling mellom Bjørnstjerne Bjørnson og Amalie Skram*, p. 127.

18. See Lene Tybjærg Schacke: 'Edvard Brandes og Amalie Skram'.

19. See Amalie Skram's article 'Optimistisk Læsemaade', in *Optimistisk Læsemaade*, p. 68.

20. Letter to Erik Skram, 15 September 1882; quoted in *Amalie Skram om seg selv*, p. 123.

21. See Elaine Showalter's discussion of 'the pervasive cultural association of women and madness' in the introduction to *The Female Malady* (p. 4). Gilbert

and Gubar: *The Madwoman in the Attic* develops the same idea differently.

22. Letter to Bjørnson, 22 April 1984; *Brevveksling mellom Bjørnstjerne Bjørnson og Amalie Skram*, p. 93.

23. Amalie Skram and Viggo Hørup's letters are collected in *Hørup i breve og digte* (Hørup in Letters and Poems), ed. Karsten Thorborg (Akademisk forlag, Copenhagen 1981).

24. Letter to Hørup, 12 August 1898; ibid., p. 345.

25. *Mennesker* is not a part of Amalie Skram's collected works; it was published in 1905, and reprinted by Pax forlag, Oslo 1976.

26. *Landsforrædere* (Gyldendalske boghandel, Copenhagen 1901), p. 7.

27. Erik Skram's letter to Amalie, 22 January 1883, quoted in *Amalie Skram om seg selv*, p. 200.

28. See Tybjærg Schacke: 'Edvard Brandes og Amalie Skram', p. 270.

29. See particularly Irene Engelstad's study of Amalie Skram's novels, *Sammenbrudd og gjennombrudd* (Breakdown and Breakthrough).

30. Letter to Peter Nansen, 8 January 1905 (*Mellom slagene*, pp. 157–8).

CHAPTER 4 Ragnhild Jølsen

1. Magdalene Thoresen published her first book at the age of forty-one and lived to be eighty-four; Aasta Hansteen published at thirty-eight and also lived to eighty-four. Of Ragnhild Jølsen's nearer contemporaries, Nini Roll Anker produced her major works after she was forty (she lived to be sixty-nine) and Sigrid Undset, although she published her first novel at the age of twenty-five, had a writing career lasting over thirty years. Cora Sandel's debut came when she was forty-six.

2. The first biography of Ragnhild Jølsen, Antonie Tiberg's *Ragnhild Jølsen i liv og digtning* (Life and Work of RJ), which was published only a year after her death, admits the fact of these affairs but understandably does not name names. Kari Christensen's *Portrett på mørk treplate* (Portrait on a Dark Wood Panel, 1989) provides biographical documentation and supplies evidence from the letters which have survived.

3. *RF* = Ragnhild Jølsen: *Romaner og fortellinger* (Novels and Stories), published in one volume (Aschehoug, Oslo 1988). Apart from her five completed books, it includes a collection of *Posthumous Writings*, published and unpublished shorter pieces edited by Antonie Tiberg. All quotations from Ragnhild Jølsen's works are taken from this volume.

4. In Kari Christensen's psychological analysis of this novel in *Portrett på mørk treplate*, the whole farm is interpreted as a metaphor for a woman's body, with its secret rooms and sealed-off passages in which little dead children are concealed.

5. Helge Nordahl, in his article 'Rytme og repetisjon. Noen tanker om sprogkunstneren Ragnhild Jølsen' ('Rhythm and Repetition. Some Thoughts about the Verbal Artistry of RJ'), has pointed out the similarity between her style and that of the Swedish author Selma Lagerlöf, who also wrote nostalgically of a lost family estate.

6. From Astrid Lorenz's postscript to the 1981 edition of *Rikka Gan*, reprinted in *Romaner og fortellinger*, pp. 186–201 (p. 194).

7. For example, Tiberg: *Ragnhild Jølsen i liv og digtning*, pp. 124–5; Astrid Lorenz: 'Kjærligheten og virkeligheten. Ragnhild Jølsens *Hollases krønike* som kvinnespeil' ('Love and Reality. RJ's *Hollases krønike* as a Women's Mirror'), p. 18.

8. For example, Per Amdam: 'En ny realisme. Historie og samtid' ('A New Realism. History and the Present'), in Edvard Beyer (ed.): *Norges litteraturhistorie*, vol. IV, p. 304.

9. Kari Christensen, in *Portrett på mørk treplate*, suggests that Ragnhild Jølsen's visit to Cologne for several months in 1896 may have been in order to bear Halvor Wiborg's child, and quotes circumstantial evidence from more than one source to the effect that the family was later informed that Ragnhild Jølsen had a daughter in Denmark. This story, if it is true, would give extra poignancy to her later descriptions of murdered babies.

10. 'Ragnhild Jølsen – romantiker og realist' ('RJ – Romantic and Realist'), in Jens Bjørneboe: *Bøker og mennesker* (Books and People), p. 201.

11. From a review by Anders Stiloff, quoted in Tiberg: *Ragnhild Jølsen i liv og digtning*, p. 101.

12. Review in *Aftenposten* 15 December 1907, quoted in Olav Solberg: 'Realisme eller romantikk, kontinuitet eller brot? – Ragnhild Jølsens *Brukshistorier*' ('Realism or Romanticism, Continuity or Break?'), p. 3.

PART II 1913–60

CHAPTER 5 On the Back Burner

1. See, for example, Nini Roll Anker: *Under skraataket* (Under the Sloping Roof, 1927); Nordahl Grieg: *Vår ære og vår makt* (Our Power and Our Glory, 1935). Both works contrast the unscrupulousness of shipowners and speculators with the harsh life of sailors and workers.

2. See 'Nansen, the Representative Norwegian', in T.K. Derry: *A History of Modern Norway 1814–1972*, pp. 336–41.

3. See Knut Mykland (ed.): *Norges historie* I–XV.

4. Anna Caspari Agerholt: *Den norske kvinnebevegelses historie*, ed. Kari Skjønsberg (1973), p. 8.

5. Irene Iversen: 'Det seierrige 20. aarhundrede' ('The Triumphant Twentieth Century'), in Irene Engelstad *et al.* (eds): *Norsk kvinnelitteraturhistorie*, vol. 2: 1900–45, p. 9.

6. Richard J. Evans: *The Feminists*, pp. 227–8.

7. Kate Millett's attack on Freud is countered by Juliet Mitchell in her study *Psychoanalysis and Feminism*, which argues that the popular view of Freud as an anti-feminist rests on a distortion of his views by his followers; he is not recommending a patriarchal society, but investigating its effects.

8. For an assessment of the work of Katti Anker Møller and other pioneers, see Kari Skjønsberg (ed.): *Mannssamfunnet midt imot. Norsk kvinnesaksdebatt gjennom tre 'mannsaldre'* (In Opposition to Male Society. Norwegian Liberation Debate through Three Generations).

9. For a fuller history of the Norwegian debate on abortion in the 1930s, see Arne Stai: *Norsk kultur- og moraldebatt i 1930–årene* (Norwegian Cultural and Moral Debates in the 1930s), pp. 100–11.

10. See Carl Joachim Hambro's review of *Den som henger i en tråd* in the conservative newspaper *Morgenbladet* (quoted by Willy Dahl in *Norges litteratur* [Norway's Literature] II, p. 394).

11. Knud Poulsen in the Danish newspaper *Politiken*; these and other similar comments are quoted by Willy Dahl in *Norges litteratur* II, p. 393.

12. For a fuller account of the debates and their background, see Stai: *Norsk kultur- og moraldebatt i 1930–årene*.

13. Leif Longum's study of Norwegian cultural radicalism between the wars, *Drømmen om det frie menneske* (The Dream of a Free Man), makes sparse reference to contributions by women. When he was challenged on this issue, he commented: 'It is a fact that very few women participated in the form of cultural debate on which I am concentrating. . . . Their criticism [Undset, Sandel] is hardly ever given expression in articles and contributions to the debate. . . . When it comes to the women who were actually members of the group around the radical trio, such as Nic Waal (the model for Evelyn in *Syndere i sommersol* [Sigurd Hoel]) – I could have said more about them, but the problem is again that there is little documentary evidence to build on.' (Private letter, 22 January 1988.)

14. For a full account of lesbian love in Scandinavian literature, see Gerd Brantenberg *et al.*: *På sporet av den tapte lyst* (On the Scent of Lost Desire).

15. Sigurd Aa. Aarnes: *Bok og lesar* (Book and Reader) includes an essay by Inger Lise Breivik on the history of *Urd*.

16. See Gerd Stahl's essay 'Dramatikken og teaterets maskineri' ('Dramatic Writing and the Machinery of the Theatre'), in *Norsk kvinnelitteraturhistorie* II, pp. 146–52.

17. Willy Dahl: *Norges litteratur* II, p. 361.

18. For a more detailed account of the effects of the occupation on literature in

Norway, see Janet Mawby: *Writers and Politics in Modern Scandinavia*.

19. Henry Notaker's collection of Resistance poetry, *Reis ingen monumenter* (Build No Monuments), devotes 61 of its 83 pages of poetry to the three major male poets. Of the other seven poets included, two are women: Inger Hagerup (3 poems) and Halldis Moren Vesaas (6).

20. See Elizabeth Rokkan: 'Cora Sandel and the Second World War', in *Scandinavica* vol.28, no. 2, November 1989, pp. 155–60.

21. See Torill Steinfeld: 'Med sans for hverdagslivets fenomener' ('A Feeling for the Stuff of Everyday Life'), in *Norsk kvinnelitteraturhistorie* III, pp. 53–9.

22. I am indebted for these figures to Willy Dahl: *Norges litteratur* III, p. 159.

23. 'Melodi' ('Melody'), from Gunvor Hofmo: *Samlede dikt* (Collected Poems) (Gyldendal, Oslo 1968), p. 13.

24. See Kari Skjønsberg (ed.): *Hvor var kvinnene? Elleve kvinner om årene 1945–60* (Where Were the Women? Eleven Women Speak about the Years 1945–60).

CHAPTER 6 Sigrid Undset

1. *Elleve år* is reprinted in Sigrid Undset: *Selvbiografiske skrifter* (Autobiographical Writings) (Aschehoug, Oslo 1989), pp. 9–10.

2. See my discussion of the grotto scenes in Camilla Collett's *The District Governor's Daughters* in Chapter 2. Nancy Friday's *My Mother My Self* is a study of the relationship between mothers and daughters, and of mothers' unwillingness to acknowledge their daughters' sexuality.

3. Gidske Anderson: *Sigrid Undset – et liv* (Sigrid Undset – A Life), pp. 61–2.

4. Virginia Woolf: *A Writer's Diary*, ed. Leonard Woolf, p. 135.

5. *Kjære Dea* (Dear Dea, in *Selvbiografiske skrifter*; see Note 1), p. 300.

6. Ibid., p. 407.

7. Sigrid Undset's novels and stories of contemporary life are collected in *Romaner og fortellinger fra nutiden (RFN)*, vols I–X (Aschehoug, Oslo 1964).

8. Gidske Anderson's account of the importance of this relationship for Sigrid Undset's writing, though dramatically expressed, is not without foundation: 'It is out of this experience of love and sexuality that Undset the author creates her great love novels. Only someone who has had a deep sexual experience can write the story of Kristin and Erlend, or the story of Jenny's temptations between father and son. From now on there is something earthy and full-blooded about her characters, in addition to the already strong sensuality. Sigrid's passionate nature has been overtaken by earthly love.' (*Sigrid Undset – et liv*, p. 181.)

9. Sandra M. Gilbert and Susan Gubar: *The Madwoman in the Attic. The Woman Writer and the Nineteenth-Century Imagination*. See especially Chapter 1: 'The

Queen's Looking Glass: Female Creativity, Male Images of Women, and the Metaphor of Literary Paternity'.

10. Sigrid Undset: *Et kvinnesynspunkt* (Aschehoug, Oslo 1982), pp. 67, 83.

11. Gidske Anderson: *Sigrid Undset – et liv*, p. 237.

12. Sigrid Undset: *Kristin Lavransdatter* I–III (Aschehougs fontenebøker, Oslo 1964). *Husfrue*, p. 376.

13. This argument is developed with reference to English society by Christine Fell: *Women in Anglo-Saxon England and the Impact of 1066*.

14. For a detailed account of the work's relationship to historical fact, and the authenticity of its settings, see Ellisiv Steen: *Kristin Lavransdatter. En estetisk studie* (Kristin Lavransdatter. An Aesthetic Study).

15. *Urd* no. 22, 1910, p. 254.

16. See Liv Bliksrud: *Natur og normer hos Sigrid Undset* (Nature and Norms in SU), pp. 257–60.

17. In her biography, Gidske Anderson suggests that this was a conscious sacrifice: 'I feel that Sigrid Undset consciously sacrificed the dearest thing she owned, her one true great possession: her art.' (*Sigrid Undset – et liv*, p. 329.)

18. See Janet Rasmussen's bibliography of research into Norwegian women's writing 1955–80, published in Åse Hiorth Lervik: *Gjennom kvinneøyne* (Through Women's Eyes), vol. II. Critical writings on Sigrid Undset take up three pages of this bibliography; the only nearly comparable authors are Amalie Skram and Cora Sandel, with two pages each.

CHAPTER 7 Cora Sandel

1. The only other Norwegian author I am aware of who is known exclusively by her pseudonym is the contemporary Mari Osmundsen.

2. Letter quoted in Odd Solumsmoen: *Cora Sandel: en dikter i ånd og sannhet* (Cora Sandel: A Writer in Spirit and in Truth), p. 191.

3. Interview in *Arbeidermagasinet*, the magazine of the left-wing newspaper *Arbeiderbladet*, no. 2, 1939.

4. My main sources of information are Odd Solumsmoen's book (see Note 2) and Janneken Øverland: *Cora Sandel om seg selv* (CS About Herself).

5. *Dyr jeg har kjent* (Animals I Have Known), *Samlede verker* V, pp. 232–4. All quotations from Cora Sandel's fiction are taken from the edition of her collected works, *Samlede verker* (= *SV*), vols I–VI (Gyldendal, Oslo 1950–51).

6. Some of Harriet Backer's paintings are reproduced in *Smiles of a Summer Night*, published by the Arts Council, London 1986.

7. Odd Solumsmoen: *Cora Sandel*, p. 98.

8. Letter to Nini Roll Anker, 31 July 1935, quoted in Janneken Øverland: *Cora Sandel om seg selv*, p. 132.

9. Quoted by Odd Solumsmoen: *Cora Sandel*, p. 123.

10. Both these stories were later printed in the collection *En blå sofa* (A Blue Sofa), to which reference is made here.

11. The best detective work on the time scale of the trilogy has been done by Åse Hiorth Lervik in *Menneske og miljø i Cora Sandels diktning* (People and Places in CS's Fiction), pp. 234–6.

12. Letter to Peter Owen, 16 September 1962; reprinted in Janneken Øverland: *Cora Sandel om seg selv*, p. 212.

13. *Barnet som elsket veier*, ed. Steinar Gimnes (Gyldendal, Oslo 1973). Of the stories which have been translated into English, most of the ones I have discussed are included in the anthology *Selected Short Stories*, transl. Barbara Wilson: 'The Child Who Loved Roads', 'The Ways of Love', 'Shit-Katrine', 'Klara', 'The Sisters', 'A Mystery', 'Thank You, Doctor', 'The Art of Murder' and 'To Lucas'. 'There's a War On' is included in the anthology *The Silken Thread*, transl. Elizabeth Rokkan, and 'Cousin Thea' in *Slaves of Love*, transl. James McFarlane (see Bibliography).

14. This story is a somewhat later one, being first published in *Kvinnen og tiden* (Women and Time) in 1947 and later included in *Barnet som elsket veier*; but in theme it is similar to many of the earlier stories.

15. Jante is the setting for many of Sandemose's novels, particularly *En flyktning krysser sitt spor* (A Fugitive Crosses His Tracks, 1933), where the ten commandments of Jante are spelt out:

    1. You shall not believe that you *are* anything.
    2. You shall not believe that you are as much as *us*.
    3. You shall not believe that you are cleverer than *us*.
    4. You shall not imagine that you are better than *us*.
    5. You shall not believe that you know more than *us*.
    6. You shall not believe that you are more than *us*.
    7. You shall not believe that *you* are any good.
    8. You shall not laugh at *us*.
    9. You shall not believe that anyone cares about *you*.
    10. You shall not believe that you can teach *us* anything.

16. 'Stivhatten' is a nickname, translated by Elizabeth Rokkan as 'Bowler Hat'.

17. Åse Hiorth Lervik: *Menneske og miljø i Cora Sandels diktning*, p. 196.

CHAPTER 8 Halldis Moren Vesaas

1. This is a claim which it is difficult to substantiate in a study based on translated material; but *nynorsk* contains more words which sound poetic to a Norwegian ear, as well as certain grammatical features such as a

single-syllable present tense (without the weak ending -er) which provides 'strong' rhyming words.

2. If she had not married Tarjei Vesaas, she later commented: 'I believe that I would have written more. It does throw your own talent into relief when you live so close to a really *great* writer.' Interview with Knut Faldbakken, *Vinduet* 2, 1975, p. 4.

3. Ibid., p. 2.

4. See Willy Dahl: *Norges litteratur* III, p. 361.

5. Otto Hageberg: 'Halldis – ei talskvinne for mange' ('Halldis – A Spokeswoman for Many'), in Leif Mæhle (ed.): *Halldis Moren Vesaas. Festskrift til 80-årsdagen 18. november 1987*, a volume of essays presented to Halldis Moren Vesaas on her eightieth birthday.

6. From the introduction to a selection of her poems, *Ord over grind* (Words over the Gate) (Den norske bokklubben, Oslo 1965), p. 4.

7. All quotations from Halldis Moren Vesaas's poems are taken from her collected poems, *Dikt i samling* (= *DS*) (Aschehoug, Oslo 1977).

8. For example, Mari Beinset Waagaard: 'Halldis Moren Vesaas', p. 41.

9. See the interview with Knut Faldbakken in the introduction to *Dikt i samling*, p. 13.

10. See David McDuff's translations of Edith Södergran's *Complete Poems* (Bloodaxe Books, Newcastle upon Tyne 1984), p. 55.

11. Interview with Knut Faldbakken (see Note 9), pp. 13–14.

12. For an analysis of the picture of rural Norway in Halldis Moren Vesaas's poetry, see the essay by Henning Sehmsdorf: 'The Poetry of Halldis Moren Vesaas and Tradition', in Leif Mæhle (ed.): *Halldis Moren Vesaas*.

13. The poem 'No plantar kvinna – ' ('Now the Woman is Planting – ') was written later than 1945, but included as a finale to *Tung tids tale* by the poet in her collected poems.

14. From the introduction to *Ord over grind*, p. 4.

15. Ibid., p. 3.

16. The bibliography in the *Festskrift* for her eightieth birthday records forty translated plays performed between 1940 and 1986.

17. *Hildegunn* (Aschehoug, Oslo 1942), p. 174.

18. *Sett og levd* (Aschehoug, Oslo 1967), p. 141.

19. Interview with Knut Faldbakken (see Note 9), pp. 19–20.

20. *I Midtbøs bakkar* (Aschehoug, Oslo 1974), p. 83.

21. *Båten om dagen* (Aschehoug, Oslo 1976), p. 60.

22. *Sett og levd*, p. 63.

23. *Så nær deg* (Aschehoug, Oslo 1987), p. 41.

24. Private letter, 10 September 1990.

25. Kore is the original name of Persephone, the daughter of the Greek goddess Demeter who was abducted by the god of the underworld and who was so

mourned by her mother that earth was covered in perpetual winter until they were reunited.

26. *Sett og levd*, p. 63.

PART III 1960–90

CHAPTER 9 The Personal is Political

1. From a conversation with a German friend, reported in an article in the German newspaper *Neue Freie Presse*, 1902.
2. T.K. Derry: *A History of Modern Norway 1814–1972*, p. 447.
3. *Our Common Future*, produced by the World Commission on Environment and Development chaired by Gro Harlem Brundtland (Oxford University Press, Oxford and New York 1987).
4. Leidulv Namtvedt (ed.): *Mini-facts about Norway 1990–91*. p. 17.
5. Ibid., p. 41.
6. Helga Maria Hernes: *Welfare State and Woman Power*. p. 27.
7. See Kari Skjønsberg (ed.): *Mannssamfunnet midt imot. Norsk kvinnesaksdebatt gjennom tre 'mannsaldre'*. (Against the Masculine Society. Debates of the Norwegian Women's Movement through Three Generations.)
8. See Randi Øverland: 'Den nye kvinnebevegelsen i Norge' ('The New Women's Movement in Norway'), in Kari Vogt *et al.* (eds): *Kvinnenes kulturhistorie* (A Cultural History of Women) vol. II, pp. 343–7.
9. Para. 1: The Aim of the Law; in *The Equal Status Act. Complete Text and Notes for Guidance*. Published by Likestillingsombudet, Oslo (not dated, but it includes amendments up to May 1988), p. 6.
10. See Tove Stang Dahl: *Women's Law*; especially the chapter 'Why Women's Law?', pp. 11–25.
11. Dahl, ibid.; Torild Skard and Elina Haavio-Mannila: 'Equality between the Sexes – Myth or Reality in Norden?', in Stephen R. Graubard (ed.): *Norden – The Passion for Equality*, Chapter 8.
12. Statistics from 'Mini-fakta om likestilling' ('Mini-facts about Equality'), a brochure published by *Likestillingsrådet*, 1989.
13. See Elina Haavio-Mannila: 'The Position of Women', in Erik Allardt *et al.* (eds): *Nordic Democracy*, pp. 555–88.
14. For a fuller discussion of the *Profil* authors, see Janet Garton: 'New Directions in Norwegian Literature', in Sverre Lyngstad (ed.): *Review of National Literatures 12: Norway*, pp. 163–84; and the same author's 'Dag Solstad and *Profil*', in Janet Garton (ed.): *Facets of European Modernism*, pp. 349–65. I have also translated some of Dag Solstad's short fiction in E.S. Shaffer (ed.): *Comparative Criticism*, vol.6 (Cambridge University Press, Cambridge 1984), pp. 229–55.

15. See Claire Duchen: *Feminism in France. From May '68 to Mitterrand*, pp. 7–8.

16. Interview with Knut Faldbakken in *Vinduet* 2, 1975, p. 3.

17. Solveig Christov: *Korsvei i jungelen* (Gyldendal, Oslo 1959), p. 113.

18. See Toril Moi's account of French feminist theory in *Sexual/Textual Politics*, Part II.

19. Solveig Christov: *Elskerens hjemkomst* (Gyldendal, Oslo 1961), pp. 181–4.

20. See Bjørg Vik's interview with Knut Faldbakken, *Vinduet* 1, 1976, pp. 53–7.

21. Willy Dahl: *Norges litteratur* III, p. 259.

22. For example, Dag Solstad: *Arild Asnes 1970* (1971); Espen Haavardsholm: *Zink* (Zinc, 1971); Tor Obrestad: *Sauda! Streik!* (Sauda! Strike!, 1972).

23. Liv Køltzow: *Hvem har ditt ansikt?* (Aschehoug, Oslo 1988), p. 252.

24. Bergljot Hobæk Haff: *Heksen* (Gyldendal, Oslo 1974), p. 63.

25. Gerd Brantenberg *et al.*: *På sporet av den tapte lyst* (On the Track of Lost Desire) traces the history of lesbian love in Scandinavian literature. The authors list only two Norwegian books with lesbianism as a major theme before 1970: Borghild Krane's *Følelsers forvirring* (Confused Feelings, 1937) and Ebba Haslund's *Det hendte ingenting* (Nothing Happened, 1948). In contrast, there are seven Danish and fifteen Swedish books.

26. Tove Nilsen: *Den svarte gryte* (Forlaget Oktober, Oslo 1985), p. 34.

27. See, for example, the analyses of nineteenth-century literature in Sandra M. Gilbert and Susan Gubar: *The Madwoman in the Attic*.

28. 'Spåkvinner, trollkjerringer – og trollmenn' ('Prophetesses, Sorceresses – and Sorcerers'), in *Skjebneveven*, Grøndahl & Søn Forlag, Oslo 1982), pp. 66–78.

29. 'Trø meg ikkje på tærne' from *Falle og reise seg att* (Gyldendal norsk forlag, Oslo 1980), p. 41.

30. See, for example, Åse Hiorth Lervik (ed.): *Kvinneaspekter i humanistisk forskning* (Feminist Aspects of Research in the Humanities), the report of a conference held in Oslo in May 1976.

31. See Toril Moi: *Sexual/Textual Politics* for an explanation of the two schools.

32. See, for example, Irene Engelstad and Irene Iversen: 'Tre tilnærmingsmåter til kvinnelitteraturen' ('Three Methods of Approach to Women's Writing'), in Mai Bente Bonnevie *et al.*: *Et annet språk* (A Different Language); and Irene Engelstad: *Sammenbrudd og gjennombrudd* (on Amalie Skram).

33. According to *Norsk teaterårbok 1975* (Norwegian Theatre Yearbook 1975), eds Tor Åge Bringsværd and Halldis Hoaas, pp. 34–41.

34. Eldrid Lunden: *hard, mjuk* (Det Norske Samlaget, Oslo 1976), p. 49.

35. Eldrid Lunden: *Gjenkjennelsen* (Recognition) (Det Norske Samlaget, Oslo 1982), p. 67.

36. 'Målsyn og kvinnesyn' ('View of Language – View of Women'), in *Essays* (Det Norske Samlaget, Oslo 1982), pp. 9–18.

37. See Øystein Rottem: *Fantasiens tiår*, a collection of articles and reviews of new literature published in the 1980s (Aschehoug, Oslo 1990).
38. Toril Brekke: *The Jacaranda Flower*, transl. Anne Born (Methuen, London 1987), p. 17.
39. (Male) political autobiographers have done exceptionally well: Einar Gerhardsen topped the best-seller list in 1978, Trygve Bratteli in 1980, Jo Benkow in 1985. See chart in Willy Dahl: *Norges litteratur* III, p. 278.
40. According to the 'New Books 1990' lists of the two largest Norwegian publishers, women wrote 11 of the 36 new works of fiction/drama/poetry for one (Gyldendal) and 14 of 31 for the other (Aschehoug).

CHAPTER 10 Bjørg Vik

1. See the interview with Knut Faldbakken in *Vinduet* 1, 1976, p. 56.
2. Interview with Inger Bentzrud, *Dagbladet*, 25 October 1985.
3. See the interview with Arngeir Berg and Espen Haavardsholm in *Partiskhet* (Taking Sides), p. 79.
4. The title of this story is a quotation from a Swedish student song.
5. *Søndag ettermiddag* (Cappelen, Oslo 1963), p. 182.
6. *Nødrop fra en myk sofa* (Cappelen, Oslo 1966), p. 7.
7. *Det grådige hjerte* (Cappelen, Oslo 1968), p. 81.
8. Interview with Knut Faldbakken (see Note 1), p. 54.
9. *Gråt elskede mann* (Cappelen, Oslo 1970), p. 68.
10. See Janneken Øverland: 'Kvinneroller – tilpasning eller opprør? Om Vigdis Stokkeliens og Bjørg Viks forfatterskap' ('Women's Roles – Adaptation or Rebellion? About the Writings of Vigdis Stokkelien and Bjørg Vik'), in Helge Rønning (ed.): *Linjer i norsk prosa* (Directions in Norwegian Prose).
11. This story has proved a fruitful source of Freudian and other interpretations. Irene Engelstad wrote a structuralist analysis using the methods of Greimas and Lévi-Strauss (in Irene Engelstad and Janneken Øverland: *Frihet til å skrive*, 1981, pp. 205–16). Toril Moi supplemented this with an analysis using methods derived from Lacan's structural psychoanalysis and Derrida's deconstructionism ('Fra skogen til skrivepulten eller faren ved den kvinnelige kreativitet' – 'From the Forest to the Writing Desk or the Dangers of Female Creativity' – in Irene Engelstad [ed.]: *Skriften mellom linjene* [Writing Between the Lines]).
12. Quotations from *An Aquarium of Women* are taken from my translation (see Bibliography).
13. From the interview in *Partiskhet* (see Note 3), p. 85.
14. Ibid., pp. 87–9.
15. *To akter for fem kvinner* (Cappelen, Oslo 1974), pp. 48–9.

16. *Fortellinger om frihet* (Den norske bokklubben, Oslo 1975), p. 10.

17. Liv Riiser: 'Småjenteskildringer i noveller av Sigrid Undset og Bjørg Vik' ('The description of girls in short stories by SU and BV'), in Anne-Cathrine Andersen *et al.* (eds): *Fra barn til kvinne* (From Child to Woman). Sigrid Undset's 'Småpiker' comes from her short-story anthology from 1918, *De kloge jomfruer* (The Wise Virgins). See Chapter 6.

18. For example, interview with Knut Faldbakken, *Vinduet* 1, 1976; interview with Astrid Brekken, *Sirene* 1, 1977.

19. Jofrid Eriksson: 'To akter for fem kvinner', *Kjerringråd* 2, 1975, p. 13.

20. *Dagbladet*, 11 July 1981.

21. *En håndfull lengsel* (Cappelen, Oslo 1979), p. 62.

22. For a detailed textual analysis of this story, see Janet Garton: 'Billedbruken i Bjørg Viks novelle "Rosa og Ruth"' ('The Use of Imagery in BV's story "Rosa and Ruth"'). I have also written a study of the collection as a whole: 'Om å snuble i sine egne lengsler' ('Tripping over One's Own Longings').

23. The radio version of *Døtre* was printed in a collection of five of Bjørg Vik's radio plays, *Det trassige håp* (Defiant Hope) (Cappelen, Oslo 1981). The English translation was printed in *New Norwegian Plays*, 1989, from which this quotation is taken (p. 56).

24. Soria Moria is the name of a cinema – but it is also the Norwegian name for the fairy-tale castle of happy-ever-after. A version of this play was shown on Norwegian television in 1983, entitled *Epleblomster og likør* (Apple-blossom and liqueur).

25. *Snart er det høst* (Cappelen, Oslo 1982), p. 202.

26. *Små nøkler store rom* (Cappelen, Oslo 1988), p. 105.

27. Elsi's story is continued in a sequel, *Poplene på St. Hanshaugen* (The Poplars on St Hanshaugen, 1991).

CHAPTER 11 Cecilie Løveid

1. Interview with Henry Notaker, 18 May 1990.

2. Interview in *Klassekampen*, 4 August 1990.

3. Interview with Henry Notaker (see Note 1).

4. See, for example, Hélène Cixous: 'The Laugh of the Medusa', *Signs*, Summer 1976.

5. Interview with Knut Faldbakken, *Vinduet* 2, 1977. p. 14.

6. Ibid.

7. Anne Marie Müller explores in detail the literary allusions in *Most* in her article 'Opplevelse og estetikk. Om komposisjonen og bildebruk i Cecilie Løveids roman *Most*.' ('Experience and Aesthetics. On the Composition and Imagery of Cecilie Løveid's novel *Most*.')

8. *Most*, reprinted in *Befri vårt daglige liv* (Free Our Daily Life) (Gyldendal, Oslo 1978), p. 75.

9. See, for example, the chapter on female images, 'Metaphors: a postlude', in Ellen Moers: *Literary Women*.

10. Irene Engelstad, Jofrid Eriksson and Irene Iversen: 'Myter og erfaring – undertrykkelsens mønstre vist av fire kvinnelige forfattere' ('Myths and Experience – the Pattern of Repression in the Works of Four Women Authors'), *Kontrast* 7, 1973, pp. 8–26.

11. Anne Marie Müller (see Note 7), p. 147.

12. *Alltid skyer over Askøy* (Gyldendal, Oslo 1976), p. 38.

13. See Kari Christensen: 'Den særegne klangen av knust språk' ('The Distinctive Ring of Shattered Language').

14. *Fanget villrose* (Gyldendal, Oslo 1977), p. 54.

15. Interview with Knut Faldbakken (see Note 5), p. 14.

16. The passage is taken from the beginning of Chapter 11 of *To the Lighthouse*, p. 72 in the Penguin Modern Classics edition (1964).

17. *Sug* (Gyldendal, Oslo 1979), p. 29.

18. See Julia Kristeva's investigation of the repercussions of Lacan's Symbolic Order for woman's identity in *La Révolution du langage poétique*, 1974.

19. For a fuller comparison of these two poems, see Janneken Øverland: 'Hva gjør du i min åker?' ('What are you doing in my field?').

20. From a lecture delivered at the University of East Anglia, Norwich, on 10 April 1991.

21. For further discussion of this problem, see Janet Garton: 'Is There Any New Norwegian Drama?', in *Norwegian Literature*, special issue of *The Norseman*, September 1990, pp. 76–80.

22. The three plays *Du, bli her!* (You, stay here!), *Måkespisere* and *Vinteren revner* were printed together in a volume called *Måkespisere* (Gyldendal, Oslo 1983).

23. See Virginia Woolf: *A Room of One's Own*, pp. 46–8.

24. The quotation is from Henning Sehmsdorff's translation, *New Norwegian Plays*, p. 293.

25. Review by Sissel Lange-Nielsen: 'Fritt efter Schønberg Erken' ('Freely Adapted from Schønberg Erken'), *Aftenposten*, 13 April 1982.

26. See Sigrun Borgersen's article 'På kant med genrene. Cecilie Løveids dramatikk' ('Inbetween Genres. CL's Plays').

27. Erik Pierstorff: 'Et rop om kjærlighet' ('A Cry for Love'), *Dagbladet*, 6 January 1983.

28. Quoted by Cecilie Løveid in an interview with Inger Bentzrud, *Dagbladet*, 15 October 1983.

29. *Balansedame* (Gyldendal, Oslo 1984).

30. For an account of the Swedish and Norwegian productions of the play

and the critical reception, see Knut Ove Arntzen: 'Cecilie Løveid og *Balansedame*', *Spillerom* 3, 1986, pp. 28–30.

31. 'Min personlige nedtur' ('My Personal Bad Trip'), interview with Kai Douglas Johnsen, *Spillerom* 3, 1986, pp. 23–6.

32. Ibid. See also Cecilie Løveid's article about the composition of the play, 'Når ideer aldri tar slutt' ('When Ideas Never Stop Coming', with the subtitle: 'The Language of Love. To Roland Barthes in Gratitude.').

33. *Fornuftige dyr* (Gyldendal, Oslo 1986, p. 42). In the printed version, the chronology has been changed so that Act III comes before Act II – a decision which the author later regretted. An unpublished translation of the play (my own) exists in manuscript.

34. There is a great difference between the printed text and the performance version of this play. The published text (Gyldendal, Oslo 1988) contains the characters Tutti and Frutti, but indicates little of their contribution to the action in purely visual terms, which is central in performance. It also – unfortunately – eliminates the singing pig from the characters because the songs s/he sings are translations and not the author's own invention.

35. See Janet Garton: 'On translating Cecilie Løveid'.

36. Cecilie Løveid's text was published together with photographs from the performance by Gyldendal (Oslo) in 1990.

37. Lecture in Norwich (see Note 20).

38. Torbjørn Egner's most popular book, *Folk og røvere i Kardemomme by*, has been published in English as *The Singing Town* (Methuen, London 1959).

39. Her participation in the Bergen Festival led to further collaboration with two experimental performing groups, *Lilith* and *Scirocco*, and resulted in the performance *Barock-Friise* (Baroque Frieze).

CHAPTER 12 From Documentary to Fantasy

1. From an interview in *Dagbladet*, 20 October 1983.

2. 'Farligheten' ('the dangerousness') is Tora's word for what Henrik does to her – an experience for which there are no words. Quotations from the trilogy are taken from the Gyldendal (Oslo) first editions: *Huset med den blinde glassveranda*, 1981 (= HBG); *Det stumme rommet*, 1983 (= SR); *Hudløs himmel*, 1986 (= HH).

3. One of the most persistent criticisms of the trilogy has been of its author's tendency to 'interfere' in the narrative with authorial commentary.

4. Irene Engelstad *et al.*: *Norsk kvinnelitteraturhistorie* III. See Rakel Christina Granaas: 'Roller, kropp og skrift. Psykologisk realisme etter 1965', pp. 177–89 (pp. 188–9); Irene Engelstad: 'Sprengning av realismen i romanen', pp. 190–203 (p. 203).

5. The fact that no woman author had won the prize since it was initiated in 1962 caused a protest in 1979, when an alternative prize – the Nordic Women's Literary Prize – was awarded to the Finland-Swedish author Märta Tikkanen for *Århundradets kärlekssaga* (*The Love Story of the Century*, 1978).

6. *Dinas bok* (Gyldendal, Oslo 1989), p. 27.

7. From an interview in *Arbeiderbladet*, 11 November 1989.

8. A literal translation of the title is 'Homosexuals of the World, Arise'. Quotations and page numbers refer to the English translation published by The Women's Press.

9. One of the explanations given for this is that it 'broke too sharply with party-political policy on sexual equality and with the relatively serious approach of organized feminism' in Norway (*Norsk kvinnelitteraturhistorie* III, p. 209). The same critic comments that it is nevertheless this novel which will probably be remembered longest.

10. See, for example, Hélène Cixous's essays on 'écriture féminine' and Mary Daly: *Gyn/Ecology*.

11. Although both Norwegian and English use the male as the dominant form, they do so in different ways, and so different strategies for revision are required. My references here are to the English version, transl. Louis Mackay in collaboration with the author.

12. *Sangen om St. Croix* (Den norske bokklubben, Oslo 1982) p. 266.

13. *Ved fergestedet* (Aschehoug, Oslo 1985), p. 30.

14. *For alle vinder* (Aschehoug, Oslo 1989), p. 281.

15. Interview with Eva Valebrokk, *Farmand* 1985.

16. 'It is almost with astonishment that one registers how indifferent one becomes to the question of homo or hetero. Sexual love is the same . . .'. Ingar Skrede in *Dagbladet*, 20 October 1983.

17. *Favntak* (Aschehoug, Oslo 1983), p. 288.

18. *Vi klarer det* (Per Sivle forlag, Oslo 1978), pp. 13–15.

19. *Wow* (Forlaget Oktober, Oslo 1982), p. 27.

20. *Gode gjerninger* (Forlaget Oktober, Oslo 1984), p. 17.

21. See Elaine Showalter's use of the term 'the wild zone' for aspects of female culture which lie outside the domain of male control, in an area of no-man's-land. 'Feminist Criticism in the Wilderness', in Showalter (ed.): *The New Feminist Criticism*, pp. 243–70, (p. 262).

22. *Familien* (Forlaget Oktober, Oslo 1985), p. 206.

23. *Arv* (Cappelen, Oslo 1988), p. 168.

24. See Øystein Rottem: *Fantasiens tiår* (The Decade of Fantasy).

Bibliography

1. GENERAL

(a) HISTORICAL, POLITICAL, SOCIAL STUDIES

Beauvoir, Simone de: *The Second Sex* (1949). Penguin Modern Classics, Harmondsworth 1983.

Dahlsgård, Inge (ed.): *Kvindebevægelsens hvem – hvad – hvor*. Politiken, Copenhagen 1975.

Daly, Mary: *Gyn/Ecology* (1978). The Women's Press, London 1979.

Duchen, Claire: *Feminism in France. From May '68 to Mitterrand*. Routledge & Kegan Paul, London, Boston, MA and Henley 1986.

Evans, Richard: *The Feminists*. Croom Helm, London and Sydney / Barnes & Noble, Totowa, NJ 1977.

Fell, Christine: *Women in Anglo-Saxon England and the Impact of 1066*. British Museum Publications, London 1985.

Friday, Nancy: *My Mother My Self* (1977). Fontana/Collins, Glasgow 1979.

Greer, Germaine: *The Female Eunuch* (1970). Paladin, London 1971.

Marks, Elaine and Isabelle de Courtivron (eds): *New French Feminisms*. University of Massachusetts Press, Amherst, MA 1980.

Mill, John Stuart: *The Subjection of Women* (1869). From *On Liberty and Other Writings*, Cambridge University Press, Cambridge 1989.

Millett, Kate: *Sexual Politics* (1969–70). Virago, London 1977.

Mitchell, Juliet: *Psychoanalysis and Feminism* (1974). Pelican, Harmondsworth 1975.

— : *Women: The Longest Revolution*. Virago, London 1984.

Rowbotham, Sheila: *Women, Resistance and Revolution*. Allen Lane, London 1972.

Showalter, Elaine: *The Female Malady: Women, Madness and English Culture 1830–1980*. Pantheon, New York 1985.

Wollstonecraft, Mary: *Vindication of the Rights of Women* (1792). Penguin Classics, Harmondsworth 1985.

Woolf, Virginia: *A Room of One's Own* (1929). Granada, St Albans and London 1977.

— : *Three Guineas* (1938). The Hogarth Press, London 1986.

(b) GENERAL LITERATURE AND LITERARY THEORY

Figes, Eva: *Sex and Subterfuge. Women Writers to 1850.* Macmillan, London and Basingstoke 1982.

Forsås-Scott, Helena: *Textual Liberation. European Feminist Writing in the Twentieth Century.* Routledge, London 1991.

Garton, Janet (ed.): *Facets of European Modernism. Essays in Honour of James McFarlane.* University of East Anglia, Norwich 1985.

Gilbert, Sandra M. and Susan Gubar: *The Madwoman in the Attic. The Woman Writer and the Nineteenth-Century Imagination.* Yale University Press, New Haven, CT and London 1979.

— : *No Man's Land. Vol.I: The War of the Words. Vol.II: Sexchanges.* Yale University Press, New Haven, CT and London 1988–9.

Heitmann, Annegret: *No Man's Land. An Anthology of Modern Danish Women's Literature.* Norvik Press, Norwich 1987.

Kristeva, Julia: *La Révolution du langage poétique.* Seuil, Paris 1974.

Moers, Ellen: *Literary Women* (1977). The Women's Press, London 1978.

Moi, Toril: *Sexual/Textual Politics.* Methuen, London and New York 1985.

Showalter, Elaine: *A Literature of Their Own.* Virago, London 1978.

— (ed.): *The New Feminist Criticism.* Virago, London 1986.

Todd, Janet: *Feminist Literary History.* Blackwell, Oxford 1988.

Woolf, Virginia: *A Writer's Diary,* ed. Leonard Woolf. Harcourt, Brace & World, New York 1953.

2. NORWAY

(a) HISTORICAL, POLITICAL, SOCIAL STUDIES

NB The place of publication is Oslo unless otherwise specified.

Agerholt, Anna Caspari: *Den norske kvinnebevegelses historie.* Gyldendal norsk forlag, 1937. (Reprinted with introduction by Kari Skjønsberg, 1973.)

Allardt, Erik *et al.* (eds): *Nordic Democracy.* Det Danske Selskab, Copenhagen 1981.

Benterud, Aagot: *Kvinnenes kamp for menneskerettighetene. Kort historikk fra oldtid til nåtid.* Norske Kvinners Nasjonalråd, 1954.

Blom, Ida: 'The Struggle for Women's Suffrage in Norway'. *Scandinavian Journal of History* vol. 5, no. 1, 1980.

— : 'A Centenary of Organised Feminism in Norway'. *Women's Studies International Forum* 5, 1982.

Blom, Ida and Gro Hagemann (eds): *Kvinner selv . . . Sju bidrag til norsk kvinnehistorie*. Aschehoug, 1977.

Bredsdorff, Elias: 'Moralists versus Immoralists: The Great Battle in Scandinavian Literature in the 1880s'. *Scandinavica* 8, no. 2, 1969 (pp. 91–111).

— : *Den store nordiske krig om seksualmoralen*. Gyldendal, Copenhagen 1973.

Bryld, Mette *et al.*: *Overgangskvinden. Kvindeligheden som historisk kategori – kvindeligheden 1880–1920*. Odense Universitetsforlag, Odense 1982.

Dahl, Tove Stang: *Women's Law. An Introduction to Feminist Jurisprudence*, transl. Ronald L. Craig. Norwegian University Press, 1987.

Derry, T.K.: *A History of Modern Norway 1814–1972*. Clarendon Press, Oxford 1973.

Graubard, Stephen R.(ed.): *Norden – The Passion for Equality*. Norwegian University Press, 1986.

Haavio-Mannila, Elina *et al.* (eds): *Unfinished Democracy. Women in Nordic Politics*, transl. Christine Badcock. Pergamon Press, Oxford 1985.

Hernes, Helga Maria: *Welfare State and Woman Power. Essays in State Feminism*. Norwegian University Press, 1987.

Holter, Harriet: *Patriarchy in a Welfare Society*. Universitetsforlaget, 1984.

Hovdhaugen, Einar: *Ekteskap og kjønnsmoral i norsk historie*. Samlaget, 1976.

Høgh, Marie (pub.) and Fredrikke Mørck (ed.): *Norske kvinder. En oversigt over deres stilling og livsvilkaar i hundreaaret 1814–1914*, I–II. Gyldendal, Kristiania 1914.

Lein, Bente Nilsen: *Kirken i felttog mot kvinnefrigjøring*. Universitetsforlaget, 1981.

Lervik, Åse Hiorth (ed.): *Kvinneaspekter i humanistisk forskning*. Norges almenvitenskaplige forskningsråd, 1976.

Lunden, Mimi Sverdrup: *De frigjorte hender. Et bidrag til forståelse av kvinners arbeid i Norge etter 1814*. (1941) Tanum–Norli, 1977.

Meyer, Ulla: *Norske kvinner. 150 portretter*. Dybwad, 1943.

Moksnes, Aslaug: *Likestilling eller særstilling? Norsk Kvinnesaksforening 1884–1913*. Gyldendal, 1984.

Moum, Sidsel Vogt: *Kvinnfolkarbeid. Kvinners kår og status i Norge 1875–1910*. Universitetsforlaget, 1981.

Mykland, Knut (ed.): *Norges historie*. I–XV. Cappelen, 1986-89.

Namtvedt, Leidulv (ed.): *Mini-facts about Norway 1990–91*. The Royal Ministry of Foreign Affairs, 1990.

Nielsen, Ragna: *Norske Kvinder i det 19de Aarhundrede*. Gyldendal, Kristiania 1904.

Olsen, Johan P.: *Organized Democracy. Political Institutions in a Welfare State – the Case of Norway*. Universitetsforlaget, Bergen 1983.

Popperwell, Ronald G.: *Norway*. Nations of the Modern World. Ernest Benn, London and Tonbridge 1972.

Schnitler, C.W.: *Slegten fra 1814*. Aschehoug, Kristiania 1911.

Skjønsberg, Kari (ed.): *Mannssamfunnet midt imot. Norsk kvinnesaksdebatt gjennom tre 'mannsaldre'*. Gyldendal, 1974.

— (ed.): *Hvor var kvinnene? Elleve kvinner om årene 1945–1960*. Gyldendal, 1979.

Stai, Arne: *Norsk kultur- og moraldebatt i 1930-årene* (1954). Gyldendal, 1978.

Vogt, Kari (ed.): *Den skjulte tradisjon – skapende kvinner i kulturhistorien*. Sigma forlag, Bergen 1982.

Vogt, Kari *et al.* (eds): *Kvinnenes kulturhistorie*. I–II. Universitetsforlaget, 1985.

(b) NORWEGIAN LITERARY HISTORY AND THEORY

Aarnes, Sigurd Aa.: *Bok og lesar*. Studia Universitetsbokhandel, Bergen 1981.

Aarseth, Asbjørn: *Romantikken som konstruksjon*. Universitetsforlaget, 1985.

—: *Realismen som myte*. Universitetsforlaget, 1981.

Aasen, Elisabeth (ed.): *'Vår bestemmelse er å giftes'. En samling tekster av kvinnelige forfattere fra 1800-tallet*. Tanum–Norli, 1978.

— (ed.): *Fra gamle dage. Memoarer, dagbøker, salmer og dikt av kvinner ca. 1660–1880*. Universitetsforlaget, 1983.

—: *Kvinners spor i skrift*. Det Norske Samlaget, 1986.

Andersen, Anne Cathrine *et al.*: *Fra barn til kvinne*. Universitetsforlaget, Tromsø 1980.

— *et al.*: *Arbeiderklassekvinner i litteraturen*. Universitetsforlaget, Tromsø 1982.

Beyer, Edvard (ed.): *Norges litteraturhistorie*. I–VI. Cappelens forlag, 1975.

Beyer, Harald and Edvard: *Norsk litteraturhistorie*. Fourth edition, Aschehoug, 1978.

Bjørneboe, Jens: *Bøker og mennesker*. Gyldendal, 1979.

Bonnevie, Mai Bente *et al.*: *Et annet språk. Analyser av norsk kvinnelitteratur*. Pax forlag, 1977.

Brantenberg, Gerd *et al.*: *På sporet av den tapte lyst*. Aschehoug, 1986.

Breivik, Inger-Lise *et al.*: *Kvinner i nynorsk prosa*. Det Norske Samlaget, 1980.

Bringsværd, Tor Åge and Halldis Hoaas (eds): *Norsk teaterårbok 1975*. Aschehoug, 1976.

Bull, Francis *et al.*: *Norsk litteraturhistorie*. I–VI. Gyldendal, 1957–63.

Dahl, Willy: *Norges litteratur*. I: Tid og tekst 1814–1884; II: Tid og tekst 1884–1935; III: Tid og tekst 1935–1972. Aschehoug, 1981–9.

Dahlerup, Pil: *Det moderne gennembruds kvinder*. Gyldendal, Copenhagen 1983.

Dale, Johs. A.: *Litteratur og lesing omkring 1890*. Det Norske Samlaget, 1974.

Doksrød, Hilde *et al.*: *Norske kvinnelige forfattere til og med 1900*. (Bibliography.) 1980.

Elster, Kristian the Younger: *Illustreret Norsk Litteraturhistorie* I–II. Gyldendalske boghandel, 1924.

Engelstad, Irene and Janneken Øverland: *Frihet til å skrive*. Pax forlag, 1981.

Engelstad, Irene (ed): *Skriften mellom linjene. 7 bidrag om psykoanalyse og litteratur.* Pax forlag, 1985.

Engelstad, Irene *et al.* (eds): *Norsk kvinnelitteraturhistorie.* I: 1600–1900; II: 1900–1940; III: 1940–1980. Pax forlag, 1988–90.

Forsås-Scott, Helene: 'Egalitarianism and Feminine Consciousness: Feminist Writing in Scandinavia'. In Helena Forsås-Scott (ed.): *Textual Liberation. European Feminist Writing in the Twentieth Century.* Routledge, London 1991.

Garton, Janet: 'Women of Letters: Nineteenth-century Norwegian Authors in their Correspondence'. *Proceedings of the Conference of Teachers of Scandinavian Studies in the British Isles,* April 1989. Edinburgh University, 1989 (pp. 94–121).

Gjernes, Erna Vibeke, Åsfrid Svensen and Jeanne Terjesen (eds): *Hvem eier drømmen din? Artikler om kvinnebevissthet og sosial forandring i nyere litteratur.* Novus forlag, 1983.

Gravier, Maurice: *Le Féminisme et l'amour dans la littérature norvégienne 1850–1950.* Minard, Paris 1968.

Hageberg, Otto: *Frå Camilla Collett til Dag Solstad.* Det Norske Samlaget, 1980.

Jensen, K.O. *et al.* (eds): *News From the Top of the World – Norwegian Literature Today,* vols 1–2. NORLA, 1988–9.

Kvinner og bøker. Festskrift til Ellisiv Steen på hennes 70-årsdag 4. februar 1978. Gyldendal norsk forlag, 1978.

Lein, Bente Nilsen *et al.*: *Furier er også kvinner. Aasta Hansteen 1824–1908.* Universitetsforlaget, 1984.

Lervik, Åse Hiorth (ed.): *Gjennom kvinneøyne.* I–II. Universitetsforlaget, 1980 and 1982. (Bibliography by Janet Rasmussen on women and Norwegian literature 1955–1980 in vol. II.)

—: *Evig din. Om kjærlighet hos kvinnelige forfattere ca. 1870–1907.* Universitetsforlaget, 1985.

Longum, Leif: *Et speil for oss selv. Menneskesyn og virkelighetsoppfatning i norsk etterkrigsprosa.* Aschehoug, 1968.

—: *Drømmen om det frie menneske.* Universitetsforlaget, Oslo–Bergen–Stavanger–Tromsø 1986.

Lyngstad, Sverre (ed.): *Review of National Literatures 12: Norway.* Griffon House Publications, New York 1983.

Mæhle, Leif: *Frå bygda til verda. Studiar i nynorsk 1900-talsdikting.* Det Norske Samlaget, 1967.

Marker, Frederick J. and Lise-Lone: *The Scandinavian Theatre. A Short History.* Blackwell, Oxford 1975.

Mawby, Janet: *Writers and Politics in Modern Scandinavia.* Hodder & Stoughton, London 1978.

Norwegian Literature 1990. Special issue of *The Norseman,* vol. 30, no. 4/5, 1990.

Notaker, Henry (ed.): *Reis ingen monumenter. Lyrikk fra okkupasjonstiden.* Gyldendal, 1969.

Palmvig, Lis: *Lysthuse. Kvindelitteraturhistorier.* Rosinante, Copenhagen 1985.

Ramnefalk, Marie Louise and Anna Westberg (eds): *Kvinnornas litteraturhistoria.* Författarförlaget, Stockholm 1981.

Rasmussen, Janet E.: 'Feminist Criticism and Women's Literature in Norway: A Status Report'. *Edda* 1980 (pp. 45–52).

Rottem, Øystein: *Fantasiens tiår.* Aschehoug, 1990.

Rønning, Helge (ed.): *Linjer i norsk prosa 1965–75.* Pax forlag, 1977.

Sverre, Turid: 'The Barrenness of Silence: The Difficult Heritage of Mothers and Daughters in Norwegian Women's Literature'. *Edda,* 1983 (pp. 329–38).

Ustvedt, Yngvar: *På tomannshånd med dikterne. Nye intervjuer med norske klassikere fra Petter Dass til Arnulf Øverland.* Gyldendal, 1976.

Zuck, Virpi (ed.): *Dictionary of Scandinavian Literature.* Greenwood Press, Westport, CT 1990.

(c) STUDIES OF INDIVIDUAL AUTHORS

NB Editions of primary texts are specified in the Notes to each chapter. The place of publication is Oslo unless otherwise specified.

Camilla Collett

Aarnes, Sigurd Aa. (ed.): *Søkelys på Amtmandens Døtre.* Universitetsforlaget, 1977.

Aarseth, Asbjørn: 'Erotisk idealism i Camilla Colletts *Amtmandens Døtre*'. *Parapraxis* 10, Lund 1978 (pp. 14–23).

Benterud, Aagot: *Camilla Collett. En skjebne og et livsverk.* Dreyers forlag, 1946.

Diktning og demokrati. Camilla Collett 150 år. Full kvinnestemmerett 50 år. 1813–1913–1963. Special issue of *Samtiden,* 1963.

Gravier, Maurice: 'Camilla Collett et la France'. *Scandinavica* 4, no. 1, 1965 (pp. 38–53).

Hareide, Jorunn: 'Grottesymbolet nok en gang: en polemisk analyse av *Amtmandens Døtre*'. *Edda* 1980 (pp. 1–13).

—: 'Forsøk på å lytte til "Grundtonen". Camilla Colletts selvbiografi *I de lange Nætter*'. *Edda* 1986 (pp. 63–80).

Møller Jensen, Elisabeth: *Emancipation som lidenskab.* Rosinante, Charlottenlund 1987.

Østerud, Erik: 'Kjerringa mot strømmen. Camilla Colletts liv og forfatterskap'. *Edda* 1987 (pp. 291–314).

Steen, Ellisiv: *Diktning og virkelighet.* Gyldendal, 1947.

—: *Den lange strid*. Gyldendal, 1954.

—: *Camilla Collett om seg selv*. Den norske bokklubben, 1985.

Amalie Skram

Amadou, Anne-Lisa: 'Madame Bovary i Constance Ring'. *Fransk i Norge*. Til Gunnar Høst på 75-årsdagen 12.8.1975. Aschehoug, 1957 (pp. 87–105).

Bjerkelund, Ragni: *Amalie Skram. Dansk borger, norsk forfatter*. Aschehoug, 1988.

Dahlerup, Pil: 'Den kvinnelige naturalist'. *Vinduet* no. 2, 1975 (pp. 30–37).

Engelstad, Irene: *Amalie Skram. Kjærlighet og kvinneundertrykking*. Pax forlag, 1978.

—: *Amalie Skram om seg selv*. Den norske bokklubben, 1981.

—: *Sammenbrudd og gjennombrudd. Amalie Skrams romaner om ekteskap og sinnssykdom*. Pax forlag, 1984.

Høgset, Gudny: *Amalie Skram 1846–1905*. Bibliography. Statens bibliotekskole, 1968.

Kjetsaa, Geir: 'Amalie Skrams mottagelse av Tolstoj og Dostojevskij'. *Edda* 1986 (pp. 335–41).

Køltzow, Liv: *Den unge Amalie Skram*. Gyldendal, 1992.

Krane, Borghild: *Amalie Skrams diktning. Tema og variasjoner*. Gyldendal, 1961.

Messick, Judith: 'Constance Ring and the Tradition of the Female Quixote'. In Sven Rossel (ed.): *Scandinavian Literature in a Transcultural Context*. University of Washington, Seattle, WA 1986 (pp. 52–6).

Rasmussen, Janet E.: 'Amalie Skram as Literary Critic'. *Edda* 1981 (pp. 1–11).

Schacke, Lene Tybjærg: 'Edvard Brandes og Amalie Skram. Til belysning af "gennembrudsmændenes" vurdering af kvindelige forfatterskaber'. *Edda* 1984 (pp. 257–73).

Tiberg, Antonie: *Amalie Skram som kunstner og menneske*. Aschehoug, Kristiania 1910.

Ragnhild Jølsen

Bjørneboe, Jens: *Drømmen og hjulet*. Aschehoug, 1964.

—: 'Ragnhild Jølsen – romantiker og realist'. In *Bøker og mennesker*, Gyldendal, 1979 (pp. 199–207).

Christensen, Kari: 'Det kvinnelige livsmønster i Ragnhild Jølsens *Rikka Gan*'. *Norsk litterær årbok*, Det Norske Samlaget, 1983 (pp. 35–46).

—: *Portrett på mørk treplate. Ragnhild Jølsens liv og forfatterskap*. Aschehoug, 1989.

Hvistendahl, Rita: 'Ragnhild Jølsens *Hollases krønike* som mytologiserende fortelling'. *Edda* 1983 (pp. 167–181).

Kinck, Hans E.: 'Ved Ragnhild Jølsens død'. *Samtiden* 19, 1908 (pp. 138–41).

Lorenz, Astrid: 'Kvinneerfaring og kjærlighetsdrøm i *Hollases krønike* av Ragnhild Jølsen'. *Vinduet* no. 2, 1980 (pp. 52–6).

—: 'Kjærligheten og virkeligheten. Ragnhild Jølsens *Hollases krønike* som kvinnespeil'. *Norsk litterær årbok*, Det Norske Samlaget, 1980 (pp. 15–32).

Nettum, Rolf Nyboe: 'Romantikk og realisme i Ragnhild Jølsens forfatterskap'. *Edda* 1972 (pp. 157–67).

Nordahl, Helge: 'Rytme og repetisjon. Noen tanker om sprogkunstneren Ragnhild Jølsen'. *Edda* 1990 (pp. 163–72).

—: . . . *tre kyss for den ensomme fugl. Syv essays om Ragnhild Jølsens diktning.* Aschehoug, 1991.

Solberg, Olav: 'Realisme eller romantikk, kontinuitet eller brot? Ragnhild Jølsens *Brukshistorier*'. *Norskrift* 53, 1987 (pp. 1–21).

Tiberg, Antonie: *Ragnhild Jølsen i liv og digtning.* Aschehoug, Kristiania 1909.

Sigrid Undset

Aasen, Elisabeth: *Sigrid Undset.* Norske forfattere i nærlys. Aschehoug, 1982.

Anderson, Gidske: *Sigrid Undset – et liv.* Gyldendal, 1989.

Anker, Nini Roll: *Min venn Sigrid Undset.* (1946) Aschehoug, 1982.

Bayerschmidt, Carl F.: *Sigrid Undset.* (In English.) Twayne Publishers, New York 1970.

Bliksrud, Liv: *Natur og normer hos Sigrid Undset.* Aschehoug, 1988.

Granaas, Rakel Christina *et al.*: *Kvinnesyn – tvisyn.* En antologi om Sigrid Undset. Novus, 1985.

Grøndahl, Carl Henrik: *Sigrid Undset 1882–1982.* Dyade/Utenriksdepartementet 1983.

Heltoft, Bente: *Livssyn og digtning. Strukturgrundlaget i Sigrid Undsets romaner.* Aschehoug, 1985.

Johnson, Pål Espolin *et al.*: *Sigrid Undset i dag.* Aschehoug, 1982.

Krane, Borghild: *Sigrid Undset. Liv og meninger.* Gyldendal, 1970.

Kvinge, Anna Brit: *Sigrid Undsets 'Jenny'.* En analyse. Novus, 1981.

McFarlane, James W.: 'Sigrid Undset'. In *Ibsen and the Temper of Norwegian Literature.* Oxford University Press, London 1960.

Packness, Ida: *Sigrid Undset bibliografi.* Universitetsforlaget, 1963.

Rieber-Mohn, Hallvard: *Sten på sten. Fem blikk på Sigrid Undset.* Aschehoug, 1982.

Sæther, Astrid: '"Dazzling Dreams and Grey Days": On the Antithesis between Ideal and Reality in Sigrid Undset's Contemporary Novels and Short Stories'. *Scandinavica* 1990 (pp. 193–205).

Steen, Ellisiv: *Kristin Lavransdatter. En estetisk studie.* Aschehoug, 1959.
Thorn, Finn: *Sigrid Undset. Kristentro og kirkesyn.* Aschehoug, 1975.
Winsnes, A.H.: *Sigrid Undset. En studie i kristen realisme.* (1949) Aschehoug, 1982. Transl. P.G. Foote as *Sigrid Undset. A Study in Christian Realism* (1953). Greenwood Press, Westport, CT 1970.

Cora Sandel

Bale, Kjersti: *Friheten som utopi. En analyse av Cora Sandels Alberte-trilogi.* Novus, 1989.
Engelstad, Irene and Janneken Øverland: *Frihet til å skrive.* (Includes four essays by Janneken Øverland on Cora Sandel.) Pax forlag, 1981.
Gimnes, Steinar: '"Tilværelsen kleber." Om kvinner og frigjering i nokre Cora Sandel-noveller'. *Norsk litterær årbok* 1976 (pp. 448–61).
—: *Cora Sandel. Norske forfattere i nærlys.* Aschehoug, 1982.
Lervik, Åse Hiorth: *Menneske og miljø i Cora Sandels diktning.* Gyldendal, 1977.
Mangset, Berit Ryen: *Alberte – fra et kvinnesynspunkt.* Novus, 1977.
Øverland, Janneken: *Cora Sandel om seg selv.* Den norske bokklubben, 1983.
Rokkan, Elizabeth: 'Cora Sandel's War Story: "Stort syn og smått syn"'. *Scandinavica* 1987 (pp. 5–12).
—: 'Cora Sandel and the Second World War'. *Scandinavica* 1989 (pp. 155–60).
Solumsmoen, Odd: *Cora Sandel. En dikter i ånd og sannhet.* Aschehoug, 1957.
Zuck, Virpi: 'Cora Sandel. A Norwegian Feminist'. *Edda* 1981 (pp. 23–33).

Halldis Moren Vesaas

Faldbakken, Knut: 'Få Dem heller en kjæreste . . .'. Interview with Halldis Moren Vesaas, Liv Køltzow and Bergljot Hobæk Haff. *Vinduet* no. 2, 1975 (pp. 2–8).
Mæhle, Leif (ed.): *Halldis Moren Vesaas. Festskriftet til 80-årsdagen 18.november 1987.* Aschehoug, 1987.
Waagaard, Mari Beinset: 'Halldis Moren Vesaas'. *Norsk litterær årbok*, Det Norske Samlaget, 1966 (pp. 18–43).

Bjørg Vik

Berg, Arngeir and Espen Haavardsholm: 'Bjørg Vik' (interview); in *Partiskhet. Samtaler med seks skandinaviske forfattere.* Gyldendal, 1975 (pp. 77–89).

Brekken, Astrid: 'Ikkje er eg så uvanleg – men det endelege målet var aldri å bli gift' (interview). *Sirene* no. 1, 1977 (pp. 5–7, 11).

Engelstad, Irene: 'En analyse av "På bussen er det fint"'; in Irene Engelstad and Janneken Øverland (eds): *Frihet til å skrive* (pp. 205–16).

— : 'Den vanskelige friheten. Et tema i Bjørg Viks noveller'. *Norsk litterær årbok*, Det Norske Samlaget, 1976 (pp. 142–56). Also printed in *Frihet til å skrive*.

Eriksson, Jofrid: 'Bjørg Vik: *To akter for fem kvinner*'. *Kjerringråd* no. 2, 1975 (pp. 11–14).

Faldbakken, Knut: 'Samtale med Bjørg Vik' (interview). *Vinduet* no. 1, 1976 (pp. 53–7).

Garton, Janet: 'Om å snuble i sine egne lengsler. Bjørg Vik: *En håndfull lengsel*'. *Norsk litterær årbok*, Det Norske Samlaget, 1983 (pp. 102–18).

— : 'Billedbruken i Bjørg Viks novelle "Rosa og Ruth"'. *Edda* 1983 (pp. 321–8).

Moi, Toril: 'Fra skogen til skrivepulten eller faren ved den kvinnelige kreativitet. En lesning av Bjørg Viks novelle "På bussen er det fint"'. In Irene Engelstad (ed.): *Skriften mellom linjene* (pp. 127–49).

Øverland, Janneken: 'Det grådige hjertes ufrihet'. *Vinduet* no. 1, 1976 (pp. 57–64).

— : 'Kvinneroller – tilpasning eller opprør? Om Vigdis Stokkeliens og Bjørg Viks forfatterskap'. In Helge Rønning (ed.): *Linjer i norsk prosa 1965–75* (pp. 241–80).

Riiser, Liv: 'Småjenteskildringer i noveller av Sigrid Undset og Bjørg Vik'. In Anne-Cathrine Andersen *et al.*: *Fra barn til kvinne* (pp. 133–46).

Waal, Carla: 'The Norwegian Short Story: Bjørg Vik'. *Scandinavian Studies* no. 2, 1977 (pp. 217–40) (includes translation of 'They Come in Small Groups').

Cecilie Løveid

See various articles in *Spillerom* no. 3, 1986 and *Kritikkjournalen* no. 2, 1990.

Borgersen, Sigrun: 'På kant med genrene. Cecilie Løveids dramatikk'. *Vinduet* no. 3, 1984 (pp. 19–23).

Christensen, Kari: 'Den særegne klangen av knust språk'. *Norsk litterær årbok* 1979 (pp. 202–13).

Engelstad, Irene, Jofrid Eriksson and Irene Iversen: 'Myter og erfaring – undertrykkelsens mønstre vist av fire kvinnelige forfattere'. *Kontrast* 42, 1973 (pp. 8–26).

Faldbakken, Knut: 'Å være med i seg selv'. Interview in *Vinduet* no. 2, 1977 (pp. 10–15).

Garton, Janet and Henning Sehmsdorf: 'Contemporary Norwegian Theatre'. *New Norwegian Plays*, Norvik Press, Norwich 1989 (pp. 9–34).

Garton, Janet: 'Cecilie Løveid: Feminist Modernist Dramatist'. In Asmund Lien (ed.): *Modernismen i skandinavisk litteratur*. Nordisk institutt, Trondheim 1991 (pp. 349–54).

— : 'On translating Cecilie Løveid'. In Janet Garton (ed.): *Proceedings of the British Association of Scandinavian Studies*, Norwich 1992 (pp. 112–17).

Løveid, Cecilie: 'Når ideer aldri tar slutt'. *Dyade* no. 1–2, 1986 (pp. 58–71).

Müller, Anne Marie: 'Opplevelse og estetikk. Om komposisjon og bildebruk i Cecilie Løveids roman *Most*'. In Erna Vibeke Gjernes *et al.* (eds): *Hvem eier drømmen din?* (pp. 123–47).

Øverland, Janneken: 'Hva gjør du i min åker?' In Irene Engelstad and Janneken Øverland: *Frihet til å skrive* (pp. 250–53).

—: 'Frihet til å oppleve de merkeligste eventyr'. Ibid. (pp. 254–63).

Herbjørg Wassmo

Granaas, Rakel Christina: 'Nødvendige mord? Herbjørg Wassmo skriver med loven i hendene: *Dinas bok*'. In Asmund Lien (ed.): *Modernismen i skandinavisk litteratur*. Nordisk institutt, Trondheim 1991 (pp. 200–6).

Hareide, Jorunn: 'Kampen for menneskeverd. Herbjørg Wassmo: *Huset med den blinde glassveranda*'. *Norsk litterær årbok* 1982 (pp. 206–19).

Isaacson, Lanae Hjortsvang: 'Fantasy, Imagination and Reality: Herbjørg Wassmo's *Huset med den blinde glassveranda*'. *Scandinavica* 1986 (pp. 177–89).

Kristjansdottir, Dagny: '"With-out." Om Tora-trilogien av Herbjørg Wassmo'. *Norskrift* no. 58, 1988 (pp. 97–107).

Moe, Karen: 'Fortsettelsens estetikk og etikk. Om Herbjørg Wassmos *Det stumme rommet*'. *Oppbrudd. Skrivende kvinner over hele verden*, Universitetsforlaget 1985 (pp. 42–7).

Norseng, Mary Kay: 'A Child's Liberation of Space: Herbjørg Wassmo's *Huset med den blinde glassveranda*'. *Scandinavian Studies* 1986 (pp. 48–66).

Vederhus, Inger: 'Tora og Herdis hos Herbjørg og Torborg. Perspektiv på romanen'. *Syn og Segn* no. 93, 1987 (pp. 329–39).

Gerd Brantenberg

Moberg, Verne: 'A Norwegian Woman's Fantasy. Gerd Brantenberg's *Egalias døtre* as kvinneskelig Utopia'. *Scandinavian Studies* 1985 (pp. 325–32).

Valebrokk, Eva: 'Gjennom ordene. Gerd Brantenberg intervjuet'. *Farmand* no. 46, 1985 (pp. 36–7).

Mari Osmundsen

Svensen, Åsfrid: 'Ordenens lov – bærer den alt i sin favn? Mari Osmundsens *Gode gjerninger*'. In Odd Martin Mæland (ed.): *Mellom tekst og tekst*, Cappelen 1988 (pp. 147–58).

3. SELECT BIBLIOGRAPHY OF ENGLISH TRANSLATIONS OF WOMEN'S WRITING

Abbreviations used for anthologies

An Everyday Story = Katherine Hanson (ed.): *An Everyday Story. Norwegian Women's Fiction*. The Seal Press, Seattle, WA 1984.

Contemporary Poets = T. Johanssen (ed.): *20 Contemporary Norwegian Poets*. Universitetsforlaget, Oslo 1984.

Scandinavian Women Writers = Ingrid Claréus (ed.): *Scandinavian Women Writers. An Anthology from the 1880s to the 1980s*. Greenwood Press, New York, Westport, CT and London 1989.

Slaves of Love = James McFarlane (ed.): *Slaves of Love and other Norwegian Short Stories*. Oxford University Press, Oxford and New York 1982.

View from the Window = Elizabeth Rokkan and Ingrid Weatherhead: *View from the Window. Norwegian Short Stories*. Norwegian University Press, Bergen 1986.

See also short excerpts from contemporary writers published in the magazine of the Office for Norwegian Literature Abroad, *News from the Top of the World* (Oslo 1988).

Anker, Nini Roll: 'A Crime' ('Gåten', from *Små avsløringer*, 1937), transl. Torild Homstad. In *An Everyday Story*.

Bøge, Kari: 'Viviann, White' (excerpt from *Viviann, hvit*, 1974), transl. Nadia Christensen. In *An Everyday Story*.

Brantenberg, Gerd: *What Comes Naturally* (*Opp alle jordens homofile*, 1973), transl. the author. The Women's Press, London 1986.

— : *The Daughters of Egalia* (*Egalias døtre*, 1977), transl. Louis Mackay. Journeyman Press, London 1985 / The Seal Press, Seattle, WA 1985.

Brekke, Toril: *The Jacaranda Flower* (*Jacarandablomsten*, 1985), transl. Anne Born. Methuen, London 1987.

Christov, Solveig: 'The Glory of Mankind' ('Menneskets herlighet', from *Jegeren og viltet*, 1962), transl. Janet Garton. In *Slaves of Love*.

— : 'The Paradise Fish' ('Paradisfisken', from *Jegeren og viltet*, 1962), transl. Nadia Christensen. In *An Everyday Story*.

Collett, Camilla: *The District Governor's Daughters* (*Amtmandens Døttre*, 1854–5), transl. Kirsten Seaver. Norvik Press, Norwich 1992.

— : 'Storyteller Sara' ('Eventyrsara og hennes Datter', from *I de lange Nætter*, 1862), transl. Janet E. Rasmussen. In *An Everyday Story*.

Haalke, Magnhild: 'Stormarja and Lillmarja' ('Stormarja og Lillmarja', from *Dragspell*, 1958), transl. Katherine Hanson. In *An Everyday Story*.

Hagen, Ingeborg Refling: 'Borrowing Fire' ('Laane varme', from *Naar elv skifter leie*, 1920), transl. Katherine Hanson. In *An Everyday Story*.

Hagerup, Inger: 'The Woman at Klepp' ('Kjærring på Klepp', 1938). Translated by Torild Homstad. In *An Everyday Story*.

— : *Helter Skelter* (*Hulter til bulter*, 1979), transl. Joan Tate. Pelham, London 1979.

— : Selected poems. In *Contemporary Poets*.

Haslund, Ebba: *Nothing happened* (*Det hendte ingenting*, 1948), transl. Barbara Wilson. The Seal Press, Seattle, WA 1987.

— : 'No Ordinary Day' ('Ingen vanlig dag'), transl. Ingrid Weatherhead. Norwegian University Press, Bergen 1986. In *View from the Window*.

— : 'Meeting in March' ('Møte i mars', from *Hver i sin verden*, 1976), transl. Tina L. Deehr. In *Scandinavian Women Writers*.

— : 'Santa Simplicitas' (from *Hver i sin verden*, 1976), transl. Katherine Hanson. In *An Everyday Story*.

Holm, Gro: 'Life on the Løstøl Farm' (Excerpts from 'Løstølsfolket', 1932–4), transl. Katherine Hanson. In *An Everyday Story*.

Holth, Åsta: 'Salt' ('Salt', from *Gamle bygdevegen: Finnskogfortellinger*, 1944), transl. Katherine Hanson. In *An Everyday Story*.

Jølsen, Ragnhild: 'Hanna Valmoen' (from *Brukshistorier*, 1907), transl. Janet Garton. In *Slaves of Love*.

— : 'The Twelfth in the Cabin' and 'Fiddle Music in the Meadow' ('Den tolvte i stua' and 'Felelåten i engen', from *Brukshistorier*, 1907), transl. Katherine Hanson. In *An Everyday Story*.

Lie, Sissel: *The Heart of the Lion* (*Løvens hjerte*, 1988), transl. Anne Born. The Orkney Press, Orkney, 1990.

Løveid, Cecilie: 'Captured Wildrose' (Excerpt from *Fanget villrose*, 1977), transl. Nadia Christensen. In *An Everyday Story*.

— : *Sea Swell* (*Sug*, 1979), transl. Nadia Christensen. Fjord Press, London and New York 1986.

— : 'Seagull Eaters' (*Måkespisere*, 1983), transl. Henning K. Sehmsdorf. In Janet Garton and Henning K. Sehmsdorf (eds): *New Norwegian Plays*, Norvik Press, Norwich 1989.

— : Selected poems. In *Contemporary Poets*.

Lundberg, Liv: Selected poems. In *Contemporary Poets*.

Lunden, Eldrid: Selected poems. In *Contemporary Poets*.

Moe, Karin: 'The Lady in the Coat' ('Dama i kåpa', from *Kjønnskrift*, 1980). 'Eagle Wings' ('Fyk 17', from *Fyk*, 1983), transl. Janet E. Rasmussen. In *An Everyday Story*.

Nedreaas, Torborg: 'Achtung, Gnädiges Fräulein' (from *Bak skapet står øksen*, 1945), transl. Elizabeth Rokkan. In *An Everyday Story*.

— : *Nothing Grows by Moonlight* (*Av måneskinn gror det ingenting*, 1947), transl. Bibbi Lee. Nebraska University Press, Nebraska 1988.

— : *Music from a Blue Well* (*Musikk fra en blå brønn*, 1960), transl. Bibbi Lee. Nebraska University Press, Nebraska 1988.

— : 'Blue Light' ('Blålys', from *Den siste polka*, 1965), transl. Katherine Hanson. In *Scandinavian Women Writers*.

Nilsen, Tove: 'Scum' ('Subb', from *Hendene opp fra fanget*, 1977), transl. Barbara Wilson. In *An Everyday Story*.

Sandel, Cora: *Alberta and Jacob* (*Alberte og Jacob*, 1926), transl. Elizabeth Rokkan. Peter Owen, London 1962 / The Women's Press, London 1980 / Ohio University Press, Athens, OH 1984.

— : *Alberta and Freedom* (*Alberte og friheten*, 1931), transl. Elizabeth Rokkan. Peter Owen, London 1963 / The Women's Press, London 1980 / Ohio University Press, Athens, OH 1984.

— : 'A Mystery' ('En gåte', from *Carmen og Maja*, 1932). 'The Child Who Loved Roads' ('Barnet som elsket veier', 1947), transl. Barbara Wilson. In *An Everyday Story*.

— : 'Cousin Thea' ('Kusine Tea', from *Mange takk, doktor*, 1935), transl. James McFarlane. In *Slaves of Love*.

— : *Alberta Alone* (*Bare Alberte*, 1939), transl. Elizabeth Rokkan. Peter Owen, London 1965 / The Women's Press, London 1980 / Ohio University Press, Athens, OH 1984.

— : *Krane's Café* (*Kranes konditori*, 1945), transl. Elizabeth Rokkan. Peter Owen, London 1968 / The Women's Press, London 1984.

— : *The Leech* (*Kjøp ikke Dondi*, 1958), transl. Elisabeth Rokkan. Peter Owen, London 1960 / The Women's Press, London 1986.

— : *Selected Short Stories*, transl. Barbara Wilson. The Seal Press, Seattle, WA 1985.

— : *The Silken Thread* (Selected short stories), transl. Elizabeth Rokkan. Peter Owen, London 1986.

Skram, Amalie: 'Karen's Christmas' ('Karens jul', 1885), transl. Janet Garton. In *Slaves of Love*.

— : *Constance Ring* (*Constance Ring*, 1885), transl. Judith Messick with Katherine Hanson. The Seal Press, Seattle, WA 1988.

— : *Betrayal* (*Forrådt*, 1892), transl. Aileen Hennes. Pandora, London 1986.

— : *Under Observation* (*Professor Hieronimus* / *På St. Jørgen*, 1895), transl. Katherine Hanson and Judith Messick. Women in Translation, Seattle, WA 1992.

—: 'Professor Hieronymus' (excerpt from *Professor Hieronimus*, 1895), transl. Alice Stronach and G.B. Jacobi, revised by Colin D. Thomson. In *Scandinavian Women Writers*.

Stokkelien, Vigdis: 'A Vietnamese Doll' ('En vietnamesisk dukke', from *I speilet*, 1973), transl. Barbara Wilson. In *An Everyday Story*.

Sveen, Karin: 'A Good Heart' ('Det gode hjertet', from *Døtre*, 1980), transl. Katherine Hanson. In *An Everyday Story*.

Takvam, Marie: Selected poems. In *Contemporary Poets*.

Undset, Sigrid: *Gunnar's Daughter* (*Fortællingen om Viga-Ljot og Vigdis*, 1909), transl. Arthur G. Chater. Cassell, London 1936.

— : *Jenny* (*Jenny*, 1911), transl. William Emmé. Fertig, New York 1920, 1974.

— : 'The Charity Ball' ('Omkring sædelighetsballet', from *Fattige skjæbner*, 1912), transl. Janet Garton. In *An Everyday Story*.

— : *Images in a Mirror* (*Splinten av Trollspeilet*, 1917), transl. Arthur G. Chater. Knopf, New York 1938.

— : *Kristin Lavransdatter* (*Kristin Lavransdatter*, 1920–22), transl. Charles Archer and J.S. Scott. Cassell, London 1930, 1969 / Pan, London 1977.

— : *The Master of Hestviken* (*Olav Audunssøn i Hestviken*, 1925; *Olav Audunssøn og hans børn*, 1927), transl. Arthur G. Chater. Knopf, New York 1928–30, 1962.

— : *The Wild Orchid* (*Gymnadenia*, 1929), transl. Arthur G. Chater. Knopf, New York 1932 / Cassell, London 1931.

— : *The Burning Bush* (*Den brændende busk*, 1930), transl. Arthur G. Chater. Knopf, New York 1932.

— : *Ida Elisabeth* (*Ida Elisabeth*, 1932), transl. Arthur G. Chater. Knopf, New York 1933.

— : *The Longest Years* (*Elleve år*, 1934), transl. Arthur G. Chater. New York 1935 / Kraus reprint, Millwood, NY 1971.

— : *The Faithful Wife* (*Den trofaste hustru*, 1936), transl. Arthur G. Chater. Cassell, London 1937.

— : *Madam Dorothea* (*Madame Dorthea*, 1939), transl. Arthur G. Chater. Cassell, London 1941.

— : *Happy Times in Norway* (*Lykkelige dager*, 1947), transl. Joran Birkeland. Knopf, New York 1943, 1961.

— : *Return to the Future* (*Tilbake til fremtiden*, 1949), transl. Henriette C.K. Naeseth. Cassell, London 1943.

— : *Four Stories*. ('Selma Brøter', 'Thjodolf', 'Miss Smith-Tellefsen', 'Simonsen'), transl. Naomi Walford. Knopf, New York 1959.

Vesaas, Halldis Moren: *Selected Poems*, transl. R. Wakefield and O. Thompson. White Pine Press, New York 1989.

— : Selected poems. In *Contemporary Poets*.

Vik, Bjørg: *An Aquarium of Women* (*Kvinneakvariet*, 1972), transl. Janet Garton. Norvik Press, Norwich 1987.

— : 'Tone – 16' (from the anthology *Så stor du er blitt*, 1981), transl. Ingrid Weatherhead. In *View from the Window*.

— : 'They Come in Small Groups' ('De kommer i små flokker', from *Fortellinger om frihet*), transl. Carla Waal. In *Scandinavian Studies* no. 2, 1977.

— : *Out of Season and other stories* (*En håndfull lengsel*, 1979), transl. David McDuff and Patrick Browne. Sinclair Browne, London 1983.

— : 'Daughters' ('Døtre', 1979), transl. Janet Garton. In Janet Garton and Henning K. Sehmsdorf (eds): *New Norwegian Plays*. Norvik Press, Norwich 1989.

Wassmo, Herbjørg: *The House with the Blind Glass Windows* (*Huset med den blinde glassveranda*, 1981), transl. Roseann Lloyd and Allen Simpson. The Seal Press, Seattle, WA 1987.

Zwilgmeyer, Dikken: 'An Everyday Story' ('En hverdagshistorie', 1885), transl. Katherine Hanson. In *An Everyday Story*.

Index